ADVANCES IN
COMPUTER
VISION
VOLUME 2

ADVANCES IN
COMPUTER
VISION

VOLUME 2

EDITED BY

CHRISTOPHER BROWN
University of Rochester

Psychology Press
Taylor & Francis Group

New York   London

First Published by
Lawrence Erlbaum Associates, Inc., Publishers
365 Broadway
Hillsdale, New Jersey 07642

Transferred to Digital Printing 2009 by Psychology Press
270 Madison Avenue, New York NY 10016
27 Church Road, Hove, East Sussex BN3 2FA

Library of Congress Cataloging-in-Publication Data

Advances in computer vision/edited by Christopher Brown.
    p.   cm.
  Bibliography: p.
  Includes indexes.
  ISBN 0-89859-648-3 (v. 1). ISBN 0-8058-0092-1 (v. 2)
  1. Computer vision.   2. Brown, Christopher M.
TA1632.A265 1988   87-27282
006.3'7——dc19   CIP

☐ CONTENTS

VOLUME 2

CONTRIBUTORS

John Aloimonos Department of Computer Science, University of Maryland, College Park, MD 20742

Dana Ballard Department of Computer Science, University of Rochester, Rochester, NY 14627

Christopher Brown Department of Computer Science, University of Rochester, Rochester, NY 14627

Allen Hanson Computer and Information Sciences Department, University of Massachusetts, Amherst, MA 01002

Robert Haralick Department of Electrical Engineering, University of Washington, Seattle, WA 98195

Alex Pentland Vision Sciences Group, Media Laboratory, Massachusetts Institute of Technology, Cambridge, MA 02139

Tomaso Poggio Artificial Intelligence Laboratory, Massachusetts Institute of Technology, Cambridge, MA 02139

Ting-Chuen Pong Department of Computer Science, University of Minnesota, Minneapolis, MN

Edward Riseman Computer and Information Sciences Department, University of Massachusetts, Amherst, MA 01002

Linda Shapiro Department of Electrical Engineering, University of Washington, Seattle, WA 98195

Allen Waxman   Electrical, Computer and Systems Engineering, College of Engineering, Boston University, Boston, MA 02215

Kwangyoen Wohn   GRASPLAB, Department of Computer and Information Science, University of Pennsylvania, Philadelphia, PA 19104

Allan Yuille   Division of Applied Sciences, Harvard University, Pierce Hall, Cambridge, MA 02139

 INTRODUCTION

VISION AND COMPUTER VISION

The series *Advances in Computer Vision* has the goal of presenting current approaches to basic problems that arise in the construction of a computer vision system, written by leading researchers and practitioners in the field. The first two volumes in the series comprise seven chapters, which together cover much of the scope of computer vision. Chapter 1 of Volume 1 is referred to as 1.1, and so forth.

In these volumes, computer vision means computer programs analyzing visual input (like a television image of a three-dimensional scene) and deriving from the image some description of the scene that is helpful to further reasoning or action concerning the scene (Pentland, 1986). The technical aspects of creating images and transferring them to the computer's memory are not addressed here: We are concerned with the techniques of computerized image analysis. Computer graphics, or the computerized production of images, is the inverse of computer vision: Graphics starts with world descriptions and produces images. Since graphics is so closely related to vision, some graphics techniques are indeed interesting to vision researchers (see chapter 2.4).

Vision is our most powerful sense. If we could endow machines with something like the power of sight, their actions and decision-making could be much more effective and efficient. Automatic navigation systems, industrial inspection, biomedical applications, consumer products, interactive systems, and a host of other areas are potential beneficiaries of breakthroughs in computer vision. Of course in a real system vision is purposive, working toward some particular goal. That means that vision is only a component of a larger system for reasoning and action. There are many hard problems yet to be solved in creating intelligent systems, even if the vision problem were overcome. Still, vision has always been a key problem in artificial intelligence (AI), and it is quite possible to make progress in vision without solving all other problems as well.

Despite our intimate association with them, our brains and minds still provide many of science's deepest and most elusive questions. Each generation applies the most powerful mechanisms it can conceive to try to describe and explain the mental functions of memory, cognition, and perception. Thus one of the currently most productive approaches to understanding mental activity and its underlying hardware is to make a computational model of the processing and then explore both its logical behavior and its implications for physical implementations. A computer program is an experimental artifact that can be used to explore theories of brain function, and the methods and representations it employs may have implications for our understanding of biological vision. The neurosciences are making great strides in describing brain structure, and there is increasing interest in relating structure to function. Thus the natural sciences and the sciences of the artificial are working together to understand general vision systems. Much has been learned, but we are a long way from knowing how to do general vision. The chapters in this volume detail aspects of the vision problem and indicate the range of issues that must be addressed.

A HISTORICAL PERSPECTIVE

The First Vision System.   Computer vision began in the mid 1960s with what today would be called a vision system that operated in the polyhedral or "blocksworld" domain (Roberts, 1965). The system started with a photographic image of a blocks scene of planar polyhedral shapes built of a small set of primitives that could be scaled, rotated, and combined by gluing. A scanning densitometer converted the photograph to an array of numbers corresponding to brightnesses. The numerical array was analyzed in several stages: Small "edge elements" were detected where the image changed brightness. These small edges were linked together into longer line segments that ideally corresponded with the images of straight edges in the polyhedral scene. The line segments were linked together at vertices that should correspond to the image of polyhedral corners. Rings of connected line segments formed polygons that delineated the blocks' faces in the image.

Topological analysis of the resulting line segments, vertices, and polygons allowed matching between the two-dimensional image and a computer-held data structure representing the three-dimensional polyhedral primitive building blocks. After matching, the program could infer how the scene was constructed from transformed and combined primitives. The final output was a line drawing of the scene from any desired viewpoint.

Besides its many technical contributions, Roberts's work provided a paradigm that in many ways still holds in computer vision: that of using a careful combination of local image evidence (e.g., edge location) and relational image evidence (e.g., how line segments touch) to make a progressive abstraction from the image signal into symbolic representations that can be used in practical jobs such as recognition or navigation.

Vision as Cognition.   After Roberts, vision systems continued to be built, but their performance seemed weak on an absolute scale, or even weak compared to the amount of work that went into them. Something was missing. One influential idea, favored also by cognitive psychologists, was that "high-level" (cognitive) processes were at the heart of vision, and that vision should be approached as some form of problem-solving (Ballard & Brown, 1982). This view has its points and also happened to fit in neatly with the economics of computing at the time—low-level vision processing was computationally very expensive. However, the cognitive vision approach faltered because automated symbolic reasoning proved to be very difficult, and because in vision, the input often does not correspond to expectation. Thus, new research directions arose.

Perception of Three-Dimensions from a Two-Dimensional Image.   The next major idea was to use physics and applied mathematics to determine the sorts of information available in an image and how it can be extracted (Horn, 1986). An important first question is how to retain and represent image information. In Volume 1, image information is usually represented as the gray-level in the image. Volume 2 presents more ideas for intermediate data representations. Chapter 2.1 discusses the representation of an image as a faceted surface, and chapter 2.2 considers the representation of an image as zero-crossings of an operator (which is something like a representation of the edges in an image).

The next step is computing "intrinsic images," or invariant physical scene parameters, from a potentially varying image signal. With general viewing conditions, the image of a scene can vary widely, while the physical scene itself, including the distance of its objects or their surface reflectance, remains the same. Understanding the physical parameters of the scene is a big step toward being able to make symbolic descriptions that can be used for tasks. By what knowledge and algorithms can the imaging process be inverted to yield a representation of the physical properties of the scene that produced the image? Particular forms of this question have been the most popular topics for computer vision research for the last decade, and have led to work on "vision modules" that might be incorporated into a complete image-understanding system. Usually these modules operate with minimal assumptions about the domain of the scene, and thus fit into a "low level" or "preattentive" role in a system. Usually research on low-level modules avoids the engineering and systems issues of an integrated system. Chapters 1.2 and 1.3 describe state-of-the-art work in extracting three-dimensional parameters from shading, stereo, and motion.

Biological and Computer Vision. Another important trend that started in the mid 1970s was to try to learn technical things about low-level computer vision from biological systems and, conversely, to try to make computational models to explain biological systems (Marr, 1982; Levine, 1985). Biological vision systems work very well compared to computer vision systems. This cross-fertilization between the neurosciences and computer sciences has been increasingly productive and promises to be a major force in the future of the field. Technology is advancing toward the goal of powerful parallel computers that can comfortably accommodate more brain-like models of computation. Chapters 2.2 and 2.3 are indicative of work at the interface between biological and computer systems.

Modern Vision Systems. Recently, in the past few years, another reaction has begun. The work on vision modules has been so productive of results that the community has turned a substantial part of its attention back to the problem of building integrated systems. This activity is resulting in autonomous land vehicles, robotic systems, and laboratory image-understanding systems. The work described in chapter 1.1 is an example of a large-scale integrated system. A system for recognizing objects must have a way to represent the objects, and one of the greatest challenges in "high-level" vision is to represent symbolically the everyday real-world objects of our visual world—objects with biological or manufactured shapes and with complex surface properties. Chapter 2.4 examines techniques for representing texture and shape that could be useful in an integrated system. Chapter 2.3 shows how a hierarchy of abstraction for polyhedral vision can be implemented with nets of neural-like simple computing units.

A FUNCTIONAL PERSPECTIVE

Another way to think about the chapters in this series is in terms of the functional components of a vision system. The organization of chapters is top-down, then bottom-up. Chapter 1.1 starts with a description of a modern vision system that is not only of considerable technical interest, but also provides an example vision system that may help the reader structure the content of the remaining chapters in the two volumes. Volume 1 then goes on in chapters 2 and 3 to concentrate on the extraction of three-dimensional physical parameters from two-dimensional images as part of early vision. Volume 2 moves from representations of the input image that are useful for further processing (chapters 1 and 2) to higher-level vision processes and three-dimensional representations (chapters 3 and 4).

Low-level Input Analysis and Image Representation.   The idea that the image can be used to suggest a few clues and then be discarded, leaving perception to cognitive levels, seems indefensible (Fodor, 1983). Chapters 2.1 and 2.2 deal explicitly with image representations. Chapter 2.2 deals with the vital question of the "natural scale" of a vision calculation: How can a system discover the proper spatial resolution in which to perform image analysis? Where is the meaningful signal in the image? Chapter 2.1 provides a scheme in which the original image information is preserved but also put into a form more accessible for later processing. Chapter 1.1 addresses these issues in the context of an integrated system.

Segmentation.   The problem of segmentation is related to the psychological phenomenon of figure-ground perception, or the perception of objecthood. Our natural and unconscious ability to see objects as unities and to delineate their boundaries has no easy implementation in a computer vision system. It is likely that biological systems use multiple sources of image information for figure-ground discrimination (motion, color, texture, and so on—see chapter 1.2). Segmentation is a hard problem that practical systems must solve. Most intrinsic image computations assume that segmentation of the scene into objects and background has been done. Certainly high-level vision (say recognition) usually assumes segmentation. Chapters 1.1, 1.3, 2.3, and 2.4 directly address the topic of segmentation.

Intrinsic Image Computations.   The purpose of these computations is to extract physical information about the scene from the image. The motivation is that the physical information will be less sensitive to irrelevant variations to which the image is prey (such as lighting effects), and thus will be a more reliable basis for practical decisions such as manipulation, navigation, or recognition. Chapters 1.2 and 1.3 are mainly concerned with intrinsic images calculation, using clues of shading, multiple cameras, and motion.

System Architecture. System architectures for vision are now being designed as part of several major projects in research centers around the country. Often the system is built around a "blackboard" that serves as communications medium, central representation, and sometimes as a form of autonomous inference or geometrical computing engine. In this volume, chapter 1 gives an explicit description of the detailed makeup of such a vision system. The neural architecture that could underlie vision and thinking in general is of course an important topic in the cognitive sciences. Chapter 2.3 outlines a hierarchy of abstractions implemented in a neural-like net of small processing units.

Hardware Architecture. There is much activity today in designing and building special-purpose hardware architectures. Low-level vision (like graphics and image processing) has long been a candidate for such work because of the simplicity and physical locality of many of the operations. Recently high-level vision, or cognitive processes in general, has influenced the development of computational models (chapter 2.3; Feldman, 1985) and actual computers (Hillis, 1986). Advances in the power and packaging of microcomputers have led to new general-purpose architectures involving many computers working in parallel. These and more special-purpose hardware architectures are very promising tools for advancing all levels of the computer vision problem. In this volume the hardware architecture issue is addressed in chapter 1.

REFERENCES

Ballard, D., & Brown, C. (1982). *Computer vision.* Englewood Cliffs, NJ: Prentice-Hall.

Feldman, J. A. Editor. (January–March 1985). *Cognitive Science 9,* 1, Special Issue on Connectionist Models.

Fodor, J. (1983). *The modularity of mind.* Cambridge, MA: MIT Press.

Hillis, D. (1985). *The connection machine.* Cambridge, MA: MIT Press.

Horn, B. K. P. (1986). *Robot vision.* Cambridge, MA: MIT Press.

Levine, M. (1985). *Vision in man and machine.* New York: McGraw-Hill.

Marr, D. (1982). *Vision.* San Francisco, CA: Freeman.

Pentland, A. P. (1986). *From pixels to predicates.* Norwood, NJ: Ablex.

Roberts, L. G. (1965). Machine perception of three-dimensional solids. In J. P. Tippet et al. (Eds.), *Optical and electro-optical information processing* (pp. 159–197). Cambridge, MA: MIT Press.

1 THE USE OF THE FACET MODEL AND THE TOPOGRAPHIC PRIMAL SKETCH IN IMAGE ANALYSIS

LINDA G. SHAPIRO
ROBERT M. HARALICK
University of Washington

TING-CHUEN PONG
University of Minnesota

INTRODUCTION

The *facet model* states that all processing of digital-image data has its final authoritative interpretation relative to what the processing does to the underlying gray-tone intensity surface. The digital image's pixel values are noisy sampled observations of the underlying surface. Thus, in order to do any processing, we must estimate this underlying surface at each pixel position. This requires a model that describes what the general form of the surface would be in the neighborhood of any pixel if there were no noise. To estimate the surface from the neighborhood around a pixel, then, amounts to estimating the free parameters of the general form. The processing that takes place is then defined in terms of the estimated parameters.

The topographic primal sketch (Haralick, Watson, & Laffey, 1983) is one possible way of representing the fundamental structure of a digital image in a rich and robust way. The basis of the topographic primal sketch is the classification and grouping of the underlying image-intensity surface patches according to the categories defined by monotonic, gray-tone invariant functions of directional derivatives. Examples of such categories are peak, pit, ridge, ravine, saddle, flat, and hillside. From this initial classification, categories can be grouped to obtain a rich, hierarchical, and structurally complete representation of the fundamental image structure. By contrast, representations of the fundamental image structure only involving edges or the primal sketch as described by Marr (1976) are impoverished in the sense that they are insufficient for unambiguous matching. They also do not have the required invariance with respect to monotonically increasing gray-tone transformations.

1

The facet approach can also be used in classical gradient-based edge detection, in image segmentation, as well as in determining the topographic primal sketch of an image. The following sections discuss the facet model for image-data specialized to the sloped facet case and its direct application to gradient-edge detection; the facet model concepts as they can apply to image segmentation, the definition of the topographic primal sketch and how the information it requires can all come from the facet-model estimates; and three-dimensional object surface-shape estimation based on the patterns of the topographic primal sketch.

THE FACET MODEL FOR IMAGE DATA

The commonly used general forms for the facet model include piecewise constant (flat facet model), piecewise linear (sloped facet model), piecewise quadratic, and piecewise cubic. In the flat model, each ideal fitting neighborhood in the image is constant in gray tone. In the sloped model, each ideal fitting neighborhood has a gray tone surface that is a sloped plane. Similarly, in the quadratic and cubic models, regions have gray tone surfaces that are quadratic and cubic surfaces, respectively.

Given a noisy defocused image, and assuming one of these models, the problem is to estimate the parameters of the underlying surface for a given neighborhood and estimate the variance of the noise. These estimates can then be used in a variety of ways: edge detection, line detection, corner detection, and segmentation. In this section we review the parameter estimation problem for the sloped facet model and illustrate its use in the classic gradient edge detector application.

Sloped Facet Parameter and Error Estimation

In this discussion we employ a least-squares procedure to estimate the parameters of the sloped facet model for a given rectangular neighborhood whose row index set is R and whose column index set is C. The facet parameter estimates are obtained for the central neighborhood of each pixel on the image. We assume that for each $(r, c) \in R \times C$, the image function g is modeled by

$$g(r, c) = \alpha r + \beta c + \gamma + \eta(r, c)$$

where η is a random variable indexed on $R \times C$, which represents noise. We will assume that η is noise having mean 0 and variance σ^2 and that the noise for any two pixels is independent.

The least-squares procedure determines an $\hat{\alpha}$, $\hat{\beta}$, and $\hat{\gamma}$, which minimize the sum of the squared differences between the fitted surface and the observed one:

$$\epsilon^2 = \sum_{r \in R} \sum_{c \in C} [\hat{\alpha}r + \hat{\beta}c + \hat{\gamma} - g(r, c)]^2.$$

Taking the partial derivatives of ϵ^2 and setting them to zero results in

$$\begin{pmatrix} \dfrac{\partial \epsilon^2}{\partial \hat{\alpha}} \\ \dfrac{\partial \epsilon^2}{\partial \hat{\beta}} \\ \dfrac{\partial \epsilon^2}{\partial \hat{\gamma}} \end{pmatrix} = 2 \sum_{r \in R} \sum_{c \in C} (\hat{\alpha}r + \hat{\beta}c + \hat{\gamma} - g(r, c)) \begin{pmatrix} r \\ c \\ 1 \end{pmatrix} = 0. \qquad (1)$$

Without loss of generality, we choose our coordinate system $R \times C$ so that the center of the neighborhood $R \times C$ has coordinates $(0, 0)$. When the number of rows and columns is odd, the center pixel, therefore, has coordinates $(0, 0)$. When the number of rows and columns is even, there is no pixel in the center but the point where the corners of the four central pixels meet has coordinates $(0, 0)$. In this case, pixel centers will have coordinates of an integer plus a half.

The symmetry in the chosen coordinate system leads to

$$\sum_{r \in R} r = 0 \text{ and } \sum_{c \in C} c = 0$$

Hence,

$$\sum_r \sum_c \hat{\alpha}r^2 = \sum_r \sum_c rg(r, c),$$

$$\sum_r \sum_c \hat{\beta}c^2 = \sum_r \sum_c cg(r, c),$$

$$\sum_r \sum_c \hat{\gamma} = \sum_r \sum_c g(r, c).$$

Solving for $\hat{\alpha}$, $\hat{\beta}$, and $\hat{\gamma}$ we obtain

$$\hat{\alpha} = \sum_r \sum_c rg(r, c)/ \sum_r \sum_c r^2,$$

$$\hat{\beta} = \sum_r \sum_c cg(r, c)/ \sum_r \sum_c c^2, \qquad (2)$$

$$\hat{\gamma} = \sum_r \sum_c g(r, c)/ \sum_r \sum_c 1.$$

Replacing $g(r, c)$ by $\alpha r + \beta c + \gamma + \eta(r, c)$ and simplifying the equations will allow us to explicitly see the dependence of $\hat{\alpha}$, $\hat{\beta}$, and $\hat{\gamma}$ on the noise. We obtain

$$\hat{\alpha} = \alpha + \left(\sum_r \sum_c r\eta(r, c) \,/\, \sum_r \sum_c r^2 \right),$$

$$\hat{\beta} = \beta + \left(\sum_r \sum_c c\eta(r, c) \,/\, \sum_r \sum_c c^2 \right),$$

$$\hat{\gamma} = \gamma + \left(\sum_r \sum_c \eta(r, c) \,/\, \sum_r \sum_c 1 \right).$$

From this it is apparent that $\hat{\alpha}$, $\hat{\beta}$, and $\hat{\eta}$ are unbiased estimators for α, β, and γ, respectively, and have variances

$$V[\hat{\alpha}] = \sigma^2 \,/\, \sum_r \sum_c r^2,$$

$$V[\hat{\beta}] = \sigma^2 \,/\, \sum_r \sum_c c^2,$$

$$V[\hat{\gamma}] = \sigma^2 \,/\, \sum_r \sum_c 1.$$

Normally, distributed noise implies that $\hat{\alpha}$, $\hat{\beta}$, and $\hat{\gamma}$ are normally distributed. The independence of the noise implies that $\hat{\alpha}$, $\hat{\beta}$, and $\hat{\gamma}$ are independent since they are normal and that

$$E[(\hat{\alpha} - \alpha)(\hat{\beta} - \beta)] = E[(\hat{\alpha} - \alpha)(\hat{\gamma} - \gamma)] = E[\hat{\beta} - \beta)(\hat{\gamma} - \gamma)] = 0$$

as a straightforward calculation shows.

Examining the squared error residual ϵ^2 we find that

$$\epsilon^2 = \sum_r \sum_c [(\hat{\alpha}r + \hat{\beta}c + \hat{\gamma}) - (\alpha r + \beta c + \gamma + \eta(r, c))]^2$$

$$= \sum_r \sum_c [(\hat{\alpha} - \alpha)^2 r^2 + (\hat{\beta} - \beta)^2 c^2 + (\hat{\gamma} - \gamma)^2 + \eta^2(r, c)$$

$$- 2(\hat{\alpha} - \alpha)r\eta(r, c) - 2(\hat{\beta} - \beta)c\eta(r, c) - 2(\hat{\gamma} - \gamma)\eta(r, c)].$$

Using the fact that

$$(\hat{\alpha} - \alpha) = \sum_r \sum_c r\eta(r, c) \,/\, \sum_r \sum_c r^2,$$

$$(\hat{\beta} - \beta) = \sum_r \sum_c c\eta(r, c) \,/\, \sum_r \sum_c c^2,$$

$$(\hat{\gamma} - \gamma) = \sum_r \epsilon R \sum_c \eta(r, c) \,/\, \sum_r \sum_c 1$$

we may substitute into the last three terms for ϵ^2 and obtain after simplification

$$\epsilon^2 = \sum_r \sum_c \eta^2(r, c) - (\hat{\alpha} - \alpha)^2 \sum_r \sum_c r^2 - (\hat{\beta} - \beta)^2 \sum_r \sum_c c^2$$

$$- (\hat{\gamma} - \gamma)^2 \sum_r \sum_c 1$$

Now notice that

$$\sum_r \sum_c \eta^2(r, c)$$

is the sum of the squares of

$$\sum_r \sum_c 1$$

independently distributed normal random variables. Hence,

$$\sum_r \sum_c \eta^2(r, c)/\sigma^2$$

is distributed as a chi-squared variate with

$$\sum_r \sum_c 1$$

degrees of freedom. Because $\hat{\alpha}$, $\hat{\beta}$, and $\hat{\gamma}$ are independent normals,

$$((\hat{\alpha} - \alpha)^2 \sum_r \sum_c r^2 + (\hat{\beta} - \beta)^2 \sum_r \sum_c c^2 + (\hat{\gamma} - \gamma)^2 \sum_r \sum_c 1)/\sigma^2$$

is distributed as a chi-squared variate with 3 degrees of freedom. Therefore, ϵ^2/σ^2 is distributed as a chi-squared variate with

$$\sum_r \sum_c 1 - 3$$

degrees of freedom. This means that $\epsilon^2/(\sum_r \sum_c 1 - 3)$ can be used as

an unbiased estimator for σ^2.

Gradient-Based Facet-Edge Detection

Suppose that our model of the ideal image is one where each object part is imaged as a region that is homogeneous in gray tone. In this case the boundary between object parts will manifest itself as jumps in gray level between successive pixels on the image. A small neighborhood on the image that can be divided into two parts by a line passing through the middle of the neighborhood and in which all the pixels on one side of the line have one gray level is a neighborhood in which the dividing line is indeed an edge line. When such a neighborhood is fitted with the sloped facet model, $\hat{\alpha}r + \hat{\beta}c + \hat{\gamma}$, a gradient magnitude of $\sqrt{\hat{\alpha}^2 + \hat{\beta}^2}$ will result. The gradient magnitude will be proportional to the gray-level jump. On the other hand if the region is entirely contained within a homogeneous area, then the true surface $\alpha r + \beta c + \gamma$ will have $\alpha = \beta = 0$ and the fitted, sloped facet model $\hat{\alpha}r + \hat{\beta}c + \hat{\gamma}$ will produce a value of $\sqrt{\hat{\alpha}^2 + \hat{\beta}^2}$ which is near zero. Hence, it is reasonable for edge detectors to use the estimated gradient magnitude $\sqrt{\hat{\alpha}^2 + \hat{\beta}^2}$ as the basis for edge detection. Such edge detectors are called "gradient based edge detectors." There are other kinds of edge detectors such as zero-crossing edge detectors. A discussion of how the facet model can be used to determine zero crossings of second directional derivatives as edges can be found in Haralick (1984).

The most interesting question in the use of the estimated gradient $\sqrt{\hat{\alpha}^2 + \hat{\beta}^2}$ as an edge detector is how large does the gradient have to be in order for it to be considered significantly different from 0. The discussion that answers this question begins by noting that $\hat{\alpha}$ has a normal distribution with mean α and variance $\sigma^2 / \sum_r \sum_c r^2$, that $\hat{\beta}$ has a normal distribution with mean β and variance $\sigma^2 / \sum_r \sum_c c^2$, and that $\hat{\alpha}$ and $\hat{\beta}$ are independent. Hence,

$$\frac{(\hat{\alpha} - \alpha)^2 \sum_r \sum_c r^2 + (\hat{\beta} - \beta)^2 \sum_r \sum_c c^2}{\sigma^2}$$

is distributed as a chi-square variate with 2 degrees of freedom. From this it follows that to test the hypothesis of no edge under the assumption that $\alpha = \beta = 0$, we use the statistic G

$$G = \frac{\hat{\alpha}^2 \sum_r \sum_c r^2 + \hat{\beta}^2 \sum_r \sum_c c^2}{\sigma^2}$$

which is distributed as a chi-squared variate with 2 degrees of freedom. If the statistic G has a high enough value, then we reject the hypothesis that there is no edge.

If the neighborhood used to estimate the facet is square, then

$$\sum_r \sum_c r^2 = \sum_r \sum_c c^2$$ so that the test statistic is a multiple of the estimated squared gradient magnitude $\hat{\alpha}^2 + \hat{\beta}^2$. Such an edge operator is the well known Prewitt edge operator. However, by knowing the conditional distribution given no edge, it becomes easier to choose a threshold. For example, suppose we want the edge detector to work with a controlled

false-alarm rate. The false-alarm rate is the conditional probability that the edge detector classifies a pixel as an edge given that the pixel is not an edge. Suppose the false-alarm rate is to be held to 1%. Then since $P(X_2^2 > 9.21) = .01$, the threshold we must use must be at least 9.21.

But to use this technique, we must know the noise variance σ^2. Fortunately we can obtain a good estimate of σ^2. Each neighborhood's normalized squared residual error,

$$\epsilon^2 / \left(\sum_r \sum_c 1 - 3 \right),$$

can constitute an estimator for σ^2. This estimator is available for each neighborhood of the image. Because there are usually large numbers (thousands) of pixels in the image, the average of $\epsilon^2 / (\sum_r \sum_c 1 - 3)$

taken over all the neighborhoods of the image is a very good and stable estimator of σ^2 if it can be assumed that the noise variance is the same in each neighborhood. If ϵ_n^2 represents the squared residential fitting error from the nth neighborhood, then we may use

$$\hat{\sigma}^2 = \frac{1}{N} \sum_{n=1}^{N} \epsilon_n^2 / \left(\sum_r \sum_c 1 - 3 \right)$$

in place of σ^2. Hence our test statistic G becomes

$$G = \frac{\hat{\alpha}^2 \sum_r \sum_c r^2 + \hat{\beta}^2 \sum_r \sum_c c^2}{\hat{\sigma}^2}$$

Under the hypothesis of no edge, G, being the ratio of two chi-squared statistics, would have an F distribution. But because the number of degrees of freedom of $\hat{\sigma}^2$ is so high, G has essentially a chi-squared distribution with two degrees of freedom. Thus if we wanted to detect edges and be assured that the false-alarm rate (the conditional probability of assigning a pixel as an edge given that it is not an edge) is less than ρ_0, we would use a threshold of θ_0 where $P(X_2^2 \geq \theta_0) = \rho_0$.

Figure 1.1a shows a controlled 100×100 image having a disk of diameter 63. The interior of this disk has gray level of 200. The background of the disk has gray level of 0. Independent Gaussian noise having mean zero and standard deviation of 40, 50, and 75 is added to the controlled image. The noisy images are shown in Figures 1.1b, 1.1c, and 1.1d, respectively.

A sloped facet model is fitted to each 5×5 neighborhood of each image and its $\hat{\alpha}$, $\hat{\beta}$, and ϵ^2 is computed. For the ideal image of Figure

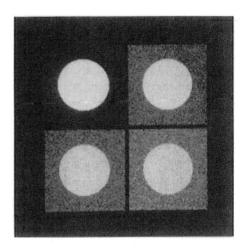

FIGURE 1.1. (a) (upper left) shows the controlled disk (background having value 0, disk having value 200) and noisy disks. (b) (the upper right) has noise standard deviation 40. (c) (the lower left) has noise standard deviation of 50. (d) (the lower right) has noise standard deviation of 75.

1.1a, the average squared residual fitting error ϵ^2, the average being taken over all neighborhoods, was 302.33. This corresponds to a standard deviation of about 17.4, which is 8.7% of the dynamic range of the image.

Obviously the fit will be perfect for all 5 × 5 neighborhoods that are entirely contained in the background or on the disk. The error must come from those neighborhoods that have some pixels from the background and some pixels from the disk. In these neighborhoods, the sloped fit is only an approximation. The neighborhood that has the worst fit is shown in Figure 1.2. The sloped fit there has an average

0	0	0	0	0
0	0	0	0	0
0	0	0	0	0
0	0	0	0	200
0	200	200	200	200

-64	-48	-32	-16	0
-28	-12	4	20	36
8	24	40	56	72
44	60	76	92	108
80	96	112	128	144

64	48	32	16	0
28	12	-4	-20	-36
-8	-24	-40	-56	-72
-44	-60	-76	-92	92
-80	104	88	72	56

observed neighborhood   slope fitted neighborhood   residual fitting errors

(a)   (b)   (c)

FIGURE 1.2. (a) illustrates a neighborhood for which the sloped fit is a relatively bad approximation. The fit produces an $\hat{\alpha} = 36$, $\hat{\beta} = 16$, and $\hat{\gamma} = 40$. The sloped fitted neighborhood is shown in (b), and the residual fitting errors are shown in (c). The total squared error from (c) is 82400. This divided by the degrees of freedom, $25 - 3 = 22$ yields an average squared error of 3746. The square root of 3746 is about 61.2, which represents the standard deviation of the residual fitting errors.

squared residual error of 3746. The standard deviation of fitting error is then 61.2, which represents 30.6% of the dynamic range.

For the noisy image of Figure 1.1b, the standard deviation of the fitting errors is $\sigma = 77.3$. This is just a little higher than the standard deviation of the noise because it takes into account the extent to which the data do not fit the model. In fact, assuming that the imperfectedness of the model and the noise are independent, we would expect to find a standard deviation of $\sqrt{17.4^4 + 75^2} = 77$, which is close to the 77.3 measured.

Figure 1.3a shows edges obtained when the statistic G computed on the ideal image of Figure 1.1a is thresholded at the value 120. Since $\hat{\sigma}^2 = 302.33$ and $\sum_r \sum_c r^2 = \sum_r \sum_c c^2 = 50$, this corresponds to selecting all neighborhoods having slopes greater than 26.94. Figure 1.3b, c, and d show the edges obtained when a 5×5 sloped facet model is employed and when the statistic G computed from each neighborhood of the noisy image of Figure 1.1d is thresholded at 4, 8, and 11. Since $\hat{\sigma}^2 = 5975.3$ for the noisy image, a threshold of 8 corresponds to selecting all neighborhoods having slopes greater than 30.92. These thresholds of 4, 8, and 11 guarantee (under the conditions of independent Gaussian noise) that the false alarm rates must be less than .1353, .01832, and .0041, respectively. The observed false-alarm rates for these thresholds are .1231, .0164, and .0042, respectively. The corresponding misdetection rates are .0205, .0820, and .1598.

As just mentioned, corresponding to each possible threshold is a false alarm rate and a misdetection rate. The misdetection rate is the conditional probability that a pixel is assigned "no edge" given that it is actually an "edge" pixel. One way to characterize the performance of an edge detector is to plot its false-alarm rate as a function of misdetection rate in a controlled experiment. Such a plot is called an "operating curve." Figure 1.4 shows two operating curves for the sloped facet edge detector.

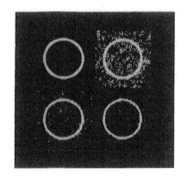

FIGURE 1.3. (a) (upper left) shows edges obtained when the statistic G computed using 5×5 neighborhoods on the ideal image of (a) is thresholded at the value 120. (b) (upper right) shows the edges obtained when the statistic G computed using 5×5 neighborhoods on the noisy image of (d) is thresholded at the value 4. (c) (lower left) and (d) (lower right) show thresholds of 8 and 11.

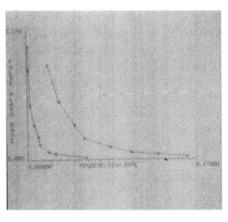

FIGURE 1.4. shows two operating curves for the 5 × 5 slope-facet gradient edge detector. The higher one corresponds to a noisy disk with noise standard deviation of 75 and the upper one corresponds to a noisy disk with noise standard deviation of 50.

The higher one corresponds to a noisy disk with noise standard deviation 75. The lower one corresponds to a noisy disk with noise standard deviation 50.

If it cannot be assumed that the noise variance is the same in each neighborhood, then the estimator using the average of the normalized squared residual errors for σ^2 is not proper. In this case, the local $\epsilon^2/(\sum_r \sum_c 1 - 3)$ can be used as an estimate of the variance in each neighborhood. However, this estimate is not as stable. It does have a higher variance than the estimate based on the average of the local variances, and it has a much lower number of degrees of freedom. Here, to test the hypothesis of no edge for the flat-world assumption, $\alpha = \beta = 0$, we use the ratio

$$F = \left(\left(\hat{\alpha}^2 \sum_r \sum_c r^2 + \hat{\beta}^2 \sum_r \sum_c c^2 \right) / 2 \right) \Big/ \left(\epsilon^2 / \left(\sum_r \sum_c 1 - 3 \right) \right),$$

which has an F distribution with

$$\left(2, \sum_r \sum_c 1 - 3 \right)$$

degrees of freedom and reject the hypothesis for large values of F.

Again notice that F may be regarded as a significance or reliability measure associated with the existence of a nonzero sloped region in the domain $R \times C$. It is essentially proportional to the squared gradient of the region normalized by

$$\epsilon^2 / \left(\sum_r \sum_c 1 - 3 \right)$$

which is a random variable whose expected value is σ^2, the variance of the noise.

EXAMPLE: Consider the following 3 × 3 region:

3	5	9
4	7	7
0	3	7

Then $\hat{\alpha} = -1.17$, $\hat{\beta} = 2.67$, and $\hat{\gamma} = 5.00$. The estimated gray-tone surface is given by $\hat{\alpha}r + \hat{\beta}r + \hat{\gamma}$ and is

3.50	6.16	8.83
2.33	5.00	7.67
1.17	3.83	6.50

The difference between the estimated and the observed surface is the error and it is

0.50	1.17	−0.17
−1.67	−2.00	0.67
1.17	0.83	−0.50

From this we can compute the squared error $\epsilon^2 = 11.19$. The F statistic is then

$$\frac{[(-1.17)^2 \cdot 6 + (2.67)^2 \cdot 6]/2}{11.19/6} = 13.67.$$

If we were compelled to make a hard decision about the significance of the observed slope in the given 3 × 3 region, we would probably call it a nonzero sloped region, since the probability of a region with true zero slope giving an $F_{2,6}$ statistic of value less than 10.6 is 0.99. 13.67 is greater than 10.6, so we are assured that the probability of calling the region a nonzero sloped region when it is in fact a zero sloped region is

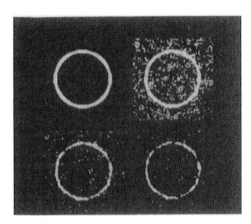

FIGURE 1.5. The edges obtained under a 5 × 5 sloped-facet model using the F statistic. (a) (upper left) shows the thresholded F statistic from the noiseless disk. (b) (upper right) shows the F statistic image of the noisy disk of (d) (noise standard deviation 75) thresholded at 2.32. (c) (lower left) and (d) (lower right) use thresholds of 5.04 and 7.06.

much less than 1%. The statistically oriented reader will recognize the test as a 1% significance level test.

Figure 1.5 shows the edges obtained when a 5 × 5 sloped facet model is employed and when the statistic F computed from each neighborhood of the noisy image of Figure 1.1d is thresholded at 2.32, 5.04, and 7.06. These thresholds should guarantee (under conditions of independent Gaussian noise) that the false-alarm rates are less than .1218, .0158, and .0042, respectively. These thresholds produce observed false-alarm rates of .1236, .0165, and .0042, indicating these were small but negligible departures from the independent Gaussian assumptions. Since these observed false-alarm rates are almost identical to the observed false-alarm rates from the Chi-square tests of Figure 1.3, we may compare the corresponding misidentification rates. The observed misidentification rates for the F test were .0792, .3224, and .5137, all of which are considerably higher than the observed misidentification of the corresponding Chi-square tests. It is obvious from a comparison of these images that the edge noise is worse in the F tests compared to the Chi-square tests. All this is to be expected because the noise meets the assumption of the Chi-square test, and the more one is able to correctly assume about reality, the better the results ought to be when the appropriate statistical test is used.

SEGMENTATION USING THE FACET MODEL

The facet model allows each neighborhood of an image to be thought of as a piecewise linear (or constant or quadratic or cubic) surface. One way in which this facet representation is useful is for image segmentation. There are a variety of approaches. We describe here one approach to determine an initial segmentation and a second approach to merge regions of an initial segmentation. The first approach was originally discussed in Haralick and Shapiro (1985) and the second approach in Pong, Shapiro, Watson, & Haralick (1984).

Determining an Initial Segmentation

To find regions of a segmentation we must look for connected sets of resolution cells that are surely on the same gray-tone intensity surface. To find edges we must look for pairs of adjacent regions having significantly different surfaces. To do segmentation, we must do both. This suggests the following hybrid linkage-combination technique. Select an appropriate-sized neighborhood. Run this neighborhood over the image. For each location where the neighborhood may be placed on the image, determine the parameters of a sloped facet-surface fit as well as the ϵ^2 error of the fit. Use this information to create an edge image.

Now perform a region-growing algorithm on the nonedge pixels. This means that no linking is performed across edge pixels, and edge pixels are not assigned to any region. Edges are barriers to the region-growing process. Such a region-growing technique is described in Haralick and Shapiro (1985). The image is scanned in usual raster-scan order: left to right and top to bottom. Each current pixel then neighbors four pixels (for 8-connectivity), which have been previously scanned. If a previously scanned pixel is not an edge pixel then it belongs to some already existing, but not necessarily completed, region segment. This not necessarily completed region segment has a mean and variance. If the value of the current pixel is not significantly different from the mean of such a neighboring region segment, the pixel is added to the segment and the mean and variance of the segment is updated. Here, significantly different means by a T test.

If there is more than one region that is close enough, then the test pixel is added to the closest region. If the means of any two competing neighboring regions are each close enough to the current pixel value and close enough to each other, then the two regions are merged and the pixel is added to the merged regions. If no neighboring region has its mean close enough, then a new segment is established containing the current pixel and having a mean value that is the value of the current pixel.

We now define the T test precisely. Let R be a segment containing N pixels and whose pixels neighbor the current pixel. The mean $\bar{X}$ and the scatter S^2 of region R are defined by

$$X = \frac{1}{N} \sum_{(r,c)\in R} I(r, c)$$

$$S^2 = \sum_{(r,c)\in R} (I(r, c) - X)^2$$

Let the current pixel have the value y.

Under the assumption that all the pixels in R and the test pixel y are independent and identically distributed normals, the statistic

$$T = \left[\frac{(N - 1)N}{(N + 1)}(y - \bar{X})^2/S^2 \right]^{1/2}$$

has a T_{N-1} distribution. If T is small enough, y is added to region R, and the mean and scatter are updated using y. The new mean and scatter are given by

$$\bar{X}_{new} \leftarrow (N\,\bar{X}_{old} + y) / (N + 1)$$

and

$$S^2_{new} \leftarrow S^2_{old} + (y - \bar{X}) + N(\bar{X}_{new} - \bar{X}_{old})^2.$$

If T is too high, the value y is not likely to have arisen from the population of pixels in R. If y is different from all of its neighboring regions then it begins its own region. A slightly stricter linking criterion can require that not only must y be close enough to the mean of the neighboring regions, but that a neighboring pixel in that region must have a close enough value to y. This combines a centroid linkage and single-linkage criterion.

To give a precise meaning to the notion of too high a difference, we use an α level statistical significance test. The fraction α represents the probability that a T statistic with $N - 1$ degrees of freedom will exceed the value $t_{N-1}(\alpha)$. If the observed T is larger than $t_{N-1}(\alpha)$, then we declare the difference to be significant. If the pixel and the segment really come from the same population, the probability that the test provides an incorrect answer is α.

The significance level α is a user-provided parameter. The value of $t_{N-1}(\alpha)$ is higher for small degrees of freedom and lower for larger degrees of freedom. Thus, region scatters considered to be equal, the

larger a region is, the closer the value of a pixel has to be to the mean of
that region in order to be merged with that region.

Note that all regions initially begin as one pixel in size. To avoid the
problem of division by 0 (for S^2 is necessarily 0 for 1-pixel regions and 0
for regions having identically valued pixels), a small positive constant can
be added to S^2. One convenient way of determining the constant is to
decide on a prior variance $V_0 > 0$ and an initial segment size N_0. The
initial scatter for a new 1-pixel region is then given by $N_0 V_0$ and the new
initial region size is given by N_0. This mechanism keeps the degrees of
freedom of the T-statistic high enough so that a significant difference is
not the huge difference required for a T-statistic with a small number of
degrees of freedom.

Region Merging

The problem with using the initial segmentation just described as input
to a higher-level algorithm attempting to recognize objects in the scene is
that the regions are too small to be meaningful. This problem motivated
us to develop a region-growing scheme that starts with an initial segmentation and produces a new segmentation having larger, hopefully more
useful regions. Such a procedure could be repeated any number of times
producing a sequence of rougher and rougher segmentations. The final
result or the entire sequence of segmentations might prove useful to a
higher-level process.

Once an initial segmentation has been produced, (either by the method previously described or some alternate method) properties of the
initial regions are computed. These resulting property vectors are used
in the region-merging process. Among the properties measured for each
region, we have used the following in our experiments.

1. *Size* is simply the number of pixels in a region.
2. *Mean gray level* is the average gray-level intensity in a region.
3. *Elongation* is a measure of the shape of a figure. It is obtained by
   finding the covariance matrix M of the distribution of $(r - \bar{r}, c - \bar{c})$
   where (r, c) represents the coordinates of a pixel in region R, and
   $(\bar{r}, \bar{c})$ is the center of mass of R.

The matrix M is defined by

$$
M = \begin{pmatrix} \sum_{(r,c) \in R} (r - \bar{r})^2 & \sum_{(r,c) \in R} (r - \bar{r}) * (c - \bar{c}) \\ \sum_{(r,c) \in R} (c - \bar{c}) * (r - \bar{r}) & \sum_{(r,c) \in R} (c - \bar{c})^2 \end{pmatrix}
$$

and $(\bar{r}, \bar{c})$ for a region R is given by

$$\bar{r} = 1/|R|i \sum_{(r,c)\epsilon R} r \text{ and } \bar{c} = 1/|R| \sum_{(r,c)\epsilon R} c.$$

Two eigenvalues can be obtained from the matrix M. Elongation is defined as the ratio of the larger eigenvalue to the smaller.

Besides the property vector for each region, a region adjacency graph that gives topological information about the regions is also generated for a segmented image. Two regions $R1$ and $R2$ are said to be *adjacent* for a segmented image if there exists some pixel in $R1$ such that its 4(8)-neighborhood intersects $R2$. The region adjacency graph has nodes corresponding to regions and edges that connect together nodes representing adjacent regions.

Now we are ready to describe the merging process. Suppose an initial segmentation is given. We group regions using an iterative scheme. Each region is represented by a property vector. At each iteration, the property vector of a region can be replaced by some function of the property vectors of the regions constituting its best fitting neighborhood of regions, a concept to be soon defined. After convergence of the iterative procedure, connected sets of regions with similar revised property vectors become the new regions.

The merging algorithm has two phases. In phase 1 the properties of each region are updated based upon the properties of its region neighborhood. In phase 2 adjacent regions that have similar updated property values are merged together. We now describe the algorithm and its several variations in detail.

Phase I

Suppose that the image-spatial domain has been divided into N non-overlapping regions labeled $r(1), \ldots, r(N)$ with corresponding property vectors $p^k(1), \ldots, p^k(N)$ at the kth iteration. Define the neighborhood of region r, $NBD(r)$, by

$$NBD(r) = \{r' \mid \text{region } r' \text{ is adjacent to region } r\}.$$

Suppose for some region r that $NBD(r) = \{r'(1), \ldots, r'(m)\}$. Then because neighboring is symmetric, r is also an element of $NBD(r'(j))$ for $j = 1, \ldots, m$. Thus region r participates in m different neighborhoods.

For a given neighborhood X, we define the variance of X, $var(X)$, by

$$var(X) = \sum_{r(j)\epsilon X} \| (p(j) - \bar{p}(X)) \|^2 /(|X| - 1)$$

where $\bar{p}(X)$ is the mean property vector of X, and $|X|$ is the cardinality of X. The best-fitting neighborhood of region r, $BF(r)$, is that one of the m neighborhoods it participates in that has lowest variance. Thus

$$BF(r) = X*$$

where $X* = NBD(r')$ for some $r' \in NBD(r)$ and

$$\text{var}(X) = \min_{r' \in NBD(r)} \text{var}(NBD(r')).$$

An iteration of the region growing algorithm starts with the set of regions $r(1), \ldots, r(N)$, with property vectors $p^k(1), \ldots, p^k(N)$, and replaces the property vector of each region by some function of the property vectors of its best-fitting neighborhood. That is,

$$p^{k+1}(n) = f(BF^k(r(n))), n = 1, \ldots, N$$

where, of course, $BF^k(r(n))$ depends on $p^k(n)$. The process is repeated until it reaches or approaches a fixed point. Then in phase 2, adjacent regions with identical or near identical property vectors are merged to form a new set of regions.

Phase 2

Suppose that we start with a segmented image whose regions are labeled $r^i(1), \ldots r^i(N_i)$. If the process for these regions reaches a fixed point at some iteration, we merge them to form a new set of regions $r^{i+1}(1), \ldots, r^{i+1}(N_{i+1})$ in the following way.

Construct a graph in which the nodes are the regions. Link together all pairs of regions (a) that are adjacent and (b) whose updated property vectors are close enough. Determine the connected components of the resulting graph. Each connected component corresponds to a subset of regions whose union constitutes one of the merged regions for the next cycle. For an image with T regions, let $n(i)$ be the number of neighbors for region i. Then the number of computations for an iteration of this algorithm is proportional to $n(1) + n(2) + \cdots + n(T)$, which gives a computational complexity $O(T \times \bar{n})$, where $\bar{n}$ is the average number of neighboring regions for all the regions. In most cases $\bar{n} \ll T$, which makes this an efficient algorithm.

Updating the Property Vectors

One of the most important steps in this region-growing algorithm is to update the property vector for each region. Three different alternatives have been tried. The first method uses the mean property vector of its best-fitting neighborhood. At iteration k, the updated property vector of a region R is given by

$$p^{k+1}(R) = \bar{p}(R*)$$

where $R* = BF(R)$. Extensions of the theorem for the flat-facet model in (Haralick & Watson, 1981) guarantee the convergence of this method.

The second way of updating the property vector of a region is to make it take on the original property vector of the region that defines the best-fitting neighborhood. That is, instead of using $p^{k+1}(R) = \bar{p}(R*)$ as in method (1), the property vector is updated by

$$p^{k+1}(R) = p^k(S)$$

where $NBD(S) = BF(R)$. Results showed that the rate of merging by this method is faster than the first. But unfortunately, this method shows oscillatory behavior for some images; it does not always lead to a fixed point.

The third alternative is to calculate the mean by weighting the property vectors of a neighborhood by their region sizes. Our results show that the first approach, using the mean property vector, is the most reliable method.

Thresholded Flat-Facet Iteration

The updating schemes described in the previous section recompute the property vector of every region at each iteration. To prevent inaccurate segmentation due to property vectors changing too much, we need to inhibit the updating if the new property vector of a region is too different from the original one. To accomplish this, the idea of a thresholded flat-facet iteration is introduced. For a flat-facet iteration with threshold e, the updated property vector of a region R is given by

$$p^{k+1}(R) = p^k(R), \qquad \text{if } \|\bar{p}(R*) - p^k(R)\| > e$$

$$= \bar{p}(R*), \text{ otherwise.}$$

The convergence of the flat facet iteration is guaranteed (Haralick & Watson, 1981). The proof that the *thresholded* flat-facet iteration also converges was given in Pong, Shapiro, & Haralick (1985).

To illustrate the region-merging technique, we begin with a busy image (Figure 1.6a) and an equally busy initial segmentation (Figure 1.6b). Figure 1.7a shows the segmentation obtained after one iteration of region merging, using only the gray-tone property and employing the first approach to updating the property vectors. After only one iteration, some order begins to appear in the cluttered segmentation. Figure 1.7.b shows the segmentation obtained after two iterations: A few meaningful

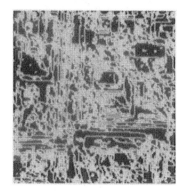

FIGURE 1.6. (a) shows an aerial image of buildings. (b) shows its initial segmentation using the techniques just described.

a

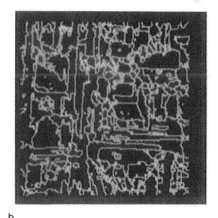

b

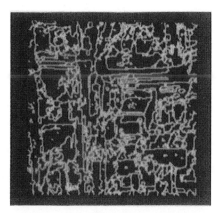

c

FIGURE 1.7. (a) shows the segmentation after one iteration of merging the regions of the segmentation of (b). (b) shows the resulting segmentation after two iterations. (c) shows the resulting segmentation after five iterations.

structures, such as streets and buildings, are now showing up. Figure 1.7c shows the segmentation obtained after five iterations. More merging has taken place and there are more meaningful regions to work with. Of course, we must remember that this is a blind, bottom-up segmentation technique. Unless it is used with a knowledge-based system that understands the semantics of some of the variations in gray tone of the original image, we cannot expect such a system to segment into meaningful objects.

THE TOPOGRAPHIC PRIMAL SKETCH

Our classification approach is based on the estimation of the first- and second-order directional derivatives. In two dimensions, the rate of change of a function f depends on direction. We denote the directional derivative of F at the point (r, c) in the direction of θ by $f'_\theta(r,c)$. It is defined as

$$f'_\theta(r, c) = \lim_{h \to 0} \frac{f(r + h^* \sin \theta, c + h^* \cos \theta) - f(r, c)}{h}$$

The direction angle θ is the clockwise angle from the column axis. It follows directly from this definition that

$$f'_\theta(r, c) = \frac{\partial f}{\partial r} (r, c) * \sin\theta + \frac{\partial f}{\partial c} (r, c) * \cos\theta.$$

We denote the second derivative of f at the point (r, c) in the direction θ by $f''_\theta(r, c)$, and it follows that

$$f''_\theta = \frac{\partial^2 f}{\partial r^2} * \sin^2 \theta + 2 * \frac{\partial f}{\partial r \, \partial c} * \sin \theta * \cos \theta + \frac{\partial f}{\partial c^2} * \cos^2 \theta.$$

The *gradient* of f is a vector whose magnitude,

$$\left(\left(\frac{\partial f}{\partial r} \right)^2 + \left(\frac{\partial f}{\partial c} \right)^2 \right)^{1/2}$$

at a given point (r, c) is the maximum rate of change of f at that point, and whose direction,

$$\tan^{-1} \left(\frac{\frac{\partial f}{\partial r}}{\frac{\partial f}{\partial c}} \right)$$

is the direction in which the surface has the greatest rate of change.

The Mathematical Properties

We will use the following notation to describe the mathematical properties of our various topographic categories for continuous surfaces. Let

∇f = gradient vector of a function f;

$\|\nabla f\|$ = gradient magnitude;

$\omega^{(1)}$ = unit vector in direction in which second directional derivativehas greatest magnitude;

$\omega^{(2)}$ = unit vector orthogonal to $\omega^{(1)}$;

λ_1 = value of second directional derivative in the direction $\omega^{(1)}$;

λ_2 = value of second directional derivative in the direction of $\omega^{(2)}$;

$\nabla f \cdot \omega^{(1)}$ = value of first directional derivative in the direction of $\omega^{(1)}$; and

$\nabla f \cdot \omega^{(2)}$ = value of first directional derivative in the direction of $\omega^{(2)}$.

Without loss of generality, we assume $|\lambda_1| \geq |\lambda_2|$.

Each type of topographic structure in our classification scheme is defined in terms of the aforementioned quantities. In order to calculate these values, the first- and second-order partials with respect to r and c need to be approximated. These five partials are as follows:

$$\partial f/\partial r, \ \partial f/\partial c, \ \partial^2 f/\partial r^2, \ \partial^2 f/\partial c^2, \ \partial^2 f/\partial r \, \partial c.$$

The gradient vector is simply $(\partial f/\partial r, \ \partial f/\partial c)$. The second directional derivatives may be calculated by forming the *Hessian* where the Hessian is a 2×2 matrix defined as

$$H = \begin{vmatrix} \partial^2 f/\partial r^2 & \partial^2 f/\partial r \, \partial c \\ \partial^2 f/\partial c \, \partial r & \partial^2 f/\partial c^2 \end{vmatrix}$$

Hessian matrices are used extensively in nonlinear programming. Only three parameters are required to determine the Hessian matrix H, since the order of differentiation of the cross partials may be interchanged. That is,

$$\partial^2 f/\partial r \, \partial c = \partial^2 f/\partial c \, \partial r.$$

The eigenvalues of the Hessian are the values of the extrema of the second-directional derivative, and their associated eigenvectors are the directions in which the second-directional derivative is extremized. This can easily be seen by rewriting f''_θ as the quadratic form

$$f''_\theta = (\sin \theta \cos \theta) * H * \begin{vmatrix} \sin\theta \\ \cos\theta \end{vmatrix}.$$

Thus

$$H\omega^{(1)} = \lambda_1\omega^{(1)}, \text{ and } H\omega^{(2)} = \lambda_2\omega^{(2)}.$$

Furthermore, the two directions represented by eigenvectors are orthogonal to one another. Since H is a 2×2 symmetric matrix, calculation of the eigenvalues and eigenvectors can be done efficiently and accurately using the method of Rutishauser. We may obtain the values of the first-directional derivative by simply taking the dot product of the gradient with the appropriate eigenvector:

$$\nabla f \cdot \omega^{(1)}$$

$$\nabla f \cdot \omega^{(2)}.$$

There is a direct relationship between the eigenvalues λ_1 and λ_2 and curvature in the directions $\omega^{(1)}$ and $\omega^{(2)}$: When the first-directional derivative $\nabla f \cdot \omega^{(1)} = 0$, then $\lambda_1/(1 + (\nabla f \cdot \nabla f))^{3/2}$ is the curvature in the direction $\omega^{(1)}$, $i = 1$ or 2.

Having the gradient magnitude and direction and the eigenvalues and eigenvectors of the Hessian, we can describe the topographic classification scheme. A peak occurs where there is a local maxima in all directions. In other words, we are on a peak if, no matter what direction we look in, we see no point that is as high as the one we are on. The curvature is downward in all directions. At a peak, the gradient is zero, and the second-directional derivative is negative in all directions. To test whether the second-directional derivative is negative in all directions, we just have to examine the value of the second-directional derivative in the directions that make it smallest and largest. A point is therefore classified as a peak if it satisfied the following conditions:

$$\|\nabla f\| = 0, \lambda_1 < 0, \lambda_2 < 0.$$

A pit is identical to a peak except that it is a local minima in all directions rather than a local maxima. At a pit the gradient is zero, and the second-directional derivative is positive in all directions. A point is classified as a pit if it satisfies the following conditions:

$$\|\nabla f\| = 0, \lambda_1 > 0, \lambda_2 > 0.$$

Ridge

A ridge occurs on a ridge-line, a curve consisting of a series of ridge points. As we walk along the ridge-line, the points to the right and left of us are lower than the ones we are on. Furthermore, the ridge-line may be flat, slope upward, slope downward, curve upward, or curve downward. A ridge occurs where there is a local maximum in one direction. Therefore, it must have negative second-directional derivative in the direction across the ridge and also a zero first-directional derivative in that same direction. The direction in which the local maximum occurs may correspond to either of the directions in which the curvature is "extremized," since the ridge itself may be curved. For nonflat ridges, this leads to the following first two cases for ridge characterization. If the ridge is flat, then the ridge-line is horizontal and the gradient along it is zero. This corresponds to the third case. The defining characteristic is that the second-directional derivative in the direction of the ridge-line is zero, while the second-directional derivative across the ridge-line is negative. A point is therefore classified as a ridge if it satisfies any one of the following three sets of conditions:

$$\|\nabla f\| \neq 0, \ \lambda_1 < 0, \ \nabla f \cdot \omega^{(1)} = 0$$

or

$$\|\nabla f\| \neq 0, \ \lambda_2 < 0, \ \nabla f \cdot \omega^{(2)} = 0$$

or

$$\|\nabla f\| = 0, \ \lambda_1 < 0, \ \lambda_2 = 0.$$

A geometric way of thinking about the definition for ridge is to realize that the condition $\nabla f \cdot \omega^{(1)} = 0$ means that the gradient direction (which is defined for nonzero gradients) is orthogonal to the direction $\omega^{(1)}$ of extremized curvature.

Ravine

A ravine (valley) is identical to a ridge except that it is a local minimum (rather than maximum) in one direction. As we walk along the ravine-line, the points to the right and left of us are higher than the one we are on. A point is classified as a ravine if it satisfies any one of the following three sets of conditions:

$$\|\nabla f\| \neq 0, \ \lambda_1 > 0, \ \nabla f \cdot \omega^{(1)} = 0$$

or

$$\|\nabla f\| \neq 0, \ \lambda_2 > 0, \ \nabla f \cdot \omega^{(2)} = 0$$

or

$$\|\nabla f\| = 0, \lambda_1 > 0, \lambda_2 = 0.$$

Saddle

A saddle occurs where there is a local maximum in one direction and a local minimum in a perpendicular direction. A saddle must therefore have positive curvature in one direction and negative curvature in a perpendicular direction. At a saddle, the gradient magnitude must be zero and the extrema of the second-directional derivative must have opposite signs. A point is classified as a saddle if it satisfies the following conditions:

$$\|\nabla f\| = 0, \lambda_1 * \lambda_2 < 0.$$

Flat

A flat is a simple, horizontal surface. It, therefore, must have zero gradient and no curvature. A point is classified as a flat if it satisfies the following conditions:

$$\|\nabla f\| = 0, \lambda_1 = 0, \lambda_2 = 0.$$

Given that the aforementioned conditions are true, a flat may be further classified as a *foot* or *shoulder*. A foot occurs at that point where the flat just begins to turn up into a hill. At this point, the third-directional derivative in the direction toward the hill will be nonzero, and the surface increases in this direction. The shoulder is an analogous case and occurs where the flat is ending and turning down into a hill. At this point, the maximum magnitude of the third-directional derivative is nonzero, and the surface decreases in the direction toward the hill. If the third-directional derivative is zero in all directions, then we are in a flat, not near a hill. Thus a flat may be further qualified as being a foot or shoulder, or not qualified at all.

Hillside

A hillside point is anything not covered by the previous categories. It has a nonzero gradient and no strict extrema in the directions of maximum and minimum second-directional derivative. If the hill is simply a tilted flat (i.e., has constant gradient), we call it a "slope." If its curvature is positive (upward), we call it a "convex hill." If its curvature is negative (downward), we call it a "concave hill." If the curvature is up in one direction and down in a perpendicular direction, we call it a "saddle hill."

A point on a hillside is an "inflection point" if it has a zero-crossing of the second-directional derivative taken in the direction of the gradient. The inflection-point class is the same as the "step edge" defined by Haralick (1984) who classifies a pixel as a step edge if there is some point in the pixel's area having a negatively sloped zero-crossing of the second-directional derivative taken in the direction of the gradient.

To determine whether a point is a hillside, we just take the complement of the disjunction of the conditions given for all the previous classes. Thus, if there is no curvature, then the gradient must be nonzero. If there is curvature, then the point must not be a relative extremum. Therefore, a point is classified as a hillside if all three sets of the following conditions are true ($'\rightarrow'$ represents the operation of logical implication):

$$\lambda_1 = \lambda_2 = 0 \rightarrow \|\nabla f\| \neq 0,$$

and

$$\lambda_1 \neq 0 \rightarrow \nabla f \cdot \omega^{(1)} \neq 0,$$

and

$$\lambda_2 \neq 0 \rightarrow \nabla f \cdot \omega^{(2)} \neq 0.$$

Rewritten as a disjunction of clauses rather than a conjunction of clauses, a point is classified as a hillside if any one of the following four sets of conditions are true:

$$\nabla f \cdot \omega^{(1)} \neq 0, \nabla f \cdot \omega^{(2)} \neq 0$$

or

$$\nabla f \cdot \omega^{(1)} \neq 0, \lambda_2 = 0$$

or

$$\nabla f \cdot \omega^{(2)} \neq 0, \lambda_1 = 0$$

or

$$\|\nabla f\| \neq 0, \lambda_1 = 0, \lambda_2 = 0.$$

We can differentiate between different classes of hillsides by the values of the second-directional derivative. The distinction can be made as follows:

Slope	if $\lambda_1 = \lambda_2 = 0$
Convex	if $\lambda_1 >= \lambda_2 >= 0, \lambda_1 \neq 0$
Concave	if $\lambda_1 <= \lambda_2 <= 0, \lambda_1 \neq 0$
Saddlehill	if $\lambda_1 * \lambda < 0$

A slope, convex, concave, or saddle hill is classified as an inflection point if there is a zero-crossing of the second-directional derivative in the direction of maximum first-directional derivative (i.e., the gradient).

Summary of the Topographic Categories

A summary of the mathematical properties of our topographic struc tures on continuous surfaces can be found in Table 1.1. The table exhaustively defines the topographic classes by their gradient magnitude, second-directional derivative extrema values, and the first-directional derivatives taken in the directions that extremize second-directional derivatives. Each entry in the table is either 0, +, −, or ∗. The 0 means not significantly different from zero on the positive side; − means significantly different from zero on the negative side, and ∗ means it does not matter. The label "Cannot occur" means that it is impossible for the gradient to be nonzero and the first-directional derivative to be zero in two orthogonal directions.

From Table 1.1 one can see that our classification scheme is complete. All possible combinations of first and second-directional derivatives have a corresponding entry in the table. Each topographic category has a set of mathematical properties that uniquely determines it.

TABLE 1.1
Mathematical Properties of Topographic
Structures

$\|\nabla f\|$	λ_1	λ_2	$\nabla f \cdot w^{(1)}$	$\nabla f \cdot w^{(2)}$	Label
0	−	−	0	0	Peak
0	−	0	0	0	Ridge
0	−	+	0	0	Saddle
0	0	0	0	0	Flat
0	+	−	0	0	Saddle
0	+	0	0	0	Ravine
0	+	+	0	0	Pit
+	−	−	−, +	−, +	Hillside
+	−	∗	0	∗	Ridge
+	∗	−	∗	0	Ridge
+	−	0	−, +	∗	Hillside
+	−	+	−, +	−, +	Hillside
+	0	0	∗	∗	Hillside
+	+	−	−, +	−, +	Hillside
+	+	0	−, +	∗	Hillside
+	+	∗	0	∗	Ravine
+	∗	+	∗	0	Ravine
+	+	+	−, +	−, +	Hillside
+	∗	∗	0	0	Cannot occur

(*Note:* Special attention is required for the degenerate case $\lambda_1 = \lambda_2 \neq 0$, which implies that $\omega^{(1)}$ and $\omega^{(2)}$ can be *any* two orthogonal directions. In this case, there *always* exists an extreme direction ω which is orthogonal to ∇f, and thus the first-directional derivative $\nabla f \cdot \omega$ is *always* zero in an extreme direction. To avoid spurious zero-directional derivatives, we choose $\omega^{(1)}$ and $\omega^{(2)}$ such that $\nabla f \cdot \omega^{(1)} \neq 0$ and $\nabla f \cdot \omega^{(2)} \neq 0$, unless the gradient is zero.)

Local Cubic Facet Model

In order to estimate the required partial derivatives, we perform a least-squares fit with a two-dimensional surface, f, to a neighborhood of each pixel. It is required that the function f be continuous and have continuous first- and second-order partial derivatives with respect to r and c in a neighborhood around each pixel in the rc plane.

We choose f to be a cubic polynomial in r, and c expressed as a combination of discrete orthogonal polynomials. The function f is the best discrete least-squares polynomial approximation to the image data in each pixel's neighborhood. More details can be found in Haralick and Watson (1981), in which each coefficient of the cubic polynomial is evaluated as a linear combination of the pixels in the fitting neighborhood.

To express the procedure precisely and without reference to a particular set of polynomials tied to neighborhood size, we will canonically write the fitted bicubic surface for each fitting neighborhood as

$$
\begin{aligned}
f(r, c) = {} & k_1 + k_2 r + k_3 c \\
& + k_4 r^2 + k_5 rc + k_6 c^2 \\
& + k_7 r^2 + k_8 r^2 c + k_9 rc^2 + k_{10} c^3,
\end{aligned}
$$

where the center of the fitting neighborhood is taken as the origin. It quickly follows that the needed partials evaluated at local coordinates (r, c) are

$$
\begin{aligned}
\partial f / \partial r &= k_2 + 2k_4 r + k_5 c + 3k_7 r^2 + 2k_8 rc + k_9 c^2 \\
\partial f / \partial c &= k_3 + k_5 r + 2k_6 c + k_8 r^2 + 2k_9 rc + 3k_{10} c^2 \\
\partial^2 f / \partial r^2 &= 2k_4 + 6k_7 r + 2k_8 c \\
\partial^2 f / \partial c^2 &= 2k_6 + 2k_9 r + 6k_{10} c \\
\partial^2 f / \partial r \partial c &= k_5 + 2k_8 r + 2k_9 c.
\end{aligned}
$$

It is easy to see that the above quantities are evaluated at the center of the pixel where local coordinates $(r, c) = (0, 0)$, only the constant terms will be of significance. If the partials need to be evaluated at an arbitrary point in a pixel's area, then a linear or quadratic-polynomial value must be computed.

THREE-DIMENSIONAL SHAPE ESTIMATION

Consider an image of a three-dimensional object illuminated by an arbitrary light source and viewed from an arbitrary position. Although ambiguities are possible, frequently the human viewer can estimate (a) the three-dimensional shape of the object, (b) the camera position, and (c) the location of the light source. The original "shape-from-shading" techniques (Horn, 1975) solve systems of differential equations to derive three-dimensional shape from gray-tone intensity variations and operate under a limiting set of restrictions. In addition to low level shading cues, we believe that the human viewer also recognizes patterns in the image that give cues leading to estimation of the shape of the object.

Extracting patterns from the original gray-tone image is, in most nontrivial cases, an impossible task. In fact, it is for this reason that syntactive pattern-recognition systems have had to first extract descriptions consisting of primitives, their properties, and their interrelationships from the image and then to parse these descriptions according to the rules of a grammar. Instead of trying to recognize patterns at the gray-tone intensity level, we propose to work at the topographic-labeling level. Our goal is to use patterns expressed in terms of ridges and valleys, peaks and pits, flats and hillsides to estimate three-dimensional shape.

Imaging Geometry

The relationship between scene coordinates and image coordinates is illustrated in Figure 1.8. We assume that the camera lens is at the origin and that the z-axis is directed toward the image plane which is in front of the lens. The image plane is placed at a distance f, the focal length of the lens, in front of the origin so that the image is oriented in the same way as the scene. As seen from Figure 1.11, the following relations hold for perspective projection:

$$u = \frac{fx}{z} \text{ and } v = \frac{fy}{z} .$$

In our discussion, the perspective projection is approximated by an orthographic projection. This approximation is good when the size of the objects being imaged is small compared to the viewing distance. In this case, appropriate coordinate systems can be chosen such that the following relations hold:

$$u = x \text{ and } v = y.$$

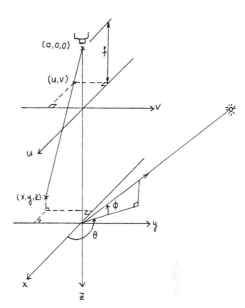

FIGURE 1.8. Relationship between scene coordinates and image coordinates.

Illumination Model

In the following discussion, we will use a simple illumination model that assumes a distant point-light source and a Lambertian reflectance model. A Lambertian surface scatters light equally in all direction. The brightness of a Lambertian surface illuminated by a distant point-light source is given by:

$$I = I_0 N \cdot L \tag{1}$$

where I_0 is a constant depending on the surface albedo and the intensity of the light source, N is the unit surface normal vector, and L is the unit vector of the illumination direction.

The unit vector which points in the direction of the light source can be specified by the two angles shown in Figure 1.11. The first is the azimuth (θ), which is the angle between the x-axis and the projection of the vector onto the x-y plane, while the second is the angle of elevation (ϕ) of the light source. If we represent this unit vector by $[a, b, c]$ then

$$a = \cos \theta \cos \phi,$$

$$b = \sin \theta \cos \phi, \text{ and,}$$

$$c = -\sin \phi.$$

In our discussion, we will consider only positive values of ϕ. Therefore, c is always less than zero.

If the height of the object surface above the x-y plane is expressed as a function of x and y,

$$z = S(x, y),$$

then the surface normal is given by the vector:

$$N = [S_x, S_y, -1]/(1 + S_x^2 + S_y^2)^{1/2}$$

where S_x and S_y denote first partials of S with respect to x and y, respectively. By carrying out the dot product in Equation 1, it follows that

$$I = I_0 \frac{aS_x + bS_y - c}{(1 + S_x^2 + S_y^2)^{1/2}}. \tag{2}$$

Shape From Topographic Patterns

There are two possible methods for determining the pattern of topographic labels that will appear, given a particular three-dimensional shape category, a particular reflectance model, a particular light source, and a particular viewpoint. The first method is to work the problem analytically, obtaining exact equations for the illuminated surface. At each point the gradient, eigenvectors, and eigenvalues can be computed in order to determine precisely which sets of points have the various topographic labels. The second method is to work the problem experimentally, using software to generate digital images of illuminated three-dimensional surfaces, to fit these images with either polynomials, splines, or discrete cosines, and to assign topograpic labels to each pixel. The first method has the advantage of exactness and the disadvantage of becoming extremely difficult for all but the simplest surfaces. The second method has the advantage of being applicable to a wide variety of surfaces and illuminating conditions and the disadvantage of yielding some inaccurate results due to possible errors in fitting the gray-tone image. We have begun to experiment with both methods, starting with very simple surfaces, the Lambertian reflectance model, and point light sources. We have worked with four simple surfaces: (a) the top half of a cylinder, (b) the upper hemisphere of a sphere, (c) the top half of an ellipsoid, and (d) the upper half of a hyperboloid. Figures 1.9 and 1.10 illustrate the cylinder and the sphere, respectively.

Method 1: The Experimental Approach

The process for topographic classification can be done in one pass through the image. At each pixel of the image, the following four steps,

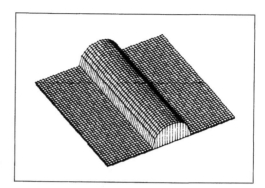

FIGURE 1.9. The cylindrical object used in our experiments.

which were discussed in detail in the previous section need to be performed.

1. Calculate the least-squares fitting coefficients of a two-dimension cubic polynomial in an $n \times n$ neighborhood around the pixel.
2. Use the coefficients calculated in step 1 to find the gradient, the gradient magnitude, and the eigenvalues and eigenvectors of the Hessian at the center of the pixel's neighborhood.
3. Search in the direction of the eigenvectors calculated in step 2 for a zero-crossing of the first-directional derivative within the pixel's area.
4. Recompute the gradient, gradient magnitude, and values of second directional derivative extrema at each zero crossing. Then classify the pixel based on Table 1.1.

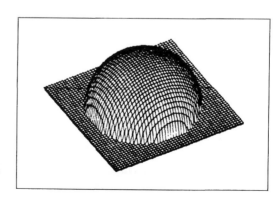

FIGURE 1.10. The spherical object used in our experiments.

Method 2: The Analytical Approach

Topographic Labels on the Cylinder

Consider a cylindrical surface given by:

$$s(x, y) = d - (r^2 - y^2)^{1/2} \text{ for } -r \leq y \leq r \tag{3}$$

where d is the distance of the x-y plane from the camera down the z-axis and r is the radius of the cylinder. This surface in which the axis of the cylinder lies along the x-axis was chosen to simplify calculations. Notice that since only the top half of the cylinder is considered, the sign of the square root in Equation 3 is taken as positive. By differentiating S with respect to x and y, we obtain

$$S_x = 0 \text{ and } S_y = y(r^2 - y^2)^{-1/2}.$$

It follows from Equation 2 that the intensity of the cylinder illuminated from direction (a, b, c) is given by:

$$I(x, y) = I_0(by - c(r^2 - y^2)^{1/2})r \tag{4}$$

After some simplifications, the first and second partials of I are found to be:

$$I_x = I_{xx} = I_{xy} = I_{yx} = 0,$$
$$I_y = I_0(b + cy(r^2 - y^2)^{-1/2})/r, \text{ and}$$
$$I_{yy} = I_0 cr(r^2 - y^2)^{-3/2},$$

where the subscripted Is denote partial differentiation with respect to the subscript(s).

Since I_x is equal to zero, the gradient magnitude ($\|\nabla f\|$) is equal to the absolute value of I_y. Therefore, $\|\nabla f\| = 0$ when

$$I_y = I_0(b + cy(r^2 - y^2)^{-1/2})/r = 0$$

which implies

$$b(r^2 y^2)^{1/2} = cy. \tag{5}$$

Upon solving Equation 5, we obtain

$$y^2 = r^2 b^2/(b^2 + c^2).$$

Because c is always negative, the sign of y is taken to be the same as that of b in order for Equation 5 to be satisfied.

To determine the second-directional derivative extrema values and the first-directional derivatives taken in the directions which extremize second-directional derivatives, we form the Hessian:

$$H = \begin{bmatrix} 0 & 0 \\ 0 & I_0 cr(r^2 - y^2)^{-3/2} \end{bmatrix}.$$

The eigenvalues of the Hessian are obtained as:

$$X_1 = I_0 cr(r^2 - y^2)^{-3/2} \text{ and} \tag{6}$$

$$X_2 = 0; \tag{7}$$

their associated eigenvectors are:

$$w_1 = (0,1) \text{ and}$$

$$w_2 = (1,0).$$

Recall that c is always negative, therefore, X_1 is always negative for $-r < y < r$. By taking the dot product of the gradient with the eigenvectors, we obtain:

$$\nabla I \cdot w_1 = I_y = I_0(b + cy(r^2 - y^2)^{-1/2}/r \text{ and}$$

$$\nabla I \cdot w_2 = 0.$$

To determine the topographic labels, we need to consider two cases: (1) zero-gradient magnitude and (2) positive-gradient magnitude.

CASE 1: Zero-Gradient Magnitude. If we let $y_0 = rb(b^2 + c^2)^{-1/2}$, it follows from Equation 5 that $\|\nabla I\| = 0$ when $y = y_0$. By Equations 6 and 7, the second directional derivative extrema values at $y = y_0$ are

$$X_1 = I_0 cr(r^2 - y_0^2)^{-3/2} \tag{8}$$

$$X_2 = 0. \tag{9}$$

Since X_1 is always less than zero, it follows directly from Table 1.1 that a ridge is located at $y = y_0$.

CASE 2: Positive Gradient Magnitude. If the gradient magnitude ($\|\nabla I\|$) is taken to be positive, then the value of the first-directional derivative in the direction of w_1 ($\nabla I.w_1$) is always non-zero because $\nabla I.w_1 = I_y$ and $\|\nabla f\| = |I_y|$. In this case, since X_1 is always negative and X_2 is always zero, it follows from row 11 of Table 1.1 that hillsides are located at those places where the gradient magnitudes are positive.

Topographic Labels on the Sphere

In the case of the sphere, the equation of a spherical surface with radius r is given by:

$$S(x, y) = d - (r^2 - x^2 - y^2)^{1/2} \quad \text{for } -r \leq x \leq r$$
$$\text{and } -r \leq y \leq r \tag{10}$$

Its intensity illuminated from direction $[a, b, c]$ is given by:

$$I(x, y) = I_0 * [ax + by - c(r^2 - x^2 - y^2)^{1/2}]/r \qquad (11)$$

After some simplifications, the first and second partials of I are found to be:

$$I_x - I_0[a + cx(r^2 - x^2 - y^2)^{1/2}]/r,$$
$$I_y = I_0[b + cy(r^2 - x^2 - y^2)^{-1/2}]/r,$$
$$I_{xx} = I_0 c(r^2 - y^2)(r^2 - x^2 - y^2)^{-3/2}/r,$$
$$I_{xy} = I_{yx} = I_0 \, cxy(r^2 - x^2 - y^2)^{-3/2}/r, \text{ and}$$
$$I_{yy} = I_0 c(r^2 - x^2)(r^2 - x^2 - y^2)^{-3/2}/r.$$

The gradient magnitude ($\|\nabla I\|$) is given by:

$$\|\nabla I\| = (I_x^2 + I_y^2)^{1/2},$$

which is zero when

$$a(r^2 - x^2 - y^2)^{1/2} + cx = 0 \text{ and}$$
$$b(r^2 - x^2 - y^2)^{1/2} + cy = 0$$

are satisfied simultaneously. By squaring and invoking the constraint $a^2 + b^2 + c^2 = 0$ on the unit vector $[a, b, c]$, the solution to the simultaneous equations is found to be:

$$x = ra \text{ and } y = rb.$$

The Hessian for the intensity surface of the illuminated sphere is given by:

$$H = \frac{I_0 c}{r(r^2 - x^2 - y^2)} * \begin{bmatrix} r^2 - y^2 & xy \\ xy & r^2 - x^2 \end{bmatrix}.$$

Its eigenvalues are found to be:

$$X_1 = I_0 cr(r^2 - x^2 - y^2)^{-3/2} \text{ and}$$
$$X_2 = I_0 c(r^2 - x^2 - y^2)^{-1/2}/r.$$

Notice that both eigenvalues are always less than zero since c is always less than zero. The eigenvector corresponding to X_1 is given by:

$$w_1 = [x(x^2 + y^2)^{-1/2}, y(x^2 + y^2)^{-1/2}]$$

and the eigenvector corresponding to X_2 is given by:

$$w_2 = [-y(x^2 + y^2)^{-1/2}, x(x^2 + y^2)^{-1/2}].$$

The dot product of the gradient with w_1 is

$$\nabla I \cdot w_1 = \frac{I_0}{(x^2 + y^2)^{1/2}} \left[x \left(a + \frac{cx}{(r^2 - x^2 - y^2)^{1/2}} \right) \right]$$

$$\left[y \left(b + \frac{cy}{(r^2 - x^2 - y^2)^{1/2}} \right) \right] \quad (12)$$

and the dot product of the gradient with w_2 is

$$\nabla I \cdot w_2 = I_0(-ay + bx)(x^2 + y^2)^{-1/2}/r. \quad (13)$$

We determine the topographic labels by considering two cases.

CASE 1: Zero Gradient Magnitude. The gradient magnitude is equal to zero when $(x, y) = (ra, rb)$. Since both eigenvalues are less than zero on the illuminated sphere, it follows directly from Table 1.1 that a peak is located at $(x, y) = (ra, rb)$.

CASE 2: Positive Gradient Magnitude. In the case when the gradient magnitude is given to be positive, since both eigenvalues are known to be negative, it follows from Table 1.1 that there is a ridge at those locations where either $\nabla f \cdot w_1 = 0$ or $\nabla f \cdot w_2 = 0$ is satisfied. We obtain from Equations 12 and 13 that

$\nabla I.w_1 = 0$ when $(ax + by)(r^2 - x^2 - y^2)^{1/2} + c(x^2 + y^2) = 0$ and

$\nabla I.w_2 = 0$ when $-ay + bx = 0$.

Table 1.1 also says that hillsides appear at places where both $\nabla f \cdot w_1$ and $\nabla f \cdot w_2$ are non-zero.

Estimation of Surface Orientation

The topographic labels along with their quantitative measurements bear a strong relationship to the surface orientation of the three-dimensional object in the scene. Consider a spherical surface as previously described. The unnormalized surface orientation of such a surface can be represented in the gradient space by the vector $[p, q, -1]$, where

$$p = \frac{x}{(r^2 - x^2 - y^2)^{1/2}} \text{ and } q = \frac{y}{(r^2 - x^2 - y^2)^{1/2}} .$$

An alternative way of specifying surface orientation is the tilt and slant representation. Tilt specifies the orientation of the projection of the surface normal onto the image plane. Slant is the angle between the surface normal and viewing direction. The tilt and slant representation and the gradient space representation can be related by the following formulas:

$$\text{Tan } \theta = q/p \text{ and}$$

$$\text{Tan } \theta = (p^2 + q^2)^{1/2} \text{ or}$$

$$\text{Cos } \theta = (1 + p^2 + q^2)^{1/2}.$$

In the case of a sphere,

$$\text{Tan } \theta = y/x \text{ and}$$

$$\text{Cos } \phi = (r^2 - x^2 - y^2)/r^2.$$

To see how the surface orientation of a spherical Lambertian surface can be derived from the topographic analysis of the image intensity surface, we need first to complete the analytical results of the previous section by considering the lower half of the sphere. The equation of the lower hemisphere of a sphere whose center is at $(0, 0, d)$ is given by:

$$S(x,y) = d + (r^2 - x^2 - y^2)^{1/2} \quad \text{for } -r \leq x \leq r$$
$$\text{and } -r \leq y \leq r.$$

Differentiating the aforementioned equation with respect to x and y, we obtain

$$p = \frac{-x}{(r^2 - x^2 - y^2)^{1/2}} \text{ and } q = \frac{-y}{(r^2 - x^2 - y^2)^{1/2}}.$$

Notice the sign difference between the surface orientations of the upper and lower hemispheres.

As for the upper hemisphere, after some simplification, we obtain for the lower hemisphere a similar set of expressions for I and its partials,

$$I = I_0[-ax - by - c(r^2 - x^2 - y^2)^{1/2}]/r,$$

$$I_x = I_0[-a + cx(r^2 - x^2 - y^2)^{-1/2}]/r,$$

$$I_y = I_0[-b + cy(r^2 - x^2 - y^2)^{-1/2}]/r,$$

$$I_{xx} = I_0 c(r^2 - y^2)(r^2 - x^2 - y^2)^{-3/2}/r,$$

$$I_{xy} = I_{yx} = I_0 cxy(r^2 - x^2 - y^2)^{-3/2}/r, \text{ and}$$

$$I_{yy} = I_0 c(r^2 - x^2)(r^2 - x^2 - y^2)^{-3/2}/r.$$

Notice that the second partials of I are the same for both halves of the sphere. Since the second partials make up the Hessian, it follows that the eigenvalues and eigenvectors for the two hemispheres are also identical. Recall that the eigenvalues and eigenvectors are given by

$$X_1 = I_0cr(r^2 - x^2 - y^2)^{-3/2},$$

$$X_2 = I_0c(r^2 - x^2 - y^2)^{-1/2}/r,$$

$$w_1 = [x(x^2 + y^2)^{-1/2}, y(x^2 + y^2)^{-1/2}], \text{ and}$$

$$w_2 = [-y(x^2 + y^2)^{-1/2}, x(x^2 + y^2)^{-1/2}].$$

If we take the ratio of the smaller over the larger eigenvalue, we obtain

$$\frac{X^2}{X^1} = \frac{(r^2 - x^2 - y^2)}{r^2} .$$

This ratio is the square root of the cosine of the surface slant. Note that the signs of both X_1 and X_2 depend only on the sign of c, which is the negative of the sine of the angle of elevation of the light source. Therefore, the ratio is always positive and its square root is always justifiable. Furthermore, the ratio is always less than or equal to one, since X_2 is the smaller eigenvalue. Thus, we can obtain surface slant by taking the arccosine of the square root of X_2/X_1. The resulting angle is determined uniquely because the surface slant for a visible surface always lies between 0 and $\pi/2$.

The remaining component to be determined for the unit surface normal is the surface tilt. By considering w_1, the eigenvector corresponding to the larger eigenvalue, we can obtain the direction θ in which the second-directional derivative of I is extremized. That is,

$$\tan \theta = \frac{y}{(x^2 + y^2)^{1/2}} \cdot \frac{(x^2 + y^2)^{1/2}}{x} = \frac{y}{x} ,$$

which is identical to the tangent of the surface tilt. Thus we have $t = \theta$ or $t = \theta + \pi$. Unfortunately, there are two possible solutions. This is expected because each solution corresponds to one half of the sphere. This shows the ambiguity in local analysis of image shading.

Without any assumption about the location of the light source, we found from the aforementioned analytical results that the topographic labels on the underlying intensity surface resulting from a spherical Lambertian surface can only be peak, pit, ridge, valley, convex, or concave hillside. This is because any combination of I_{xx}, I_{yy}, and I_{xy} resulting from a spherical Lambertian surface can produce only either a semipositive or seminegative definite Hessian. Therefore, not all combinations of I_{xx}, I_{yy}, and I_{xy} are possible.

Furthermore, if we approximate three-dimensional surfaces locally by spherical surfaces, it is expected that the radii of the approximating spheres for points or a spherical surface are constant. Recall that the radius, r, and the eigenvalues, X_1 and X_2, of a spherical Lambertian surface are related by the following expressions:

$$X_1 = \frac{I_0 cr}{(r^2 - x^2 - y^2)^{3/2}} \text{ and } X_2 = \frac{I_0 c}{r(r^2 - x^2 - y^2)^{1/2}} .$$

We obtain from the expression from X_1

$$(r^2 - x^2 - y^2)^{1/2} = \frac{I_0 c}{X_2 r} .$$

We then have from the expression for X_2

$$X_1 = I_0 cr \left(\frac{I_0 c}{X_2 r} \right)^{-3} ,$$

or

$$r^4 = \frac{X_1 I_0^2 c^2}{X_2^3} .$$

Since I_0 and c are fixed, we conclude that X_1/X_2^3 is constant for a spherical Lambertian surface. Therefore, an image point can be determined as resulting from a point on a spherical Lambertian surface only if it is labeled as a peak, pit, ridge, valley, convex hillside or concave hillside, and the radii of the approximating spheres at pixels within the neighborhood around that point are similar enough. What this suggests is that we should estimate surface tilt and surface slant locally from the eigenvalues and eigenvectors of the Hessian of the underlying intensity surface only if the underlying intensity surface is compatible with that of a spherical Lambertian surface.

It can be observed from the expressions of the eigenvalues that a pit, valley, and convex-hillside classification of the intensity surface of a spherical Lambertian surface corresponds to a positive c. This implies a light source below the object surface. Although this is physically possible, such illuminating condition can usually be ignored when solving practical problems. We thus further assume that a spherical Lambertian surface can only result in peak, ridge, and concave-hillside classifications.

Classification of Object Surfaces

We propose here a scheme for partial classification of three-dimensional object surfaces. The basic goal of this classification scheme is to group together pixels that are likely to come from the same surface patch. We limit our consideration to five types of object surfaces. They are planar, developable, spherical, elliptical, and hyperbolic surfaces.

Based on the previous discussions, it is evident that topographic labels together with the signs and magnitudes of their second directional derivatives bear a strong relationship to the nature of the three-dimensional object surface in the scene. This evidence leads to the assumption that maximally connected sets of pixels having the same topographic label belong to the same surface patches. A feature-extraction process is employed to extract these connected sets of topographic structures. The resulting structures are arcs, regions, and topographic labels. The desired topographic structures are then determined by applying a connected-components algorithm to the topographic labels within each region segment.

The assembled topographic structures may be divided into three categories: (1) areal structures, which consist of convex hillsides, concave hillsides, saddle hillsides, flat surfaces, and sloped surfaces; (2) arc structures, which include edges, ridges, and valleys; and (3) point structures, which include peaks, pits, and saddle points. In what follows, we suggest hypotheses that can be made about the three-dimensional objects based on the analytical results that we have derived and the results of the experiments that we have performed. We believe that three-dimensional object shape can be inferred by feeding this knowledge into a hypothesis-based reasoning system.

Areal Structures

Flat. A flat is a simple surface with zero gradient and no curvature. That is, the gray-level intensity is constant in a connected flat structure. Since the surface-normal vectors within a planar surface are constant, we can be almost certain that pixels belonging to a connected flat structure come from the same planar surface. Although this may not hold for shadow areas, we can usually separate shadow areas by identifying flat structures with relatively low intensity averages.

Hillsides. We first hypothesize that a concave/convex hillside assembly is part of a spherical, elliptical, or developable surface, and a saddle hillside assembly is part of a hyperbolic surface. Our first hypothesis is driven by the analytical and experimental results of the cylindrical, spherical, elliptical, and hyperbolic surfaces that we considered.

We further postulate that a concave/convex hillside assembly is part of a developable surface if it is adjacent to a straight and horizontal ridge. In particular, it is part of cylindrical surface if it is concave and the second-directional derivative of the hillside in the direction of the ridge is zero.

As a result of the previous section, a hillside assembly can be considered as part of a spherical surface if it is concave and the radii of the approximating spheres within the hillside assembly are similar enough. We have not been able to derive a complete classification scheme for all the areal structures. Nonetheless, since the assembled regions are likely to come from the same surface patches, they are good starting regions for shape-from-shading approaches.

Line and Point Structures

While edges are considered to be good indications of the discontinuities, peaks and ridges are found to be significant structures in the images of the conic surfaces that we have considered. The following observations are gathered from the topographic structures of the conic surface:

1. The ridge arcs obtained from the images of the sphere are found to be symmetrical around the peaks.
2. Ridges for the images of the ellipsoid and the hyperboloid are found to be symmetrical around the peaks only if the projection of the light vectors are parallel to one of the axes of these conic surfaces.
3. Straight ridge lines are found in the images of the cylinder. The gray-tone intensities along the ridge lines are found to be constant.
4. While the ridges around the peaks found in the image of the ellipsoid curve away from the light sources, those of the hyperboloid curve toward the light sources.
5. The peaks located in the images of the conic surfaces correspond to locations where the surface normals are pointing toward the light sources.

Results

We will show the analytical and experimental results of the topographic patterns on the cylinder and sphere. See Pong, Shapiro, and Haralick (1985) for results on other surfaces. Three illumination conditions are considered for each surface: (1) the light direction is $(0, 0, -1)$, which means directly above the center of the surface; (2) the light direction is $(0, \sqrt{3}/2, -1/2)$, which translates to azimuth $0°$ and elevation $30°$; (3) the light direction is $(1/2, 1/2, -1/\sqrt{2})$, which translates to azimuth $45°$ and elevation $45°$. The illuminated surfaces of the cylinder and the sphere are shown in Figure 1.11 and Figure 1.12 respectively.

FIGURE 1.11. Shaded images of the cylinder of Figure 1.9.

Analytical Results for the Cylinder

When the light direction is from azimuth 0°, elevation 90°, analytical results indicate a ridge parallel to the axis of the cylinder and running along the center of the top half as shown in Figure 1.13. When the light direction is from azimuth 0° and elevation 30°, the ridge appears as in Figure 1.13. When the light direction is from azimuth 45° and elevation 45°, the ridge appears as in Figure 1.13. In all three cases, the remaining points of the cylinder are hillsides.

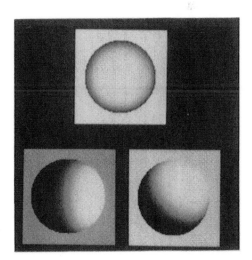

FIGURE 1.12. Shaded images of the sphere of Figure 1.10.

Analytical Results for the Sphere

When the light source is directly above the center of the sphere, the gradient magnitude is zero at $(0, 0)$; therefore, a peak is located at the center of the sphere. The gradient magnitude is positive and the first-directional derivative in the direction w_2 is zero at the remaining points of the sphere. It follows from our analytical results that ridges locate at these points.

When the light direction is $(0, \sqrt{3}/2, -1/2)$, a peak is found at $(0, \sqrt{3}r/2)$. At the remaining points,

$$\nabla I.w_1 = 0 \text{ when } (x^2 + y^2) = \sqrt{3}/2y(r^2 - x^2 - y^2)^{1/2} \text{ and}$$

$$\nabla I.w_2 = 0 \text{ when } x = 0.$$

Therefore, there are ridges when either one of these two equations is satisfied and hillsides otherwise.

Similarly, a peak is found at $(r/2, r/2)$ when the light direction is $(1/2, 1/2, -1/\sqrt{2})$. Ridges can be located at places where either

$$\sqrt{2}(x^2 + y^2) = (x + y)(r^2 - x^2 - y^2)^{1/2} \text{ or}$$

$$x = y \text{ is satisfied.}$$

At the remaining points, hillsides are the correct categories. Figure 1.14 shows the topographic labels for the illuminated spheres.

Experimental Results

Experimentally, we are working in the GIPSY (General Image Processing System) environment. There currently exist GIPSY commands to

FIGURE 1.13. The analytically derived topographic labeling of the cylinder.

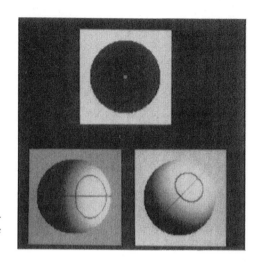

FIGURE 1.14. The analytically derived topographic labeling of the sphere.

construct three-dimensional surfaces, to produce images of these surfaces from various viewpoints and light directions, to fit these images with either cubic polynomials, splines, or discrete cosines, and to calculate the topographic labelings. Figures 1.15 and 1.16 show experimental results for the cylinder and sphere using cubic polynomial surface fitting. Experimental results show very good correspondence with the analytical results, except for the sphere when the light direction is $(0, 0, -1)$. In this case, when points are labeled *ridge* and have neighboring points in a direction orthogonal to the gradient that are also labeled *ridge,* our software reclassifies these ridge continuums as hillsides.

FIGURE 1.15. The experimental results for the cylinder.

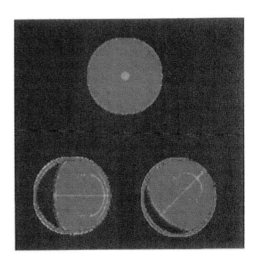

FIGURE 1.16. The experimental
results for the sphere.

In addition to the images of the two simple surfaces, a synthetic image
of a more complex surface was also used in testing. The surface is composed of cylindrical and spherical surface patches. Figure 1.17 shows the
image of the surface when illuminated from azimuth 45° and elevation
45°. Figure 1.18 illustrates the topographic labels that resulted from the
experimental method. Most of the resulting topographic labels are located at places where they are predicted by the analytical method.

Our results show that the most informative features found in the
images of the cylinder and sphere are ridges and peaks. While the ridges
found in the cylinder images are intuitive, the ellipse-like ridges found in
the sphere images are unexpected. Although most ridge points found in
the sphere images are weak ridges, experimental results show that these
ridges are detectable. These ellipse-like ridges will be a definite clue to

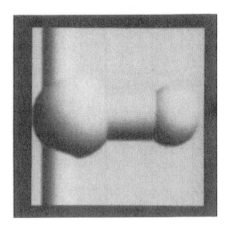

FIGURE 1.17. Gray-tone image of the
synthetic object illuminated from azimuth 45° and elevation 45°.

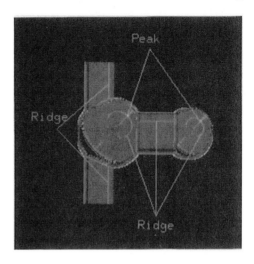

FIGURE 1.18. The topographic labeling of the synthetic object image.

three-dimensional surface identifications. Once the shape of the three-dimensional surface is hypothesized as cylindrical or spherical, information such as the direction of the light source and the cylinder/sphere radius may also be estimated by examining the topographic labels.

SUMMARY

The facet model for image processing estimates the underlying surface of a gray-tone intensity image and uses this estimate in processing the image. The facet model has been used in edge detection, several kinds of segmentation algorithms, and to construct the topographic primal sketch of the image. The topographic primal sketch, a pixel classification scheme, has been used to aid in the estimation of three-dimensional shape from two-dimensional views of shaded objects. In all of these different algorithms, the facet model has been shown to be a robust model for understanding and processing images.

REFERENCES

Haralick, R. M., "Digital step edges from zero crossing of second directional derivatives," *IEEE Transactions on Pattern Analysis and Machine Intelligence, PAMI-6* (1), Jan. 1984, pp. 58–68.

Haralick, R. M., & L. G. Shapiro, "Image segmentation techniques," *Computer Vision, Graphics, and Image Processing, 29*(1), Jan. 1985, pp. 100–132.

Haralick, R. M., & L. T. Watson, "A facet model for image data," *Computer Graphics and Image Processing, 15,* 1981, pp. 113–129.

Haralick, R. M., L. T. Watson, & T. J. Laffey, "The Topographic Primal Sketch," *International Journal of Robotics Research, 2* (1), 1983, pp. 50–72.

Horn, B. K. P., "Obtaining shape from shading information," *The Psychology of Computer Vision,* P. H. Winston (Ed.), McGraw-Hill, New York, 1975, pp. 115–155.

Marr, D., "Early processing of visual information," *Philosophical Transactions Royal Society of London, B, 275,* 1976, pp. 483–534.

Pong, T. C., L. G. Shapiro, L. T. Watson, & R. M. Haralick, "Experiments in segmentation using a facet model region grower," *Computer Vision, Graphics, and Image Processing,* Jan. 1984, pp. 1–23.

Pong, T. C., L. G. Shapiro, & R. M. Haralick, "Shape Estimation from Topographic Primal Sketch," *Pattern Recognition, 18,* (5), 1985, pp. 333–348.

2 SCALING AND FINGERPRINT THEOREMS FOR ZERO-CROSSINGS

ALAN L. YUILLE
TOMASO POGGIO
Massachusetts Institute of Technology

We characterize some properties of the zero-crossings of the Laplacian of signals—in particular images—filtered with linear filters, as a function of the scale of the filter, extending recent work by A. Witkin (1983). We review our two main results. First, we have proven that in any dimension the only filter that does not create generic zero-crossings as the scale increases is the Gaussian. This result can be generalized to apply to level-crossings of any linear differential operator: It applies in particular to ridges and ravines in the image intensity. Second, we have proven that the scale map of the zero-crossings of almost all signals filtered by a Gaussian of variable size determines the signal uniquely, up to a constant scaling. Exceptions are signals that are antisymmetric about all their zeros, for instance, infinitely periodic gratings. Our proof provides a method for reconstructing almost all signals from knowledge of how the zero-crossing contours of the signal, filtered by a Gaussian filter, change with the size of the filter. The proof assumes that the filtered signal can be represented as a polynomial of finite, albeit possibly very high, order. The result applies to zero- and level-crossings of signals filtered by Gaussian filters. The theorem is also valid in two dimensions, that is, it applies to images. Thus, extrema (for instance of derivatives) at different scales are a complete representation of a signal. Finally we discuss the new results proven by Curtis (1985) for two- and higher-dimensional functions.

INTRODUCTION

In most physical phenomena, changes in spatial or temporal structure occur over a wide range of scales. Images are no exception: Changes in light intensity reflect the many spatial scales at which visible surfaces are organized. It seems intuitive that a great deal of information can be gained by an analysis of the changes in a signal at different scales. For instance, graphs of one-dimensional functions are a very effective tool for describing complex systems. An important reason is that they allow direct visual access to important properties of the data, chiefly to their changes over different scales.

The idea of scale is critical for a symbolic description of the significant changes in images or other types of signals. Changes must be detected at different levels of detail and over different extents. In general different physical processes may be associated with a characteristic behavior across different scales. In an image, changes of intensity take place at many spatial scales depending on their physical origin. A multiscale analysis, tracing the behavior of some feature of the signal across scales, can reveal precious information about the nature of the underlying physical process. In images, for instance, spatial coincidence at all scales of zero-crossings in the Laplacian of the intensity values filtered with a Gaussian mask, may signal a physical "edge," distinct from surface markings or shadows. Not only is it necessary to detect and describe changes in a signal at different scales, but in addition, much useful information can be obtained by combining descriptions across scales.

The importance of this idea has been clearly realized in the field of vision. One of the main contributions of visual psychophysics in the last 10 years was, indeed, to show that visual information is processed in parallel by a number (perhaps a continuum) of spatial-frequency-tuned channels (Campbell & Robson, 1968). The bulk of the data demonstrates that the visual system analyses the image at different resolutions. Physiological experiments are consistent with the psychophysics. They suggest that in the visual pathway, spatial filters of different size operate at the same location. Furthermore, psychophysics, physiology, and anatomy all show that the spatial grain of analysis continuously changes from foveal to peripheral locations. Receptive and dendritic field sizes of both retinal and cortical neurons increase monotonically with eccentricity, in agreement with the dependency on eccentricity of the psychophysical channels.

In the field of computer vision, Rosenfeld was one of the first to propose explicitly an edge detection scheme-based on multixcale analysis performed with filters of different sizes (Rosenfeld & Thurston, 1971). A similar algorithm was suggested by Marr (1976), though with different goals and motivations. More recently, he has strongly advocated the use of derivatives of Gaussian-shaped filters of different sizes with the goal of detecting changes in intensity at different scales (Marr, 1982). The idea was first proposed in the context of a theory of stereomatching (Marr & Poggio, 1979). In that scheme, analysis at the different scales was effectively kept separate. Later, Marr and Hildreth (1980) proposed some

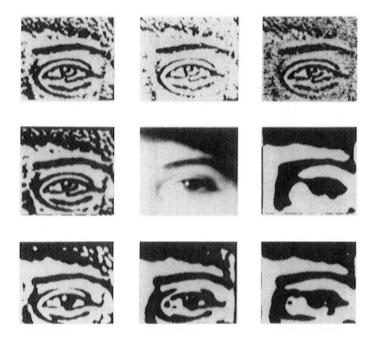

FIGURE 2.1. The image is the face shown in the central square. We show the sign values of the image convolved with the Laplacian of a Gaussian at different scales. The scale is largest at the extreme right center square and decreases in the clockwise direction.

heuristical rules to combine information from the different channels. However, the important problem of how to combine effectively the different scales of analysis at this early level has remained open, although recent work by D. Terzopoulos (1982) has successfully applied multilevel algorithms to the problem of reconstructing visual surfaces (see also Canny, 1983; Crowley, 1982; Richards, Nishihara, & Nielson, 1982). Figure 2.1 shows the zero-crossings of a photograph of a face at different scales.[1]

Recently a new way of describing zero-crossings across scale was suggested by Witkin (1983). A one-dimensional signal is smoothed by convolution with a small (large) Gaussian filter and the zeros of the second derivative are localized and followed as the size of the filter increases (decreases). This procedure originates a plot of the zero contours in the x-σ plane (where σ measures the size of the Gaussian filter).[2] In this way, Witkin was able to classify and label zero-crossings achieving an effective

---

[1]Courtesy of H. Vorhees.

[2]J. Stansfield first described the idea of plotting zero-crossings over scale—for analysing commodities trends (Stansfield, 1980)—but did not develop it.

description of a signal for purposes of recognition and registration. This is possible mainly because the geometry of the zero-crossings contours is surprisingly simple. Zero-crossings contours are either lines from small to very large scale or closed, bowl-like shapes. Zero-crossings are never created as the scale increases. Babaud, Witkin and Duda (1983) obtained the striking result that the Gaussian filter is the only filter with this remarkable property in one-dimension.

This property of the Gaussian filter is interesting for two reasons: First, it allows *coarse-to-fine tracking* of zero-crossings in scale space and, second, it ensures that the scale-space diagram contains in some sense a minimal number of zero-crossings (for $\sigma = 0$ the number of zero-crossing is determined by the signal, see condition 3 following).

We have independently succeeded in obtaining a proof of this result and extended it to two dimensions (and in fact any number of dimensions). We have also obtained related results for zero- and level-crossings of other differential operators, in particular, for ridges and ravines in the image intensity. The work described here was first reported in (Yuille & Poggio, 1983a).[3]

The two-dimensional result seems important because it:

1. lays the necessary mathematical foundation for using multiresolution labels for classifying zero-crossings for a symbolic description of intensity changes.
2. justifies the use of Gaussian filters and an associated linear derivative because of their "nice" properties under changes in scale.

In this chapter, we first state and prove the one-dimensional result. We then show that only a specific two-dimensional extension is valid. Zero-crossing of linear derivatives have the "nice scaling behavior" if and only if the image is filtered by a two-dimensional rotationally symmetric Gaussian. In particular, the Laplacian-of-a-Gaussian filter suggested by Marr and Hildreth has nice scaling behavior. The second-directional derivative along the gradient, however, does not: No filter exists that can ensure a nice scaling behavior of the zeros of this derivative (Yuille & Poggio, 1986). We have then the following results:

1. For linear derivative operations—in particular, for the Laplacian—the Gaussian is the only filter with a nice scaling behavior.

---

[3]In an interesting manuscript, which only recently came to our attention, Koenderink, Huys and Toet (pers. comm.) discussed multi-scale resolution of images using the Gaussian filter and the diffusion equation. More recently Koenderink (1984) has obtained similar results to ours by exploiting properties of the diffusion equation.

2. For the nonlinear directional derivative, no filter will give nice scaling behavior (the proof can be found in Yuille & Poggio, 1983a).

In the second part of this chapter we address another question, namely, how much information is represented by the scale-space diagram. Ideally one would like to establish a unique correspondence between the changes of intensity in the image and the physical surfaces and edges that generate them through the imaging process. A more restricted class of results that does not exploit the constraints dictated by the signal or image generation process has been suggested by work on zero-crossings of images filtered with the Laplacian of a Gaussian. Logan (1977) had shown that the zero-crossings of a one-dimensional signal ideally bandpass with a bandwidth of less than an octave determine uniquely the filtered signal (up to scaling). The theorem has been extended—only in the special case of oriented bandpass filters—to two-dimensional images (Poggio, Nishihara, Nielsen, 1982; Marr, Poggio, & Ullman, 1979), but it cannot be used for Gaussian-filtered signals or images, since they are not ideally bandpass. Nevertheless, Marr et al. (1979) conjectured that the zero-crossing maps, obtained by filtering the image with the second derivative of Gaussians of variable size, are very rich in information about the signal itself (see also Grimson, 1981; Marr, 1982; Marr & Hildreth, 1980; Marr & Poggio, 1977; for multiscale representations see also Crowley, 1982; Rosenfeld, 1982). Curtis (1985) has very recently proved that in two or more dimensions, zero-crossings allow full reconstruction (up to an overall scaling factor) provided the function is bandlimited in two or higher dimensions and some other conditions are satisfied (the most important is that $f(x, y)$ should not be factorizable as $f(x, y) = n(x)m(y)$). Her theorems are therefore stronger than ours for two and higher dimensions. We will discuss her results later on in the chapter.

In this chapter we prove *completeness* property: The map of the zero-crossing across scales determines the signal uniquely for almost all signals (in the absence of noise). The scale maps obtained by Gaussian filters are true *fingerprints* of the signal. Our proof shows how the original signal can be reconstructed by information from the zero-crossing contours across scales. It is important to emphasize that our result applies to level-crossings of any arbitrary linear (differential) operator of the Gaussian, since it applies to functions that obey the diffusion equation. These results were originally reported in Yuille and Poggio (1983b). The proof is constructive and applies in both one-dimensional and two-dimensional.

Reconstruction of the signal is, of course, not the goal of early signal processing. Symbolic primitives must be extracted from the signals and used for later processing. Our results imply that scale-space fingerprints are complete primitives, that capture the whole information in the signal and characterize it uniquely. Subsequent processes can therefore work on this more compact representation instead of the original signal.

Our results have theoretical interest in that they answer the question as to what information is conveyed by the zero- and level-crossings of multiscale Gaussian-filtered signals. From a point of view of applications, the results in themselves do not justify the use of the fingerprint representation. *Completeness* of a representation (connected with Nishihara's *sensitivity*) is not sufficient (Nishihara, 1981). A good representation must, in addition, be *robust* (i.e., *stable* in Nishihara's terms) against photometric and geometric distortions (the general point of view argument). It should also possibly be *compact* for the given class of signals. Most importantly, it should make *explicit* the information that is required by later processes.

This chapter divides naturally into two parts. The first part describes the scaling behavior and the scaling theorems and the second part, the outline the proof of uniqueness of the representation.

SCALING THEOREMS: ASSUMPTIONS AND RESULTS

We will consider filtering the image I with a suitable filter F and then consider the behavior of the zero-crossings as we change the scale of the filter. We make five assumptions about the filter, and impose them as conditions.

1. Filtering the shift-invariant and, hence, a convolution. We write this as

$$F * I(\underline{x}) = \int F(\underline{x} - \zeta)I(\zeta)d\zeta.$$

2. The filter has no preferred scale. In two dimensions standard results of dimensional analysis (Bridgman, 1922) give $F(\underline{x}, \sigma) = \frac{1}{\sigma^2} f(\underline{x}/\sigma)$, where σ is the scale of the filter. The factor $\frac{1}{\sigma^2}$ ensures that the filter is properly normalized at all scales.

3. The filter recovers the whole image at sufficiently small scales. This is expressed by $Lim_{\sigma \to 0}, F(\underline{x}, \sigma) = \delta(\underline{x})$, where $\delta(\underline{x})$ denotes the Dirac delta function.

4. The position of the center of the filter is independent of σ. Otherwise, zero-crossings of a step edge would change their position with change of scale.

5. The filter goes to zero as $|\underline{x}| \to \infty$ and as $\sigma \to \infty$.

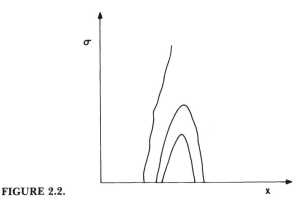

FIGURE 2.2.

As will become apparent, our results are independent of scaling the *x*-axis. We usually require that we scale this axis so that the filter is radially symmetric and state theorems for radially symmetric filters. However, we can relax this requirement by rescaling the axes.

Figure 2.2 shows the typical scaling behavior of zero-crossings in one dimension observed by Witkin. Figure 2.3 shows some possible behavior of zero-crossings, which are never empirically observed when the filter is a Gaussian. The generic properties of the zero-crossing curves in the *x*, σ plane can be derved from the Implicit Function Theorem (Chillingworth, 1978). To yield a C^r curve (i.e., with continuous derivatives up to the $r - th$ order) the theorem requires that the Laplacian of the filtered image is C^r. Therefore the filter must be reasonably smooth. Observe that filtering with a Gaussian will ensure a C^∞ output for all images, because solutions of the heat equation are entire functions and the Gaussian kernel is the Green function of the heat equation. The Implicit

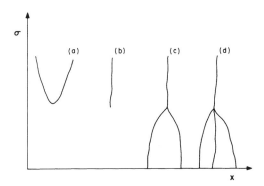

FIGURE 2.3. Case (a) can never occur for a Gaussian filter. Cases (b) and (c) cannot occur for any filter. Case (d) only occurs for Gaussian filters in special conditions, these are described later in this chapter.

Function Theorem may break down at degenerate critical points when all first derivatives of the filtered image vanish together with the Hessian.[4] These points are nongeneric in the sense that a small perturbation in the signal will destroy them. Observe that "true" zero-crossings (i.e., "simple" zeros, see Logan, 1977) can only disappear in pairs in the x, σ plane. Only trivial zeros that do not cross zero can disappear by themselves. They are, however, nongeneric. In this chapter, we consider only generic zero- and level-crossings.

In one dimension, the zero crossings in the second derivative of f obey

$$0 = \int_{-\infty}^{\infty} f'' \left(\frac{x - \zeta}{\sigma} \right) I(\zeta) d\zeta. \tag{2.1}$$

where f'' is the second derivative of f.

This equation gives x as an implicit function of σ, that is, $x = x(\sigma)$. If we vary x and σ so that Equation 2.1 is still satisfied, we obtain

$$\frac{dx}{d\sigma} = \frac{\int_{-\infty}^{\infty} \left(\frac{x - \zeta}{\sigma} \right) f''' \left(\frac{x - \zeta}{\sigma} \right) I(\zeta) d\zeta}{\int_{-\infty}^{\infty} f''' \left(\frac{x - \zeta}{\sigma} \right) I(\zeta) d\zeta} \tag{2.2}$$

So the tangent to the curve is uniquely defined at a point, as are all the higher order derivatives. This prevents the behavior shown in Figures 2.3b, 2.3c (Fig. 2.3d is meant to trigger some thoughts in our readers) with the possible exception of the nongeneric cases, when the Implicit Function Theorem breaks down.

The curve in Figure 2.3(a) is more interesting because it corresponds to a pair of zero crossings being "created" as the scale (i.e., σ) increases. The Implicit Function Theorem does not rule out this case. It therefore seems natural to require a filter such that this never occurs. In the following three sections, we will prove some theorems showing that such a filter can only be a Gaussian and, moreover, that not all differential zero-crossings operators can have this property. More precisely, we prove:

Theorem 1. In one dimension, with the second derivative, the Gaussian is the only filter obeying our five conditions that never creates zero-crossings as the scale increases.

Theorem 2. In two dimensions, with the laplacian operator, the Gaussian is the only filter obeying the conditions which never create zero-crossings as the scale increases.

---

[4]Zeros of the Hessian correspond to zeros of the Gaussian curvature.

Theorem 3. In two dimensions, with the directional derivative along the gradient, there is no filter obeying the conditions that never creates zero-crossing as the scale increases.

Later in this chapter, we show that results similar to Theorems 1 and 2 can be extended to all linear-differential operators (in particular, directional derivatives) and, therefore, to other features of the image, such as ravines and ridges (but not peaks) in the image-intensity function. They will also apply to level-crossings of the image. These theorems can be extended to any dimension, but we will not give these extensions here.

It should be emphasized that, although zero-crossings can only annihilate themselves in pairs as σ increases, the intensity change corresponding to a zero-crossing could become arbitrarily smaller with increasing sigma. The zero-crossing would then become so weak that for practical purposes the curve terminates.

THE ONE-DIMENSIONAL CASE

Let the image be I and the filter be F. We consider the zero crossings in the filtered image.

$$F * I(x) = \int_{-\infty}^{\infty} F(x - \zeta)I(\zeta)d\zeta \qquad (3.1)$$

Denote $\dfrac{d^2}{dx^2}(F * I)$ by E. Hence the zero crossings are the solutions of

$$E(x) = 0 \qquad (3.2)$$

These form curves in the $x - \sigma$ plane. The condition that zero crossings are not created at larger scales is that for all such curves $\sigma(x)$ the extrema of $\sigma(x)$ are not minima. Hence, for all points x_0 such that $\sigma'(x_0) = 0$, we require that $\sigma''(x_0) < 0$.

Let t be a parameter along a curve in $\sigma - x$ space. Then

$$\frac{dE}{dt} = \frac{\partial E}{\partial x}\frac{dx}{dt} + \frac{\partial E}{\partial \sigma}\frac{d\sigma}{dt} . \qquad (3.3)$$

On a curve of zero-crossings, $E = 0$, and so $\dfrac{dE}{dt} = 0$ along the curve.

We can choose the parameter t to be x. Then, using the Implicit Function Theorem, we obtain:

$$\frac{d\sigma}{dx} = \frac{-E_x}{E\sigma} . \qquad (3.4)$$

This derivative vanishes at x_0 if and only if

$$E_x(x_0) = 0, \tag{3.5}$$

and we calculate, at places where Equation 3.5 holds,

$$\frac{d^2\sigma(x_0)}{dx^2} = \frac{-E_{xx}(x_0)}{E_\sigma(x_0)} . \tag{3.6}$$

Thus, our filter must be such that if

$$E(x_0) = E_x(x_0) = 0 \tag{3.7}$$

then

$$\frac{E_{xx}(x_0)}{E_\sigma(x_0)} > 0. \tag{3.8}$$

The heat equation can be written as

$$\frac{\partial^2 E}{\partial x^2} = \frac{1}{\sigma} \frac{\partial E}{\partial \sigma} . \tag{3.9}$$

Note that by the substitution $t = \frac{\sigma^2}{2}$, we obtain the standard heat equation. If the filter F is a Gaussian,

$$F(x) = \frac{1}{\sigma} \exp\left\{ \frac{-x^2}{2\sigma^2} \right\}, \tag{3.10}$$

then it will obey the heat equation of which it is the Green function and hence $E(x)$ will also obey the equation. Thus, $E_{xx}/E_\sigma = 1/\sigma$ and so a Gaussian filter will always satisfy the conditions in Equations 3.7 and 3.8.

We now show that the Gaussian is the *only* filter that satisfies the conditions and obeys the conditions specified in the first section of this chapter.

Consider an image that is the sum of delta functions:

$$I(\zeta) = \sum_{i=1}^{n} A_i\delta(\zeta - \zeta_i). \tag{3.11}$$

It is possible to generate any image in this way by taking the limit as $n \rightarrow \infty$.

Set

$$T(x) = F_{xx}(x). \tag{3.12}$$

Equations 3.7 and 3.8 yield

$$\sum_{i=1}^{n} A_i T(x_0 - \zeta_i) = 0 \tag{3.13}$$

$$\sum_{i=1}^{n} A_i T_x(x_0 - \zeta_i) = 0 \qquad (3.14)$$

and

$$\frac{\sum_{i=1}^{n} A_i T_{xx}(x_0 - \zeta_i)}{\sum_{i=1}^{n} A_i T_\sigma(x_0 - \zeta_i)} > 0. \qquad (3.15)$$

We can construct a counter example if we can solve the simultaneous equations for any $x_0, \zeta_1, \ldots, \zeta_n$ and any positive ℓ^2:

$$\sum_{i=1}^{n} A_i T(x_0 - \zeta_i) = 0. \qquad (3.16)$$

$$\sum_{i=1}^{n} A_i T_x(x_0 - \zeta_i) = 0. \qquad (3.17)$$

$$\sum_{i=1}^{n} A_i T_{xx}(x_0 - \zeta_i) = -\ell^2. \qquad (3.18)$$

$$\sum_{i=1}^{n} A_i T_\sigma(x_0 - \zeta_i) = 1. \qquad (3.19)$$

We can write these as a matrix equation:

$$\begin{pmatrix} T(x_0 - \zeta_1) & \cdots & T(x_0 - \zeta_n) \\ T_x(x_0 - \zeta_1) & \cdots & T_x(x_0 - \zeta_n) \\ T_{xx}(x_0 - \zeta_1) & \cdots & T_{xx}(x_0 - \zeta_n) \\ T_\sigma(x_0 - \zeta_1) & \cdots & T_\sigma(x_0 - \zeta_n) \end{pmatrix} \begin{pmatrix} A_1 \\ \cdot \\ \cdot \\ A_n \end{pmatrix} = \begin{pmatrix} 0 \\ 0 \\ -\ell^2 \\ 1 \end{pmatrix} \qquad (3.20)$$

Using Appendix A at the end of this chapter, a necessary and sufficient condition for it to be impossible to solve these equations for any values of $x_0, \zeta_1 \ldots \zeta_n$ is that there exists a vector $\lambda = (\lambda_1, \lambda_2, \lambda_3, \lambda_4)$ independent of x such that

$$\lambda_1 T(x) + \lambda_2 T_x(x) + \lambda_3 T_{xx}(x) + \lambda_4 T_\sigma(x) = 0 \qquad (3.21)$$

and

$$-\lambda_3 \ell^2 + \lambda_4 \neq 0 \qquad (3.22)$$

Equation (3.22) will be satisfied for all positive ℓ^2 if and only if ($\lambda_3 = 0$ and $\lambda_4 = 0$ can be ruled out because of the conditions)

$$\lambda_3 \lambda_4 < 0 \qquad (3.23)$$

Our condition in Equation 2 means that $F(x)$, and hence $T(x)$ cannot depend on any scale length. The λ's are independent of x, and so to make Equation 3.21 dimensionally correct (Bridgman, 1922) we set

$$\lambda_1 = \frac{a}{\sigma^2} , \lambda_2 = \frac{b}{\sigma} , \lambda_3 = c, \lambda_4 = \frac{-d}{\sigma} \tag{3.24}$$

and rewrite it as

$$\frac{aT}{\sigma^2} + \frac{bT_x}{\sigma} + cT_{xx} = \frac{d}{\sigma} T_\sigma \tag{3.25}$$

Condition in Equation 3.23 implies that $\frac{d}{c}$ is positive.

Now $T = \frac{d^2F}{dx^2}$ so F will also satisfy Equation 3.25. Although it is possible to add a term ϕ to F where $\frac{d^2\phi}{dx^2} = 0$, according to Condition 5 ϕ can only be the zero function.

Thus, we have shown that we can always construct a counter example *unless* our filter F obeys to the equation

$$\frac{aF}{\sigma^2} + \frac{b}{\sigma} F_x + cF_{xx} = \frac{d}{\sigma} F_\sigma \tag{3.26}$$

with $\frac{d}{c}$ positive. It is shown in Appendix B at the end of this chapter that the only solution of this equation obeying the conditions is the Gaussian, thus proving Theorem 1.

THE TWO-DIMENSIONAL CASE

We now consider the two-dimensional case when the zero crossing operator is the laplacian ∇^2 and the image depends on $\underline{x} = (x, y)$. Again, we consider the filtered image

$$F * I(\underline{x}) = \int_{-\infty}^{\infty} \int_{-\infty}^{\infty} F(\underline{x} - \underline{\zeta})I(\underline{\zeta})d\underline{\zeta} \tag{4.1}$$

We set

$$E(\underline{x}) = \nabla^2\{F * I(\underline{x})\} \tag{4.2}$$

The zero-crossings are solutions of $E(\underline{x}) = 0$ and form surfaces in the three-dimensional $(\underline{x}, \sigma)$ space. Our requirements that zero crossings are

not created at larger scales is satisfied if the extrema of these zero crossing surfaces are either maxima or saddle points. Minima are forbidden.
Thus, if we have a surface $\sigma(x, y)$ and there is a point (x_0, y_0) with

$$\sigma_x(x_0, y_0) = \sigma_y(x_0, y_0) = 0 \tag{4.3}$$

we cannot have $\sigma_{xy} = 0$ and both

$$\sigma_{xx} > 0, \sigma_{yy} > 0. \tag{4.4}$$

The axes are chosen to be along the lines of curvature at the extrema:
Thus, σ_{xx}, σ_{yy} are eigenvalues of the Hessian.
Let t be a parameter of a curve of the surface $E(\underline{x}) = 0$. Then,

$$\frac{dE}{dt} = \frac{\partial E}{\partial x} \frac{dx}{dt} + \frac{\partial E}{\partial y} \frac{dy}{dt} + \frac{\partial E}{\partial \sigma} \frac{d\sigma}{dt} \tag{4.5}$$

Since we are on the zero-crossing surface, we have $\frac{dE}{dt} = 0$ and setting $t = x$ and then $t = y$, we obtain

$$\sigma_x = \frac{-E_x}{E_\sigma} \tag{4.6}$$

$$\sigma_y = \frac{-E_y}{E_\sigma} \tag{4.7}$$

Suppose we are at an extremum (x_0, y_0). Choose the x- and y-axes so
that they coincide with the directions of principal curvature at (x_0, y_0).
Then we calculate

$$\sigma_{xx}(x_0, y_0) = \frac{-E_{xx}(x_0 y_0)}{E_\sigma(x_0, y_0)} \tag{4.8}$$

$$\sigma_{yy}(x_0, y_0) = \frac{-E_{yy}(x_0 y_0)}{E_\sigma(x_0, y_0)} \tag{4.9}$$

It should be emphasized that Equations 4.8 and 4.9 are true only at an
extremum of $\sigma(x, y)$ and only if the x- and y-axes are taken along the
directions of the lines of curvature (this ensures $\sigma_{xy} = 0$)
It follows, as in the one-dimensional case, that the conditions in Equations 3 and 4 will always be satisfied if E obeys the heat equation. If
$\sigma_{xx}(x_0, y_0)$ and $\sigma_{yy}(x_0, y_0)$ are both positive. Equations 4.8 and 4.9 imply
that $\dfrac{E_{xx}(x_0 y_0)}{E_\sigma(x_0, y_0)}$ and $\dfrac{E_{yy}(x_0, y_0)}{E_\sigma(x_0, y_0)}$ are both negative. Thus, a Gaussian filter
will always obey our condition.
We now show that if the filter is not a Gaussian, we can construct a

counter-example. The argument is a generalization of the proof of Theorem 1. Let

$$I(\zeta) = \sum_{i=1}^{n} A_i \delta(\underline{\zeta} - \underline{\zeta}_i) \tag{4.10}$$

Set

$$T(\underline{x}) = \nabla^2 F(\underline{x}) \tag{4.11}$$

We can construct a counter-example if we can solve the matrix equation for any $x_0, \zeta_1 \ldots, \zeta_n$ and any positive ℓ_1^2 and ℓ_2^2:

$$
\begin{pmatrix}
T(x_0 - \zeta_1) & \cdots & T(x_0 - \zeta_n) \\
T_x(x_0 - \zeta_1) & \cdots & T_x(x_0 - \zeta_n) \\
T_y(x_0 - \zeta_1) & \cdots & T_y(x_0 - \zeta_n) \\
T_{xx}(x_0 - \zeta_1) & \cdots & T_{xx}(x_0 - \zeta_n) \\
T_{xy}(x_0 - \zeta_1) & \cdots & T_{xy}(x_0 - \zeta_n) \\
T_{yy}(x_0 - \zeta_1) & \cdots & T_{yy}(x_0 - \zeta_n) \\
T_\sigma(x_0 - \zeta_1) & \cdots & T_\sigma(x_0 - \zeta_n)
\end{pmatrix}
\begin{pmatrix}
A_1 \\
\cdot \\
\cdot \\
\cdot \\
\cdot \\
A_n
\end{pmatrix}
=
\begin{pmatrix}
0 \\
0 \\
0 \\
-\ell_1^2 \\
0 \\
-\ell_2^2 \\
1
\end{pmatrix}
\tag{4.12}
$$

Using Appendix A, a necessary and sufficient condition for no solution to exist for all $x_0, \zeta_1, \ldots, \zeta_n$ is that we can find $\underline{\lambda} = (\lambda_1, \ldots, \lambda_5)$ such that

$$\lambda_1(x) + \lambda_2 T_x(x) + \lambda_3 T_y(x) + \lambda_4 T_{xx}(x) + \lambda_7 T_{xy}(x) + \lambda_5 T_{yy} + \lambda_6 T_\sigma(x) = 0 \tag{4.13}$$

and

$$-\ell_1^2 \lambda_4 - \ell_2^2 \lambda_5 + \lambda_6 \neq 0 \tag{4.14}$$

Equation 4.14 can be satisfied for all positive ℓ_1^2 and ℓ_2^2 if and only if (because of the conditions)

$$\lambda_4 \lambda_5 > 0, \lambda_4 \lambda_6 < 0. \tag{4.15}$$

Again, Condition 2 implies the λs are of form

$$\lambda_1 = \frac{a}{\sigma^2} , \lambda_2 = \frac{b_1}{\sigma} , \lambda_3 = \frac{b_2}{\sigma} , \lambda_4 = c_1, \lambda_5 = c_2, \lambda_6 = \frac{-d}{\sigma} , \lambda_7 = c_3 \tag{4.16}$$

and T satisfies

$$\frac{aT}{\sigma^2} + \frac{b_1}{\sigma} T_x + \frac{b_2}{\sigma} T_y + c_1 T_{xx} + c_2 T_{yy} + c_3 T_{xy} = \frac{d}{\sigma} T_\sigma \tag{4.17}$$

with $c_1 c_2 > 0$ and $c_1 d > 0$[5].

---

[5] We can obtain restrictions on c_3 by requiring that the curvature at the extreme points is negative. This means that elliptic operators—and hence, a skewed Gaussian filter—will also have the desired scaling properties. We are not interested in these since we will require the filter to be symmetric (see later).

F will satisfy Equation 4.17 up to a term ψ with $\nabla^2\psi = 0$, but because of Condition 5 ψ can be taken to be zero.

It is shown in Appendix B that the only solution of Equation 4.17 that obeys our conditions is the product of 2 one-dimensional Gaussians. If we make the additional assumption of symmetry, we obtain a two-dimensional symmetric Gaussian. Hence, the Gaussian is the only filter that satisfied our condition, and we have proven Theorem 2.

There is an additional property of Gaussian filters: allowed zero-crossing surfaces in (x, y, σ) space cannot have saddle points with positive mean curvature *H*, because $H = \dfrac{\sigma_{xx} + \sigma_{yy}}{2}$. The result of this section forbids the existence of upside-down mountains or pits [in the (x, y, σ) plane] and also of upside-down volcanos. Sections of the zero-crossing surfaces normal to the (x, y) plane may appear as suggesting that lines of zero-crossings are created. In fact, because of saddle points of the surface, zeros can be traced *continuously* along the zero-crossing surface to smaller and smaller scales.

FURTHER RESULTS

It is clear that the methods of proof we have developed do not only apply to zero crossings. For example, consider the one-dimensional case and look for solutions of

$$\frac{d}{dx} (F * I) = 0 \qquad (5.1)$$

These correspond to maxima and minima of the filtered signal, which we call "peaks" and "troughs." If we set $E = \dfrac{d}{dx} (F * I)$ and duplicate the arguments discussed earlier in this chapter we find that having a Gaussian filter is a necessary and sufficient condition for peaks and troughs not to be created.

More generally, if $L(\underline{x})$ is a differential operator in any dimension that commutes with the diffusion equation, then solutions of

$$L(F * I) = const \qquad (5.2)$$

will not be created if and only if the filter is Gaussian. Zeros of all linear-differential operators can be encompassed by Theorem 1.

In particular, in two dimensions, surfaces obeying $\frac{d}{dx}(F * T) = 0$ can only be created by a non-Gaussian filter. Thus, ridges and ravines whose creation necessarily involves creation of zeros along some direction can only be created, as the scale increases, by a non-Gaussian filter. The argument, however, does not apply to extremum points (nondegenerate critical points, such as peaks and pits, where all derivatives vanish simultaneously).

These results also apply to level-crossings of signals. To see this, observe that the level-crossings of a signal are equivalent to the zero-crossings of a modified signal.

INTERSECTIONS OF ZERO CROSSINGS

We now consider the possibility of having two zero-crossing contours that intersect. This is illustrated in figure 2.3d. First observe that the only place where two zero-crossings of a signal $u(x, t)$ can intersect is at a saddle point of $u(x, t)$. This can br thought of intuitively as two contour lines on a mountain intersecting at a saddle point. Figure 2.4 shows an example of the intersection of two zero-crossing curves.[6]

Suppose we have a signal $u(x, t)$, which has a saddle point. We show that this imposes restrictions on how the zero-crossing contours can cross. First, from the analytical properties of the Gaussian filter, we can expand $u(x, t)$ as a Taylor series in x. As we expand in x we impose that the $u(x, t)$ obeys the diffusion equation. This is possible because of the analytic properties of Gaussian-filtered functions, and hence of $u(x, t)$. So at a particular point, which without loss of generality we take to be the origin, we can expand

$$\begin{aligned}
u(x, t) = Ex &+ \alpha \langle x^2 + 2t \rangle + \beta \langle x^3 + 6xt \rangle \\
&+ \gamma \langle x^4 + 12x^2t + 12t^2 \rangle \\
&+ \delta \langle x^5 + 20x^3t + 60xt^2 \rangle + 0(x^6)
\end{aligned} \tag{6.1}$$

Now we require that $u(x, t)$ has a saddle point at the origin $(0, 0)$. First we need

$$\frac{\partial u}{\partial x} = \frac{\partial u}{\partial t} = 0 \tag{6.2}$$

This imposes that $E = 0$ and $\alpha = 0$. The Condition 6.2 ensures that (x, t) is an extremum. To be a saddle point, we need

$$\left\langle \frac{\partial u^2}{\partial x^2} \frac{\partial^2 u}{\partial t^2} - \left(\frac{\partial u}{\partial x \partial t} \right)^2 \right\rangle < 0 \tag{6.3}$$

$$(x, t) = (0, 0).$$

Now for a saddle point we have

$$\begin{aligned}
u(x, t) = \beta(x^3 &+ 6xt) \\
&+ \gamma \langle x^4 + 12x^2t + 12t^2 \rangle \\
&+ \delta \langle x^5 + 20x^3t + 60xt^2 \rangle.
\end{aligned} \tag{6.4}$$

---

[6]Courtesy of H. Vorhees.

FIGURE 2.4. The signal is a sine wave subtracted from a regular sawtooth pattern. The lower diagram shows the sign value of the signal convolved with the second derivative of a Gaussian in scale space. The upper diagram shows the intersections of the zero-crossings curves. Note that the zero crossings intersect at saddle points of the convolved signal.

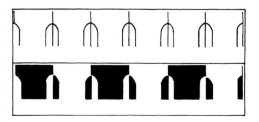

To find the possible directions for zero-crossings at a saddle point we write $u(x, t)$ as a Taylor series

$$u(x, t) = u(0, 0) + x^2 \frac{\partial^2 u}{\partial x^2} |(0, 0) + t^2 \frac{\partial^2 u}{\partial t^2} |(9, 0) \qquad (6.5)$$

$$+ 2xt \frac{\partial^2 u}{\partial x \partial t} |(0, 0)$$

From Equation 6.4 we have

$$\frac{\partial^2 u}{\partial x^2} |(0, 0) = 0 \qquad (6.6)$$

$$\frac{\partial^2 u}{\partial x \partial t} = 6\beta \qquad (6.7)$$

$$\frac{\partial^2 u}{\partial t^2} = 24\gamma \qquad (6.8)$$

So if we expand in x and t we have

$$u(x, t) = 6\beta xt + 12\gamma t^2 + 0(3) \qquad (6.9)$$

We see from Equation 6.6 that $(0,0)$ is automatically a saddle point. We are interested in the lines which are solutions of

$$u(x, t) = 0 \qquad (6.10)$$

From equation 6.9 we see that to first order they are given by

$$(\beta x + 2\gamma t)t = 0 \qquad (6.11)$$

The higher-order terms will not contribute to the tangent vectors of these lines at $(0, 0)$. So we see from Equation 6.11 that, at places where zero-crossings cross, one line must have tangent vector $(1, 0)$ and the other $(-2\gamma, \beta)$. Since β and γ can have arbitrary values, the tangent $(-2\gamma, \beta)$ can point in any direction. However, we have the constraint that at a zero-crossing intersection, one of the zero-crossing lines must be parallel to the x-axis. From our previous results we know that this must correspond to a maximum.

It is easy to construct a signal whose zero-crossings will intersect in scale-space. For example $f(x) = x^3 - x$ has zeroes at $\pm 1, 0$. Convolving with a Gaussian gives $f(x, t) = x^3 + (6t - 1)x$, this has three zeros for $t <$ 1/6 and one for $t > 1/6$. Hence the zero-crossing contours must cross at $x = 0, t = 1/6$. Note that even if zero-crossings intersect it is still possible to do coarse to fine tracking of the signal since the two contours are still continuous when they cross. The results above also show that at such a saddle point one of the zero-crossing contours will be parallel to the x-axis and will therefore correspond to a maximum.

One may apply Catastrophe theory to the expansion (Equation 6.1) to study other interesting special cases.

FINGERPRINT THEOREMS: ASSUMPTIONS AND RESULTS

Again we consider the zero-crossings of a signal $I(x)$, space-scale filtered with the second derivative of a Gaussian, as a function of x, σ. Let E be defined by

$$E(x, \sigma) = I * G''$$

$$E(x, \sigma) = I(x) * [G(x, \sigma)''] = \int I(\zeta) \frac{1}{\sigma} \frac{d^2}{dx^2} exp - \frac{(x - \zeta)^2}{2\sigma^2} d\zeta. \quad (7.1)$$

Notice that $E(x, \sigma)$ obeys the diffusion equation in x and σ:

$$\frac{\partial^2 E}{\partial x^2} = \frac{1}{\sigma} \frac{\partial E}{\partial \sigma} . \quad (7.2)$$

We restrict ourselves to images, or signals, P such that E can be expressed as a finite Taylor series of arbitrarily high order and such that E is not antisymmetric about all its zeros. Observe that any filtered image can be approximated arbitrarily well in this way, because of the classical Weierstrass approximation theorem. Functions that are antisymmetric about all their zeros, such as sinusoid functions, are discussed in detail in a forthcoming paper (Yuille & Poggio, 1986). It is shown that these are the only functions for which the zero-crossing contours are independent of scale (i.e., the contours go straight up in the scale-space fingerprint). Additional information about the gradient of the function on the zero-crossings or knowledge of the level-crossings is sufficient to determine the signal. Note that, for a finite-order polynomial, functions antisymmetric about all their zeros have only one zero-crossing contour.

We will show that the local behavior of the zero-crossing curves [defined by $E(x, \sigma) = 0$] on the $x - \sigma$ plane determines the image. Our reconstruction scheme provides the image I in terms of Hermite polynomials. The proof of this result can be generalized to two-dimensional and extended to zero- and level-crossings of linear (differential) operators. More precisely we have proven the following theorem:

Theorem 1: The derivatives (including the zero-order derivative) of the zero-crossing contours defined by $E(x, \sigma) = 0$, at two distinct points at the same scale, uniquely determine a signal of class P up to a constant scaling (except on a set of measure zero).

Note that the theorem does not apply to signals that do not have at least two distinct zero-crossing contours. Yuille and Poggio (1983b) have extended Theorem 1 to the two-dimensional case.

The theorems do not directly address the *stability* and the numerical conditioning of this reconstruction scheme. The first question concerns stability of the reconstruction of the *filtered* function $E(x, \sigma)$ at the σ where the derivatives are taken. Note that our result relies only on two points on the zero-crossing contours. Exploitation of the whole zero-crossing contours should make the reconstruction considerably more robust. The second question is about the stability of the recovery of the unfiltered signal $I(x)$ from $E(x, \sigma)$. This is equivalent to inverting the diffusion equation, which is numerically unstable since it is a classically ill-posed problem. Reconstruction is, however, possible with an error depending on the signal to noise behavior (see Yuille & Poggio, 1983b).

Outline of the One-Dimensional Proof

We summarize here the one-dimensional proof from a slightly different point of view that clarifies its bare structure.

The proof starts by taking derivatives along the zero-crossing contours at a certain point. Such derivatives split into combinations of x and t derivatives (where $t = \sigma^2/2$). Because the filter is assumed to be Gaussian, however, derivatives can be expressed in terms of x derivatives. This is a key point: Since the filtered signal $E(x, t)$ satisfies the diffusion equation, the t derivatives can be expressed in terms of the x derivatives simply by $E_t = E_{xx}$. The next stage is to find the x derivatives of $E(x, t)$ up to an arbitrary degree n from such derivatives along the zero-crossing contours in the $x - t$ plane. We show that this can be done by using two points on two contours. (It is possible that one point is sufficient, but we are as yet unable to prove this.) Since $E(x, t)$ is entirely analytic because of the Gaussian filtering, it can be represented by a Taylor series expansion in x. Since we know the values of the n derivatives of $E(x, t)$ with respect to x, we know its Taylor series expansion and hence $E(x, t)$. The unfiltered signal $I(x)$, $(E(x, t) = I(x) * G(x, t))$ can then be recovered in the ideal noiseless case by deblurring the Gaussian. A particularly simple way of doing this is provided by a property of the function ϕ_n, in which we will expand the function F: The coefficients of an expansion of $I(x)$ in terms of ϕ_n are equal to the coefficients of the Taylor series expansion of $E(x, t)$. In the presence of noise, the recovery of $I(x)$ from $E(x, t)$ is obviously unstable, since it is a classically ill-posed problem. It is limited by S/N ratio since high spatial frequencies in the signal are masked by the noise for increasing t. (For instance, if $F(x) = \Sigma a_\mu e^{i\mu x}$, the filtered signal is $E(x, t) = \Sigma a_\mu e^{i\mu x} e^{-\mu^2 t}$.) Note that since the zero-crossing contours are available at all scales, a reconstruction scheme that exploits more than two points will be significantly more robust. As one would expect, the reconstruction of the unfiltered signal is therefore affected by noise. The reconstruction of the filtered signal $E(x, t)$ is likely to be considerably more robust.

PROOF OF THE THEOREM IN ONE-DIMENSION

Our proof can be divided into three main steps. The first shows that derivatives at a point on a zero-crossing contour put strong constraints on the "moments" of the Fourier transform of $E(x, \sigma)$ (see Equation 8.11.4). The second relates the "moments" to the coefficients of the expansion of $I(x) = E(x, 0)$ in functions related to the Hermite polynomials. Finally the "moments" can be uniquely determined by the derivatives on a second point of a different zero-crossing contour. We outline here only the first part of the proof, which is given in full in Yuille and Poggio (1983b).

THE "MOMENTS" OF THE SIGNAL ARE CONSTRAINED BY THE ZERO-CROSSING CONTOURS

Let the Fourier transform of the signal $I(x)$ be $\tilde{I}(\omega)$ and the Gaussian filter be $G(x, \sigma) = \dfrac{1}{\sigma} e^{\frac{-x^2}{2\sigma^2}}$ with Fourier transform $\tilde{G}(\omega) = e^{\frac{-\sigma^2 \omega^2}{2}}$.

The zero-crossings are given by solutions of $E(x, t) = 0$. Using the convolution theorem we can express $E(x, t)$ as

$$E(x, t) = \int e^{-\omega^2 t} e^{i\omega x} \tilde{I}(\omega) d\omega. \tag{8.11.1}$$

and $t = \sigma^2/2$. The Implicit Function theorem gives curves $x(t)$, which are C^∞ (this is a property of the Gaussian filter and of the diffusion equation, see Yuille & Poggio, 1983a,b). Let ζ be a parameter of the zero-crossing curve. Then

$$\frac{d}{d\zeta} = \frac{dx}{d\zeta}\frac{\partial}{\partial x} + \frac{dt}{d\zeta}\frac{\partial}{\partial t}. \tag{8.11.2}$$

On the zero-crossing surface, $E = 0$ and $\frac{d^n}{d\zeta^n}E = 0$ for all integers n.

Knowledge of the zero-crossing curve is equivlent to knowledge of all the derivatives of x and t with respect to ζ.

We compute the derivatives of E with respect to ζ at (x_0, t_0). The first derivative is:

$$\frac{d}{d\zeta}E(x, t) = \frac{dx}{d\zeta}\int e^{-\omega^2 t}e^{i\omega x}(i\omega)\tilde{I}(\omega)d\omega$$
$$+ \frac{dt}{d\zeta}\int e^{-\omega^2 t}(-\omega^2)e^{i\omega x}\tilde{I}(\omega)d\omega \tag{8.11.3}$$

and is expressed in terms of the first and second moments of the function $e^{-\omega^2 t}e^{i\omega x}I(\omega)$. The moment of order n is defined by:

$$M_n = \int_{-\infty}^{\infty}(i\omega)^n e^{-\omega^2 t}e^{i\omega x}\tilde{I}(\omega)d\omega. \tag{8.11.4}$$

The second derivative is

$$\frac{d^2}{d\zeta^2}E(x, t) = \frac{d^2x}{d\zeta^2}\int e^{-\omega^2 t}e^{i\omega x}(i\omega)\tilde{I}(\omega)d\omega$$

$$+ \frac{d^2t}{d\zeta^2}\int e^{-\omega^2 t}(-\omega^2)e^{i\omega x}\tilde{I}(\omega)d\omega$$

$$+ \left(\frac{dx}{d\zeta}\right)^2\int e^{-\omega^2 t}e^{i\omega x}(-\omega^2)\tilde{I}(\omega)d\omega \tag{8.11.5}$$

$$+ 2\frac{dx}{d\zeta}\frac{dt}{d\zeta}\int e^{-\omega^2 t}(-\omega^2)e^{i\omega x}(i\omega)\tilde{I}(\omega)d\omega$$

$$+ \left(\frac{dt}{d\zeta}\right)^2\int e^{-\omega^2 t}(\omega^4)e^{-i\omega x}\tilde{I}(\omega)d\omega.$$

Since the parametric derivatives along the zero-crossing curve are zero, Equation 8.11.3 is a homogeneous linear equation in the first two moments. Similarly, (8.11.5) is a homogeneous linear equation in the first four moments. In general, the nth equation, $\frac{d^n}{d\zeta^n}E(x, t) = 0$, is a homogeneous equation in the first $2n$ moments. We choose our axes such that

$x_0 = 0$. We can then show that the moments of $e^{-\omega^2 t} I(\omega)$ are the coefficients a_n in the expression of the function $I(x)$ in Hermite polynomials. So we have n equations in the first $2n$ coefficients a_n. To determine the a_n uniquely, we need n additional and independent equations, which can be provided by considering a neighboring zero-crossing curve at (x_1, t_0) (see Yuille & Poggio, 1983b).

CURTIS' THEOREM

Since our results were published (Yuille & Poggio, 1983b), Curtis (1985) has proven a set of somewhat different and stronger theorems to which we have referred earlier. For completeness we give here a brief description of her results. The basic theorem is

Curtis theorem: Let $f(x, y)$ and $g(x, y)$ be real, two-dimensional, doubly-periodic, bandlimited functions with sign $f(x, y) = $ sign $g(x, y)$, where $f(x, y)$ takes on both negative and positive values. If $f(x, y)$ and $g(x, y)$ are nonfactorable when expressed as polynomials in the Fourier series representation then $f(x, y) = cg(x, y)$.

An intuitive way to understand its meaning is the following. Consider a Fourier polynomial in one-dimension. Reconstructing it is equivalent to computing its Fourier coefficients, which are finite in number because of the bandlimiting property. Assume that the polynomial has zero-crossings, x values at which the function crosses zero. For each zero-crossing an equation can be written (putting the polynomial equal to zero for the value of x). Thus, there is a system of linear equations from which, in principle, the Fourier coefficients can be calculated. It is fairly easy to see that in order to have enough equations for the number of unknowns, the Fourier polynomial has to be bandpass with a bandwidth of less than an octave (one knows that there are at least as many zero-crossings as twice the lower cut-off). This is an extension of Logan's theorem to Fourier polynomials (see Poggio, 1982a, where it is shown under which, rather technical conditions, this set of equations is independent). Consider now the equivalent two-dimensional case: The Fourier polynomial is still determined by a finite number of coefficients. The number of zero-crossing points is now, however, infinite (zero-crossings are curves). An infinite number of equations can therefore be written without any bandpass condition on the function! Curtis' theorems make precise this informal equation-counting argument.

This result has been extended to more general bandlimited functions than Fourier polynomials (Curtis, 1985). The theorem says that for bandlimited functions that satisfy the nonfactorability condition, zero-crossings or level-crossings determine the function uniquely in two, or more, dimensions. The assumptions are different from ours. We do not need the function to be bandlimited. We must however filter it through a Gaussian. Curtis' result is stronger because it does not require information at different scales. One can show that our theorems are then a special case for the functions to which Curtis' theorem applies. Curtis' theorems do not apply in one dimension, where zero-crossings determine uniquely the underlying function only for functions that are bandpass with one octave bandwidth or less and satisfy some other more technical condition (Logan, 1977). For more general functions in one-dimension, it seems therefore that information at several scales is needed, as required by our theorems.

It is important to notice that Curtis' results give a constructive way of computing the function from the zero-crossings. The method, however, is likely to be, in general, ill-conditioned. This issue was not analyzed by Curtis.

An Application

We will indicate here how one can use Curtis' theorem to give a simpler proof of our one-dimensional result. Consider a polynomial one-dimensional function $I(x)$. Construct the two-dimensional function $E(x \; \sigma)$ defined by

$$E(x, \sigma) = I * G$$

that is

$$E(x, \sigma) = I(x) * [G(x, \sigma)] = \int I(\zeta) \frac{1}{\sigma} exp \; \frac{-(x - \zeta)^2}{2\sigma^2} \; d\zeta.$$

It is a straightforward consequence of the diffusion equation that $E(x, t)$ is a polynomial in x and t. Consider now the zero-crossings of $E(x, t)$. In deriving her results Curtis makes use of the following theorem:

Theorem: Let $f(x, y)$ and $g(x, y)$ be real, two-dimensional polynomials of degrees r and s with no common factors, then there are at most rs distinct pairs (x, y) where:

$$f(x, y) = g(x, y) = 0.$$

This theorem can be used to give a simpler proof of our results: If the scale space diagrams of two polynomials are the same, then the polynomials are identical or have common factors. We are interested in polynomials of form $f(x, t) = G * I(x)$ and $g(x, t) = G * J(x)$. It is clear that they can have common factors only if $I(x)$ and $J(x)$ are identical. Hence, the zero-crossings uniquely specify one-dimensional polynomial signals, up to scaling.

A CONNECTION WITH PSYCHOPHYSICS?

We now illustrate the use of scale space by analyzing a psychophysical experiment.

The analysis of spatial structures at different spatial resolution has been a fashionable theme in visual psychophysics for the last 15 years. It is natural to ask whether the fingerprint results have any connection with psychophysics. In this section, we briefly describe psychophysical experiments by Henning, Hertz, & Broadbent (1975) and a possible interpretation in terms of fingerprints.

Henning et al. (1975) measured discriminability of a sinusoidal grating of the type shown in Figure 2.5a against the pattern of figure 5b, which is the same as 5a but with sidebands. They found that the discriminability was markedly reduced by adding a low-frequency grating as shown in figure 2.6c and 2.6d. They concluded that this finding is inconsistent with the hypothesis that the visual system analyzes spatial patterns in independent, narrowly-tuned bands of spatial frequency.

Figures 2.5, 2.6, and 2.7, however, show that the finding is consistent with the idea that the visual system use fingerprints (i.e., zero-crossings at different scales). The fingerprints of Figure 2.5a and 2.5b are quite different; those of figure 2.6c and 2.6d are almost indistinguishable.

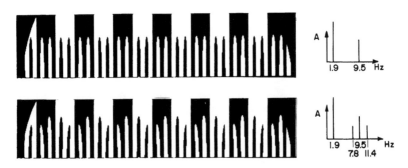

FIGURE 2.5. Figure (a) shows the scale space diagram of a sinusoid signal with period 9.5 Hz. Figure (b) shows the scale space diagram of the signal superimposed with two sinusoids of frequencies 7.8 and 11.4 Hz.

FIGURE 2.6. Figure (a) shows the scale space diagram of the signal in Figure 2.5a with an additional sinusoid at 1.9 Hz. Figure (b) shows the scale space diagram of the signal in Figure 2.5b with an additional sinusoid at 1.9 Hz.

CONCLUSIONS

The behavior of the zero- (or level-) crossings is more complex in two dimensions than in one dimension. In the two-dimension case, two zero-crossing contours can merge into one closed contour as the scale increases. The zero-crossing surface has a one-dimensional cross section (for given y, say) that corresponds to an allowed one-dimensional case. In two-dimensions, however, the "complementary" situation can also occur:

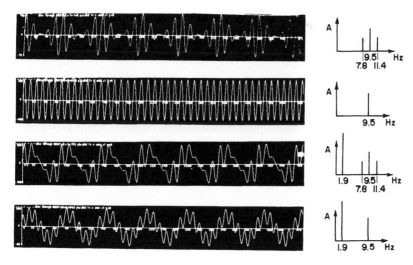

FIGURE 2.7. Figures (a), (b), (c) and (d) show the signals in Figures 2.5(b), 2.5(a), 2.6(b), and 2.6(a) respectively.

A closed zero-crossing contour can split into two as the scale increases, just as the trunk of a tree may split into two branches. This occurs at saddle points of the zero-crossing surface. This case would correspond in one-dimension to the "creation" of a zero-crossing (imagine a one-dimensional section of the zero-crossing surface) which is forbidden. In two-dimensions, however, no new zero-crossing is created, since the corresponding surface is continuous down to zero scale. We have constructed two-dimensional examples of both these two cases, using the Gaussian filters. Both examples would also work for all other filters.

Several other functions have been proposed for filtering images. We expect that they only give a nice scaling behavior for values of σ for which they approximate the solution of the diffusion equation. The DOG (difference of Gaussians) *does not* satisfy the diffusion equation, but is a good approximation except when σ is very small. One-dimensional real Gabor functions (the product of a Gaussian and a sine or a cosine) approximate the solution of the diffusion equation only for large values of σ. Our conditions are violated even more by the sine function, which only satisfies the diffusion equation at best in a weak asymptotic sense. It is interesting that our proof implies that the heat equation is the only linear equation that has a nice scaling behavior of its solutions, with suitable boundary conditions.

In summary, we have shown here that the Gaussian is the only filter that guarantees a nice scaling behavior of the zero- and level-crossings of linear differential operators. (Notice that the Gaussian need not be symmetric: Elongated directional filters, obtained by stretching the axes, also have a nice scaling behavior).

We conclude with a brief discussion of a few issues that are raised by this chapter and that will require further work.

1. *Stability of the reconstruction.* Although we have not yet rigorously addressed the question of numerical stability of the whole reconstruction scheme, there seem to be various ways for designing a robust reconstruction scheme. The first step to consider is the reconstruction of the *filtered* signal $E(x, t)$. One could exploit the derivatives at n points—at the given t—and then solve the resulting highly constrained linear equations with least squares methods. Alternatively, it may be possible to fit a smooth curve through several points on one contour, and then obtain the derivatives there in terms of this interpolated curve. The same process must be performed on a second separate zero-crossing contour. This scheme provides a rigorous way of proving that instead of derivatives at two points, the location of the whole zero-crossing contour across scales can be used directly to reconstruct the signal.

The second step involves the reconstruction of the unfiltered signal

$I(x)$. This reconstruction step is unstable if only one scale is used, but it can be regularized and effectively performed in most situations, especially by using information from zero-crossings at smaller scales.

2. *Degenerate fingerprints.* Our uniqueness result applies to *almost* all signals: A restricted but well known class of signals with vertical zero-crossings in the scale-space diagram correspond to nonunique fingerprints. These signals, which will be discussed in a forthcoming paper (Yuille and Poggio, 1986), and which correspond to functions antisymmetric about all their zeros, do not belong to the class P introduced in Theorems 1 and 2. Interestingly, elements of this class can be distinguished by level-crossing (with a level different from zero) or by knowledge of the gradient (Yuille and Poggio, 1986). As we mentioned already, the results of Curtis (1985) extend significantly our theorems in the case of images (two-dimensional functions).

3. *Extensions.* Our main results apply to zero- and level-crossings of a signal filtered by a Gaussian filter of variable size. They also apply to transformations of a signal under a linear space-invariant operator—in particular, they apply to the linear derivatives of a signal and to linear combinations of them. In both one-dimension and two-dimensions, local information at just two points is sufficient. In practice, since many derivatives are needed at each point, information about the whole contour, to which the point belongs, is in fact exploited.

4. *Are the fingerprints redundant?* The proof of our theorem implies that two points on the fingerprint contours are sufficient. As we mentioned earlier, several points are probably required to make the reconstruction robust and to ensure the avoidance of a nongeneric pair of points. Curtis' results imply that (for bandlimited, two-dimensional functions) zero-crossings at just one scale ($t = 0$) are indeed sufficient for a reconstruction (in general, however, ill-conditioned).

5. *Implications of the results.* As we discussed in the introduction, our results imply that the fingerprint representation is a *complete* representation of a signal or an image. Zero- and level-crossings across scales of a filtered signal capture full information about it. Note that the fingerprint theorems do not constrain or characterize in any way the differential filter that has to be used. The filter may be just the identity operator, provided of course that enough zero-crossing contours exist. Independent arguments, based on the constraints of the signal formation process, must be exploited to characterize a suitable filter for each class of signals. For images, second derivative operators such as the Laplacian are suggested by work that takes into account the physical properties of objects and of the imaging process (Grimson, 1983; Torre and Poggio, 1984; Yuille, 1983).

6. *Zero-crossings and slopes.* A natural question to ask is whether gradient information across scales at the zero-crossings, in addition to their location, can be used to reconstruct the original. Hummel (1984, personal communication) has recently shown that this is the case, as one would expect in the light of our results (Yuille and Poggio, 1983b, 1986). We have been able to simplify and extend the elegant proof by Hummel and obtain the following result: *Knowledge of zero-crossing surfaces and magnitude of the x − t gradient over a finite, nonzero interval of the zero-crossing surface is sufficient to determine the image.*

Finally we can use the uniqueness results of Curtis (1985) in two dimensions to obtain a new proof of uniqueness in one dimension that has implications for inverting the heat equation. This is discussed in Yuille and Poggio (1986).

APPENDIX A

If we have a matrix equation

$$B\underline{x} = \underline{a} \tag{1}$$

the necessary and sufficient condition for the existence of a solution is that

$$rank \begin{pmatrix} b_{11} & \cdots & b_{1n} \\ . & \cdots & . \\ b_{m1} & . & b_{mn} \end{pmatrix} = rank \begin{pmatrix} b_{11} & \cdots & b_{1n} & a_1 \\ . & \cdots & . \\ b_{m1} & \cdots & b_{mn} & a_m \end{pmatrix} \tag{2}$$

Hence, a necessary and sufficient condition for the nonexistence of a solution is that we can find a vector $\underline{\lambda} = (\lambda_1, \ldots, \lambda_m)$, such that

$$\lambda_1(b_{11}, \ldots, b_{1n}) + \ldots + \lambda_m(b_{m1}, \ldots, b_{mn}) = 0 \tag{3}$$

but for which

$$\lambda_1 a_1 + \ldots + \lambda_m a_m \neq 0. \tag{4}$$

APPENDIX B

Suppose we have a generalized diffusion equation of form

$$a\,\frac{F}{\sigma^2} + \frac{bF_x}{\sigma} + cF_{xx} = \frac{dF_\sigma}{\sigma}. \tag{1}$$

We can remove the first term by the scaling $F \to \sigma^{-(a/d)}F$. Consider the remaining terms

$$\frac{bFx}{\sigma} + cF_{xx} = \frac{dF_\sigma}{\sigma} . \tag{2}$$

We write

$$F(x, \sigma) = \frac{1}{\sqrt{2\pi}} \int f(\omega, \sigma)e^{-i\omega x}d\omega \tag{3}$$

where $f(\omega, \sigma)$ is the Fourier transform of $F(x, \sigma)$ with respect to x. Combining Equations 3 and 2 we obtain

$$\frac{b(-i\omega)}{\sigma} f + c(-\omega^2)f = \frac{d}{\sigma} \frac{\partial f}{\partial \sigma} . \tag{4}$$

We integrate and get

$$f(\omega, \sigma) = g(\omega)\{e^{\frac{-i\omega b\sigma}{d}} e^{\frac{-c\omega^2}{d} \frac{\sigma^2}{2}}\} \tag{5}$$

where $g(\omega)$ is a function of integration independent of σ.
Hence, substituting Equation 5 into 3 gives us

$$F(x, \sigma) = \frac{1}{\sqrt{2\pi}} \int g(\omega)\{e^{\frac{-i\omega b\sigma}{d}} e^{\frac{-c\omega^2}{d} \frac{\sigma^2}{2}}\}e^{-i\omega x}d\omega. \tag{6}$$

Note that we are considering equations for which c/d is positive, and so the integral is well defined. We now apply the convolution theorem to Equation 6 and get

$$F(x, \sigma) = \frac{1}{\sqrt{2\pi}} \int \lambda(x - \zeta, \sigma)\mu(\zeta)d\zeta \tag{7}$$

where $\mu(\zeta)$ is the Fourier transform of $g(\omega)$ and $\lambda(x, \sigma)$ is the Fourier transform of $\{e^{\frac{-i\omega b\sigma}{d}} e^{\frac{-c\omega^2\sigma^2}{2d}}\}$. We calculate

$$\lambda(x, \sigma) = \sqrt{\frac{d}{c}} \frac{1}{\sigma} e^{\frac{-d}{2c\sigma^2} (x+b\sigma)^2} \tag{8}$$

Thus the general solution to (1) is of form

$$F(x, \sigma) = \frac{1}{\sqrt{2\pi}} \sigma^{\frac{a}{d}-1} \sqrt{\frac{d}{c}} \int e^{\frac{-d}{2c\sigma^2} (x-\zeta+b\sigma)^2} \mu(\zeta)d\zeta \tag{9}$$

We now impose the conditions stated in the beginning of the chapter. First, note that $\lambda(x, \sigma)$ is a Gaussian with centre $x = -b\sigma$. The requirement that the center of the filter does not move implies that $b = 0$. Write

$$F(x, \sigma) = \sigma^{\frac{a}{d}} \int \frac{1}{\sqrt{2\pi}} \sqrt{\frac{d}{c}} \frac{1}{\sigma} e^{\frac{-d}{2c\sigma^2} (x-\zeta)^2} \mu(\zeta)d\zeta \tag{10}$$

and consider the limit as σ tends to 0. Now,

$$Lim_{\sigma \to 0} \frac{1}{\sqrt{2\pi}} \sqrt{\frac{d}{c}} \frac{1}{\sigma} e^{\frac{-d}{2c\sigma^2} (x-\zeta)^2} = \delta(x - \zeta) \tag{11}$$

where δ denotes the Dirac delta function. If $\left(\frac{a}{d}\right)$ is nonzero the limits of $F(x, \sigma)$ will either be undefined or zero. Hence, our condition (Equation 3) forces $a = 0$. Moreover, substituting into Equation 10 we obtain

$$Lim_{a \to 0} F(x, \sigma) = \mu(x) \tag{12}$$

and condition of Equation 3 means that $\mu(x)$ must be the delta function. Hence, on substituting this back into Equation 10 the only solutions of Equation 1 that satisfies our condition is the Gaussian

$$G(x, \sigma) = \frac{1}{\sqrt{2\pi}} \sqrt{\frac{d}{c}} \frac{1}{\sigma} e^{\frac{-d}{2c} \frac{x^2}{\sigma^2}} . \tag{13}$$

This analysis can be extended to the two-dimensional generalized diffusion equation

$$\frac{aF}{\sigma^2} + \frac{b_1 F_x}{\sigma} + \frac{b_2 F_y}{\sigma} + c_1 F_{xx} + c_2 F_{yy} + c_3 F_{xy} = \frac{d}{\sigma} F\sigma \tag{14}$$

A similar argument shows that the only solution obeying the condition in a two-dimensional space is with $c_3 = 0$ because of the symmetry requirements given in the beginning of the chapter.

$$G(x, y, \sigma) = \frac{1}{\sqrt{2\pi}} \sqrt{\frac{d}{c_1}} \sqrt{\frac{d}{c_2}} \frac{1}{\sigma^2} e^{\frac{-d}{2c_1} \frac{x^2}{\sigma^2}} e^{\frac{-d}{2c_2} \frac{y^2}{\sigma^2}} \tag{15}$$

We again use the symmetry requirement at the beginning of the chapter to set $c_1 = c_2$. Then we obtain

$$G(x, y, \sigma) = \frac{1}{2\pi} \frac{d}{c} \frac{1}{\sigma^2} e^{\frac{-d}{2c} \frac{(x^2 + y^2)}{\sigma^2}} . \tag{16}$$

We can scale the σ axis by $\sqrt{\frac{c}{d}}$ and write Equations 13 and 16

$$G(x, \sigma) = \frac{1}{\sqrt{2\pi}} \frac{1}{\sigma} e^{\frac{-x^2}{2\sigma^2}} \tag{17}$$

and

$$G(x, y, \sigma) = \frac{1}{2\pi} \frac{1}{\sigma^2} e^{\frac{-(x^2 + y^2)}{2\sigma^2}} , \tag{18}$$

respectively. This ensures that σ is the standard deviation of the function.

ACKNOWLEDGMENTS

Support for work performed at the Artificial Intelligence Laboratory of the Massachusetts Institute of Technology is provided in part by the Advanced Research Projects Agency of the Department of Defense under Office of Naval Research contract N00014-80-C-0505 and by the Hughes Aircraft Corporation. We are grateful to C. Koch and M. Brady for useful suggestions and especially to V. Torre and M. Kass for many discussions with one of us (T. P.). We are especially grateful to D. Terzopoulos and to J. Marroquin for very useful comments on our proofs. Carol Bonomo did no more than type the equations.

REFERENCES

Babaud, J., Witkin, A., & Duda, R., "Uniqueness of the Gaussian kernel for scale-space filtering," Fairchild TR 645, Flair 22, 1983.

Bridgman, P. W., *Dimensional Analysis,* Yale University Press, 1922.

Campbell, F. W. C., & Robson, J. "Application of Fourier analysis to the visibility of gratings," *Journal of Physiology (Lond.), 197,* 417–424, 1968.

Canny, J. F. "A variational approach to edge detection," submitted to AAAI Conf., Washington, DC, Sept., 1983.

Chillingworth, D. R. J., *Differential Topology with a view to Applications,* Research Notes in Mathematics Series 9, Pitman Publishing, London, 1978.

Crowley, J. L. "A representation for visual information," CMU-RI-TR-82-7, Robotics Institute Carnegie-Mellon University, 1982.

Curtis, S. R. "Reconstruction of multidimensional signals from zero crossings," Research laboratory of electronics (tech. report 509). Dept. of Electrical Engineering and Computer Science. MIT, Cambridge, MA, 1985.

Grimson, W. E. L. *From Images to surfaces,* MIT, Cambridge, MA, 1981.

Grimson, W. E. L. "Surface consistency constraints in vision," *Computer Vision Graphics and Image Processing, 24,* 28–51, 1983.

Henning, G. B., Hertz, B. G., & Broadbent, D. E. "Some experiments bearing on the hypothesis that the visual system analyses spatial patterns in independent bands of spatial frequency," *Vision Research* (Vol. 15). pp 887–897. Pergamon Press, 1975.

Koenderink, J. J. "On the Structure of Images," Journal of Biological Cybernetics, 50. 363–370, 1984.

Logan, B. F. "Information in the Zero Crossings of Bandpass Signals." *Bell Systems Technical Journal, 56, 4, 487–510, 1977.*

Marr, D. "Early processing of visual information," *Transactions of the Royal Society of London,* 275:483–519, 1976.

Marr, D. *Vision, A computational investigation into the human representation & processing of visual information.* W. H. Freeman & Co., San Francisco, 1982.

Marr, D., & Hildreth, E. "Theory of edge detection," *Proceedings of the Royal Society of London B, 207,* 187–217, 1980.

Marr, D., & Poggio, T. 1979. "A computational theory of human stereo vision," *Proceedings of the Royal Society of London B, 204,* 301–328.

Marr, D., Poggio, T., & Ullman, S. "Bandpass channels, zero-crossings and early visual information processing," *Journal of the Optical Society, 70,* 868–870, 1979.

Nishihara, H. K. 1981. "Intensity, visible-surface, and volumetric representations," *Artificial Intelligence, 17,* 265–284.

Poggio, T. "Trigger features or Fourier analysis in early vision: A new point of view." In *The Recognition of Pattern Form,* edited D. Albrecht, Springer, 88–99, 1982a.

Poggio, T., Nishihara, H. K., & Nielsen K. R. K. "Zero-crossings and spatiotemporal interpolation in vision: aliasing and electrical coupling between sensors," Artificial Intelligence memo 675, May 1982b.

Richards, W., Nishihara, H. K., & Dawson, B. "Cartoon: A biologically motivated edge detection algorithm." M.I.T. Artificial Intelligence Lab Memo No. 668, Cambridge, MA, 1982.

Rosenfeld, A. "Quadtrees and Pyramids: Hierarchical representation of images," TR 1171, University of Maryland, 1982.

Rosenfeld, A., & Thurston, M. "Edge and curve detection for visual scene analysis," *IEEE Transactions Computers, C-20,* 562–569, 1971.

Stansfield, J. L. "Conclusions from the commodity expert project," MIT Artificial Intelligence Lab Memo No. 601, Cambridge, MA, 1980.

Terzopoulos, D., "Multi-level reconstruction of visual surfaces," MIT Artificial Intelligence Memo 671, Cambridge, MA, 1982.

Torre, V. and Poggio, T., "On Edge Detection," MIT Artificial Intelligence Memo 768, Cambridge, MA, 1984.

Witkin, A. "Scale-Space Filtering," Proceedings of International J Conference on Artificial Intelligence, 1019–1021, Karlsruhe, 1983.

Yuille, A. L. "Zero-crossings and lines of curvature," MIT Artificial Intelligence Memo 718, Cambridge, MA, 1983.

Yuille, A. L., & Poggio, T. "Scaling theorems for zero-crossings," MIT Artificial Intelligence Memo 722, Cambridge, MA, 1983a.

Yuille, A. L., & Poggio, T. "Fingerprints theorems for zero-crossings," MIT Artificial Intelligence Memo 730, Cambridge, MA, 1983b.

Yuille, A. L., & Poggio, T. "New theorems for scale-space," MIT Artificial Intelligence Memo 751, Cambridge, MA, in preparation, 1986.

FORM PERCEPTION USING
TRANSFORMATION NETWORKS: POLYHEDRA

DANA H. BALLARD
The University of Rochester

In order to navigate and manipulate objects in the environment, one must have a model of oneself and the surroundings. The key issues are: What form should these models take? How are they constructed from visual input? and How are they used? We argue that the use of object-centered coordinate frames to find transformations is an essential ingredient in such models. Furthermore, such transformations can be economically computed in terms of a hierarchical network where levels in the network represent discrete functional values of geometrical constraints.

INTRODUCTION

For a long time research in the computational problem of perception has struggled with the basic questions of extracting explicit descriptions from mostly visual input. However, as these problems become better understood and formative solutions are available, the more basic questions of the *goals* of vision and motor actions start demanding attention. One useful function of vision is to allow us to interact with our geometric environment. There are several ways that this can happen. In *navigation*, the goal is to keep track of our relation to a geometric reference. *Motion perception* may be viewed as a kind of navigation described by the temporal change of the relation to a reference object. In *segmentation*, the goal is to isolate the parts of the visual field that belong to a reference object. *Object identification* is a memory task in which an isolated visual subfield must be correctly matched to a stored object representation.

Object acquisition is the task of relating the visual subfield to the internal representation.

Studying the goals of vision may elucidate additional helpful constraints on what the visual system can usefully compute and how the motor system can take advantage of such information. Above all, the need is for basic organizing principles that can simplify the immense computational problems in visuo-motor coordination. One such organizing principle is based on geometric transformations (Ballard, 1981; Hinton, 1981). This chapter suggests that the aforementioned vision problems may all be solved by computing geometric transformations between object-centered memory features and retinotopically-indexed features. Such transformations can form the basis of more complicated sequential strategies for realizing different goals.

The choice of features is important as it dictates not only what can be computed but the computational efficiency. We argue that a natural primitivization is that of a geometric reference frame. The reasoning behind such a choice is as follows. The world is composed of objects that can be modeled by collections of surfaces. Geometric reference frames at a point on a surface, aligned with surface curvature, describe the surface uniquely. Although this complete notion of surface is mathematically useful, for visual perception it is more useful to keep track of reference frames only at special locations, termed *surface invariances*. A surface invariance can be a boundary between two surfaces, such as a polyhedral edge or a homogeneous surface patch, such as that of a cylinder. These frames usually can be chosen in a way that the environment is described by a discrete set of modest size. In other words, such frames are natural properties of the environment in the sense conveyed by Gibson's notion of affordances (Gibson, 1977). While the mathematical notion of a coordinate frame does not restrict its choice, the structure of the world is such that only a relatively few possibilities for geometric frames suggest themselves in any given scene.

Of the possible frames, we postulate that, at any given moment, one is selected as the focus of attention. Such a frame is termed a *task frame*. A task frame is a coordinate frame for the immediate task that is chosen from environmental features, features of the robot, and features of the task itself. The main advantage of such a description is that it provides a central reference for relating visual, somatic, and proprioceptive information that allows complex actions to be encoded in a small set of parameters.

The task frame ideas are developed within the following model of the human and environment. A binocular vision system is mounted on a head. The eyes have two rotational degrees of freedom (dof) with respect to the head, which in turn has three rotational dofs with respect to the shoulders. In addition, there is a six dof arm, which is attached to the shoulder. This arrangement is shown in Figure 3.1. Such a model allows us to represent various problems in visuo-motor coordination. The properties that are important are: more than one eye; the ability of the eyes to focus and track a particular point; known transformations between the eyes; and a known transformation between the arm and the eyes. Additionally, the world is assumed to consist only of rigid polyhedral objects. The advantages of this restriction are developed later in this chapter.

The notion of describing the world in terms of geometric transformation has been the subject of much study in the psychological literature. Apparent motion can be succinctly modeled by rigid coordinate transformations between alternate views (Shepard, 1984). Internal shape models have several levels of detail, but only one can be imaged at any one time (Kosslyn, 1980). A complex geometric reasoning task can be broken down into a sequence of geometric transformations (Just & Carpenter, 1985). All these studies support the hypothesis that the human visual system computes using three-dimensional coordinate systems in a very direct way.

Since the first attempts at a computational model (Ballard, 1981; Hinton, 1981; Hinton and Lang, 1985), there have been several other attempts to compute object identity using the transformational approach (Linnainmaa, Harwood, & Davis, 1985; Silberberg & Davis, 1984; Stockman & Esteva, 1984). These recent methods, however, are aimed at the

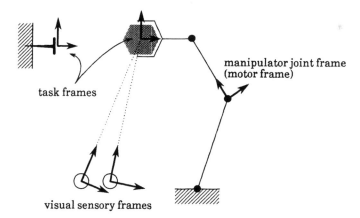

FIGURE 3.1. The essential robot for visuo-motor coordination (top view). Two eyes with vergence control are related to each other. A manipulator is related to the eyes via mechanical links. The figure shows three kinds of coordinate frames: (1) sensory frames; (2) a motor frame; and (3) task frames (for this example of turning a hexagonal nut with a wrench or hammering a nail).

task level. That is, they do not address the question of computing directly on a parallel architecture. Tackling the issue directly leads to radically different computational approaches that are directed toward the human visual system. In particular, our models are compatible with human performance data (Triesman & Gelade, 1980) and certain architectural features of the cerebral cortex (Ballard, 1986a).

Object-Centered Coordinate Frames

In visuo-motor coordination, objects are manipulated under visual guidance to bring about certain relationships between them. From a computational standpoint, these operations are potentially complex, and any description of how this is accomplished must include object geometry. In particular, it must explain: (a) how an object is recognized; and (b) how relationships between objects can be brought about.

A crucial element in the descriptive process is the choice of coordinate frame used for the object geometry. Transformations between coordinate frames are trivial mathematically but not so when using actual visual data; different reference frames can have a large effect on the accuracy and efficiency of computations. To obtain a general idea of the effect of different coordinate frames, refer to Figure 3.1.

This figure shows the important coordinate frames used in visual-motor coordination. They are as follows.

1. *Retinotopic frames* are used to describe the early visual input (early in the sense of low levels of the abstraction hierarchy). A necessary property of a retinotopic frame is that when the eye moves, the description changes.

2. *Motor frames* (or joint frames in robotics parlance) can be used to compute muscle lengthening and contracting signals to bring about desired positions and forces at certain positions in a linked skeletal system.

3. *Object frames* can be used to create invariant descriptions of an object, i.e., descriptions that *do not vary with the viewpoint.*

4. *Task frames* can be used to solve changes in geometry required to bring about relationships among objects in the image. Task frames can be seen as a subset of object-centered frames.

Objects are perceived in an image-centered or retinotopic frame. Such a viewpoint has the disadvantage that the description of the object changes with the viewpoint. For this reason it is more useful to use object-centered or intrinsic frames. Such a frame is attached to the object itself (Hinton, 1981). Experiments with human subjects suggest that they chose different object-centered frames depending on the viewpoint (Hinton, 1979). Marr (1982) used object-centered coordinate frames for generalized cylinders. Such frames can also be used for polyhedral objects and spheres as well, as shown in Figure 3.2. In fact, we can also associate a coordinate system with any surface patch based on its axes of curvature.

While a surface description based on local coordinate frames is complete, it is too general to be useful; instead, coordinate frames must be garnered from special points on the environment (Hrechanyk & Ballard, 1983). Our model is currently developed for a polyhedral world. This simplification has one particularly nice property in that the description of polyhedra is in terms of frame primitives. Polyhedral vertices can be viewed as candidate frame origins, and edges can be viewed as candidate frame orientations. (Some care has to be taken to avoid surface ambiguities, Brown, 1981). Also, the set of such transformations is finite for any given scene.

The use of frame primitives has an important advantage in that any of the frames contains the requisite information that allows it to become the current task frame. Put another way, given a set of frames, any one can be chosen as the task frame by applying its inverse to itself and all the other frames in the set.

The advantage of coordinate transformations is that they allow one to compute invariant descriptions of the environment. The advantage of invariant descriptions in recognition is that the task of recognizing a

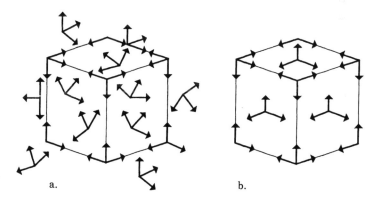

a.   b.

FIGURE 3.2. An infinite number of reference frames are possible (a) but only a few suggest themselves (b). Such frames may be defined by discontinuities in surface structure or axes of symmetry.

previously encountered object is enormously simplified if one can relate an arbitrary view to a canonical (object-centered) view.

Computing Object-Centered Frames from Visual Input

Given only two frames, one representing a viewer-centered or reti- notopic feature, and another an object-centered feature, where the two are known to correspond, the problem of computing the transformation between them is completely determined. The main problem is that in general, *a set of frames* for the prototype is given together with *a set of frames* for the retinotopic description, and the correspondence between individual features is not known. This is an instance of the central prob- lem in vision known as the *correspondence problem.* Three other problems are that any measurements will be noisy, that parts of the retinocentric description will be missing owing to occlusion, and that the monocular retinocentric description is two-dimensional.

A general way of solving the correspondence problem is to test all possible correspondences to see if they agree with a particular model. If there is a significant consensus among the image-model pairs, then that model is selected. An efficient way of performing this test is known as the Hough transform (Ballard, 1984a; Duda & Hart, 1972). In terms of the coordinate frame matching problem just mentioned, one can pair all the coordinate frames in the retinocentric description with all those in the object-centered description and test whether a subset has the same *rigid transformation parameters.* The general method can also be applied to the problem of building the three-dimensional description from binocular input. The method is described in (Ballard & Tanaka, 1985) and has two basic levels, as shown in Figure 3.3.

The essence of the method is to compare data in two coordinate frames (or views) to see if a subset of the data can be characterized as having a rigid transformation. This way of relating sensory and memory data allows several qualitatively different operations to be handled with the same underlying computational structure. Consider *image segmenta- tion.* In our view this process identifies the portions of a potentially large number of image features that are consistent with a single internal model. If that internal model is a geometric prototype, then transforma- tional mapping will compute the image primitives that can be rigidly transformed into the object-centered prototype. *Object recognition* can be seen as the case where many different object descriptions in the first view are matched against a single segmented structure in the retinotopic view. If a transformational mapping can be built between the segmented im-

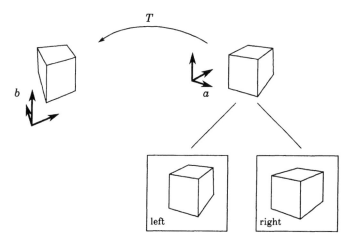

FIGURE 3.3. Generalized matching paradigm. Two simultaneous two-dimensional views, for example, left and right, of an object can be combined to obtain a three-dimensional description *a*. Three-dimensional descriptions, for example, *a* and *b*, can be tested to see if the difference can be described by a rigid transformation *T*.

age and one of the prototypes, the object in the image has been identified. *Navigation* matches frames from one space-time point against those from another space-time point. The transformation itself is the answer in this case. *Object model acquisition* consists of (a) choosing an object-centered frame as the reference; and (b) matching additional views against this description. Matching additional views adds to the model those features occluded in the initial view of the object. Note that step (a) is easy to do since the primitives are coordinate frames themselves; thus any one of these can be selected as the base frame. These different cases are shown in Figure 3.4; all are based on the ability to compute a rigid transformation by consensus matching.

Computing Goal Transformations with Task Frames

The previous discussion focused on tasks that use a single-memory object or single-image object. Now consider the more complicated case of two objects such as a tool and an object on which the tool is to be used. Given an object and a tool in an image-centered coordinate frame, in principle, one can directly compute the transformation to place the tool against the object in the appropriate way by using just the image-centered data. However, we argue that such a direct computation is very

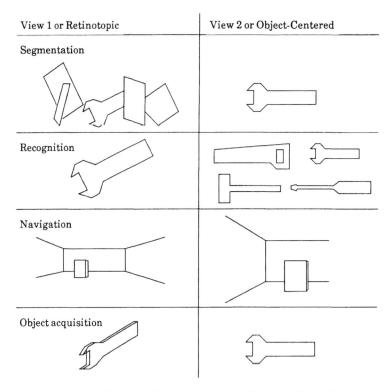

View 1 or Retinotopic	View 2 or Object-Centered
Segmentation	
Recognition	
Navigation	
Object acquisition	

FIGURE 3.4. The generalized two-view matching paradigm subsumes several important cases as variants. Each of the above cases may be solved by computing a transformation between two views. In *segmentation* the transformation is between a memory object and the scene. In *recognition* the transformation is between one of many memory objects and the scene. In *navigation* the transformation is between two views of the scene taken at different times. In *object acquisition* the transformation is between a partially recorded view of an object and a new view which might include extra parts.

inefficient for at least two reasons. It does not consider the larger contexts of (a) interfacing that transformation with a symbolic reasoner and (b) using the transformation in a motor system.

When all these constraints are taken together, the computation of the transformation to place the wrench on the nut can be done in a different way. The method has the following components (Figure 3.5a and b).

1. *Relating symbolic actions to object frame description.* Suppose we have the symbolic action "Attach the wrench to the nut." Each of the

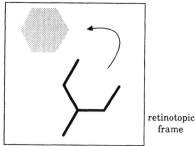

FIGURE 3.5a. Transformation in a view-centered frame. The problem of planning a transformation to attach the wrench to the nut can be seen as one of computing a transformation in view-centered coordinates, but in general this is difficult to do.

retinotopic frame

various ways that this may be carried out in the world involves selecting geometric parts of the two objects to be mated.

2. *Object-frame transformation.* A ubiquitous use of tools requires a male–female type of fit. In other words, the parts of the tool and object that are supposed to fit together define complementary sur-

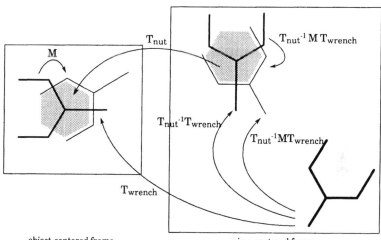

object-centered frame   view-centered frame

FIGURE 3.5b. Transformations in mating a tool and a part. The object-centered frame contains representations of the models of both the wrench and the nut as well as the desired position (relative to the nut) of the wrench when it is mated with the nut. M accomplishes the transformation from the model to this desired position. T_{nut}, T_{wrench} transforms the views of the nut and wrench, respectively, back into the object-centered frame. $T_{nut}^{-1} M T_{nut}$ is the view-centered version of M and, composed with $T_{nut}^{-1} T_{wrench}$, accomplishes $T_{nut}^{-1} M T_{wrench}$, the mating transformation in the view-centered frame. This scheme takes advantage of the fact that M can be precomputed and stored and used with the techniques used later in the chapter that computed T_{wrench} and T_{nut}.

faces. By selecting these complementary surfaces as in 1 above, the transformation, M, required for mating in the object frame can be easily computed. This is the transformation that specifies how to change the object-frame position of the tool so that it mates with the object-frame position of the part. Furthermore, it can be computed by the consensus technique of matching the parts.

A reason for explicitly computing this transformation is so that information specific to this particular mating operation can be stored. For example, it may be useful to derive and remember the approach vector required for the mating operation.

3. *Transformation between image-centered and object-centered frames.* This step is described later in the chapter. T_{nut} and T_{wrench} transform the nut and the wrench from the image-centered frame to their respective object-centered frames.

4. *Relative transformation.* The two view transforms describe how each of the two objects are related to their respective object-centered descriptions. The transformation $T_{nut}^{-1}T_{wrench}$ makes the wrench have the same position relative to the nut in the image-centered frame as it has in the object-centered frame. This is shown by the arrangement at the top of the view-centered frame in Figure 3.5.

5. *Control transformation.* Finally, consider that the composition of the two transformations computed in steps 2 and 4 is the desired answer. The transformation in step 2 represents the desired change in the relationship between the two parts in the object-centered frame. In the view-centered frame this transformation is $T_{nut}^{-1} M T_{wrench}$. The transformation in step 4 represents the change necessary to produce that relationship in the object-centered frame. Thus the composition of these two transformations, $T_{nut}^{-1} M T_{wrench}$, represents the change that the tool has to undergo to mate with the part.

The key strategy here is the specification of desired relationships as transformations between objects in an object-centered frame. This allows the relationship of symbolic and geometric information. Thus the specification of the task at hand can be done independently of the location of the objects in the world.

Rationale and Overview

The preceding description has been at the *task level* (using Marr's, 1982, scheme of task, algorithmic, and implementation levels). However, the form of the theoretical description has been hierarchical, and this turns out to be a particularly useful property that allows a straightforward realization of the task-level theory at the implementational level.

The implementation of the theory in terms of polyhedra forms a major portion of this chapter. The general theory has been described previously (Ballard, 1981a; 1986a; 1986b) and is summarized in the following section. The format is very close to that of Hopfield (1982, 1984) networks with the exception that units form hierarchies connected by *nonsymmetric, ternary* weights. Also, another important assumption is that the threshold function has a quasi-linear form.

The number of units required to simulate a system of reasonable size places severe demands on a sequential computer. To that end a special simulator was developed that takes advantage of properties of the networks. By doing so, the simulator can accurately model a virtual network of appropriate size by dynamically manipulating different parts of the network. This technique is described later in the chapter.

Also demonstrated is how the problems of polyhedral form perception can be realized in terms of the formalism of the following section.

The entire network simulates one restricted case of mapping a portion of an image to a prototype. In order to explain the functions described previously, some additional control structure is required. We speculate on what this control structure might be.

We also summarize a test simulation with the complete network comparing actual and computed values of key parameters and discuss the merits and demerits of the current approach, as well as possibilities for future work.

BACKGROUND:
HIERARCHIES OF PARAMETER NETWORKS

Our principal hypothesis is that: *A major function of the perceptual system is to compute collections of invariants at different levels of abstraction.* The value of computing these invariants is that they are increasingly concise descriptions of the environment with respect to the agent. At the most abstract level, this means that the agent can plan actions in a concise space of possibilities. Also, as the invariants become more abstract, they are true for larger portions of space and time. Thus they give the agent time to consider more elaborate actions.

An entity may be described as an invariant with respect to its component parts. Thus, a two-dimensional line is an invariant with respect to its component edge elements. A vertex is invariant with respect to specific collections of intersecting two-dimensional lines. The key notion is that the invariant is constant over many possible different collections of its components. Our concern is with invariants that can be described with a small number of parameters, typically less than 10. The usefulness of small-parameter descriptions that describe a large number of different situations is primarily computational. Small parameters descriptions have been shown to be easily computed by distributed network models. These models have been termed *connectionist* to denote that the fundamental description of the problem is in the particular connections in the network. Previous papers have suggested a model for the visual system in terms of representations and computational strategies that make the computation of invariants efficient (Ballard, 1984a, 1986a; Feldman, 1985; Feldman & Ballard, 1982).

The Value-Unit Principle

We have picked a specific representation first suggested by Barlow (1972) that is geared to solving parallel processing problems. This representation is termed *value units*. Value units are a general way of representing different kinds of *multi-dimensional variables and functions* without requiring that the output of each unit have a large bandwidth. Value units break up the ranges of a variable into intervals and represent each interval with a separate unit. These intervals can be organized in many different ways. One straightforward way is to represent a variable $v = (v_1, \ldots, v_k)$ isotropically by allocating a unit for each of N^k discrete values. These values are the center of intervals of width Δv ($\Delta v_1, \ldots, \Delta v_k$). The value k is the *dimensionality* of the variable. We will use the term *parameter* to refer to a scalar component of a variable, that is, one of the v_i.

Let us compare the value-unit encoding with variable representation in conventional Von Neumann computers. In a Von Neumann machine, variables only access one value at any instant and acquire these values by assignment statements. For example, $x := 3; y := 4$ assigns values 3 and 4 to x and y, respectively. Since a sequential computer can only access one value of a variable at a time, the notion of unique values for each variable at any instant is particularly appropriate. However, a parallel computer typically requires access to many values of a variable at the same time, and thus requires a different encoding scheme. A value unit representation such as an array of possible (x, y) values allows this parallel access. This difference is shown in Figure 3.6a and b.

An important advantage of the value unit organization is that complex functions can be easily constructed, for example, $f(x, y) = e\sqrt{x} \cdot \Pi^{1/y}$ are easily constructed by a table look-up strategy. Suppose one has such a function $f(x, y)$. Let us allot units for each interesting *value* of x and have a

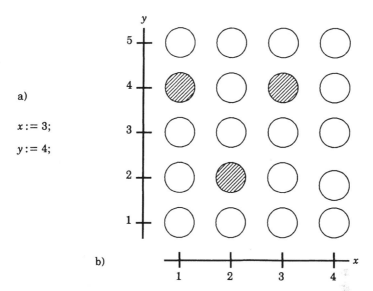

a)

$x := 3;$

$y := 4;$

b)

FIGURE 3.6. (a) Von Neumann encoding assigns a single value to a variable at any instant. (b) In contrast, value-unit encoding allows many values of the same variable to be accessed simultaneously by having individual processors (units) for each of a discrete set of values. In the figure, in addition to (3, 4), (1, 4) and (2, 2) are represented.

similar set for the interesting y values. One can think of these different values as very similar to just-noticeable differences. Then the outputs of these units can be used pairwise to construct the function by connecting them to units representing appropriate values of f. We assume that both members of a pair of connections must be on before the unit representing a specific value of f registers input. This type of input has been termed a *conjunctive connection* (Feldman & Ballard, 1982).

Computing with Value Units

To illustrate how value units can solve problems in parallel, we will describe the solution to a very specific problem. Consider the simple map in Figure 3.7a with four regions. The problem is to color the map so that no two adjacent countries have the same color. Each region may be colored with one of the colors shown. This problem is representative of a ubiquitous class of problems which can be posed as: "satisfy the largest set of compatible constraints" (Freuder, 1978; Hummel & Zucker, 1983; Prager, 1980; Rosenfeld, Hummel, & Zucker, 1976; Ullman, 1979). When this problem is translated to value unit notation, the color of each region is a separate value unit. If a particular color is compatible with the

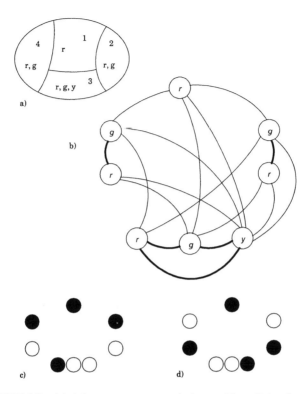

FIGURE 3.7. (a) A four-country map coloring problem: Color the map with the colors shown (r = red, g = green, y = yellow) so that adjacent countries have different colors. The numbers designate the different countries. (b) A value-unit representation of the map-coloring problem. A separate unit is allocated for each color of every country. Symmetric inhibitory connections are denoted by boldface links; other lines represent symmetric excitatory links. Other designs are possible; for example, one could use inhibitory connections between incompatible colors in neighboring countries. The particular design keeps inhibition local to individual countries. (c) A particular starting configuration where dark units are on and light units are off. (d) The correct solution achieved by iteration using the state modification rule described in the text.

currently chosen value units representing neighboring colors, then that unit is likely to be chosen to represent its corresponding region's color. The constraints are represented as links between units. There are many different ways to do this. We choose to let connections between locally incompatible colors be inhibitory (negative weights) and connections between compatible colors be excitatory (positive weights). These links are shown in Figure 3.7b.

Networks of value units compute as follows. One can think of the ith

unit as having a small amount of information, $(s_i, \mathbf{w}_i)$, where s_i is the state and $\mathbf{w}_i = \{w_{i1} \ldots w_{in}\}$ is the synaptic weight vector. Where the weights are symmetric (i.e., $w_{ij} = w_{ji}$), there are several algorithms to minimize the "energy" functional

$$E = - \sum_i \sum_j w_{ij} s_i s_j \tag{2.1}$$

where s_i is the binary state of a unit, either *on* (0) or *off* (1), and w_{ij} is a real number that describes a particular constraint (Hopfield, 1982). Adopting a technique developed by Kirkpatrick, Gelatt, and Vecchi (1983), termed *simulated annealing,* Hinton and Sejnowski (1983) have provided an algorithm for finding the global minimum of Equation 1. Eventual convergence to a global minimum has been proved for a variant of this technique by (Geman & Geman, 1985). In our example it is easy to spot check that the correct solution is an energy minimum by directly computing values of E for different states, for example,

$$E(r1, g2, y3, g4) = -10$$

$$E(r1, g2, y3, g3, g4) = -8$$

$$E\ (\Phi = 0$$

$$E(r1, g2, g3, g4) = -6$$

In this notation, "$g2$" denotes that the green unit for country 2 is on, and so forth.

This simple case can be handled with binary states and a gradient minimization rule:

$$s^{k+1} := 1 \text{ if } p_i^k > 0, \text{ else } 0$$

where

$$p_i^k := \sum_j w_{ij} s_j^k$$

While we will not offer a formal proof that the network just shown converges, informally, one can see that if the inhibitory links are weighted at least twice as great as excitatory links, the preponderance of excitatory links at the appropriate units will favor the solution just described. The example has been simulated and has proven stable to variations in the initial state.

The points behind the map-coloring problem are threefold. First, the problem is characteristic of other constraint-satisfaction problems in that empirical tests show that larger-scale versions do not require appreciably more time (although this has yet to be quantified). This controversial statement about problem scaling is currently based on empirical tests.

Kirkpatrick et al. (1983) argued that convergence is based on how "frustrating" (incompatible) the constants are. The second point is that the kinds of constraints that we used are extremely general and can characterize a broad range of perceptual and cognitive situations (Ballard, 1986c; Ballard & Hayes, 1984; Feldman, 1985; Hinton, Sejnowski, & Ackley, 1984). In particular, problems in visual gestalt recognition can be described as trying to satisfy an appropriately weighted collection of local constraints (Ballard, Hinton, & Sejnowski, 1983; Feldman, 1985). The third lesson of constraint satisfaction is that *local* constraints can imply a *global* solution.

Learning algorithms that are also compatible with our formalism have also been published recently. These include supervised learning algorithms [Ackley, Hinton, & Sejnowski, 1985; Rumelhart, Hinton, & Williams, 1985] and an associative learning algorithm [Rumelhart & Zipser, 1985].

The energy minimization can also be done with *analog* units (Hopfield, 1984; Hopfield & Tank, 1985). The formulation with analog units allows the state to vary continuously in the interval (0, 1). Although the current algorithm with analog units is not guaranteed to find a global minimum, the limited testing that has been done shows that it produces good solutions for perceptual problems. The algorithm is:

Algorithm Analog Energy Minimization
State equations evolve according to

$$dp_i/dt = -p_i/\tau + \Sigma \, w_{ij} s_j \qquad (2.2)$$

$$s_i = 1/(1 + e^{-p_i})$$

Hierarchical Architectures

The use of value units together with an energy minimization computational engine does not commit one to a hierarchical architecture; but for a host of reasons, some of which were mentioned earlier and others of which are developed in (Ballard, 1984a; 1986a), such organizations are desirable. The structure that we use and that is also advocated by others (Rumelhart & Zipser, 1985; Smolensky, 1986) contains well-defined layers of units, each having a given semantics, (e.g., "optical flow units"). Connections between layers have positive weights, and connections within a layer have negative weights, as shown in Figure 3.8.

We have proposed to crudely characterize the hierarchical structure in Figure 3.9a by associating it with the corresponding semantic hierarchy, as shown in Figure 3.9b. These tokens have qualitatively different

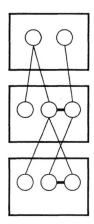

FIGURE 3.8. A hierarchical architecture.

mathematical properties, as in Figure 3.9c. At the most abstract level, the tokens represent discrete values of discrete processes, for example, the color red for a particular country as captured by the map-coloring example. The idealization of this representation is that its members can be characterized abstractly as a set of discrete elements. This model is also suited to the abstract entities in models of cognition, for example, beliefs, plans, actions, relations, and objects. At the *lowest* level, the information is in the form of continuous values of continuous processes. The constraints at this level are captured by the classical Shannon sampling theorem and other more biologically-motivated variants. The idealization of this representation is that of continuous function of a set of variables, for example, an image function $f(x, y, t)$.

In between these two extremes, we argue for an intermediate level

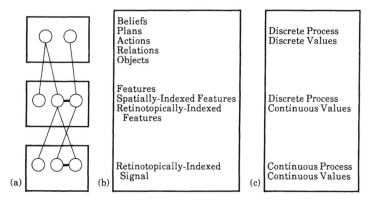

FIGURE 3.9. (a) A hierarchical architecture; (b) an interpretation of its possible semantics; and (c) mathematical characteristics.

that can be characterized as requiring continuous values of discrete processes. For example, the rotation of the visual field can be characterized by rotational values of a single rigid body-motion process. There is only one process, but the actual parameter values that describe that process are numerical and vary over continuous intervals. Since this level is qualitatively different from the more abstract (discrete-discrete) and less abstract (continuous-continuous) levels, one might suspect that the mathematics required to model it would be qualitatively different also.

Although the values of a process in the intermediate level are continuous, the representation in which they are embedded is composed of discrete units. Here, there seems at first to be a problem when accurate quantities are needed but only discrete values are represented. However, an obvious solution is to interpolate between discrete values (Ballard, 1986b; Saund, 1986).

Discrete Processes with Continuous Values

To understand the need for interpolation, we first need to broadly characterize how the stimuli "look" at this level of representation. Our abstract model of the way data is acquired for an invariant represented as a parameter value in a parameter space is as follows. The general character of the world is that within a parameter space, for any perceptually relevant space–time interval, only a small distinct set of values will occur. These values may be idealized as points in the parameter space. The idealization is a model of the world. What is actually sensed is not the ideal point but a value that is usually corrupted by noise. This noise may arise from the world process itself or from sensor errors or both. This situation is described in Figure 3.10. In addition to these noise sources,

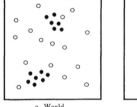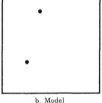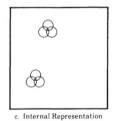

a. World   b. Model   c. Internal Representation

FIGURE 3.10. Our description of the modeling problem for features (discrete processes, continuous values). An environment, as represented by sensors, contains background noise (open circles) and discrete processes (closed circles). The closed circles are scattered about a mean because of noise. The goal is to represent the central value of such processes, and remove background noise. Processes are interconnected in terms of networks, and because of an overall relaxation process, the central values may migrate.

there may be background noise from other world processes that only partially fit the parameter model. The main problem is to estimate a small set of values for the idealized model, given the noisy measurements.

This problem is made difficult both by the fact that the measurements are noisy and by the fact that the internal representation is discrete. The latter difficulty forces the use of units that are sensitive to the stimulus in an area that is generally referred to as its receptive field. Thus, the internal representation approximates the ideal situation of the world model by interpolating across overlapping receptive fields, as shown in Figure 3.5c.

Since the model consists of sets of point processes, it is qualitatively different from the Shannon model and other models that regard the model as a continuous function over the domain. Instead, the model can be defined as a collection of delta functions, that is,

$$\delta(x - x_i) \text{ for } i = 1, \ldots M$$

where $\delta(x) = \{1 \text{ for } x = 0, \text{ and } 0 \text{ for } x \neq 0\}$.

The internal representation represents this information in terms of projections into (Lagrangian) basis functions. Note that the signal is not bandlimited, yet we will be able to show that under certain conditions, it can be unambiguously recovered.

Interpolation and Minimization

This qualitative description can be related to the formal models introduced earlier. Consider the equations for the analog model. In this system the potential p_i and state s_i change according to Equation 2.2. Let us simplify this equation and just look at the steady state value as $t \rightarrow \infty$. In this case

$$p_i = \tau \sum_j w_{ij} s_j$$

Notationally, to relate this model to value units, it is helpful to use the discrete value itself as the unit index instead of i. Thus, for a discrete value of a parameter x we will write $p[x_i]$ instead of p_i. Given this notation, we can make the following interpretation (which will be substantiated in latter development):

$s_j = s[x_j] \equiv$ the "evidence for" measurement x_j

$w_{ij} = w[x_i, x_j] \equiv$ the weight required by the interpolation formula where x_j is evidence for x_i

$\langle s_i x_i \rangle =$ the interpolated value of x using "local" values of x_i

($\langle \rangle$ denotes averaging over the index i.)

Interpolation and the Hough Transform

Now let us return to the problem of estimating precise numerical values from discrete samples. The previous method for doing this used rounding (Ballard, 1984a; Duda & Hart, 1972; Li, Levin, & LeMaster, 1985). The primary problem with the rounding method is that it is tied to the grain size of the quantization. The value can only be reported to within plus or minus one grid unit. Furthermore, the following dilemma occurs. If the grain size is small to minimize the effects of roundoff error, the individual measurements do not fall in the same quantized cell; whereas if the grain size is large, the roundoff error prohibits accurate localization. While these problems might be solvable at one level of abstraction, they can become much worse with the incorporation of hierarchies, since truncation errors can propagate up the hierarchies.

Our solution is to use a particular form of Lagrangian interpolation (Davis, 1963; Jaeger & Starfield, 1974). Instead of voting unity for a single discrete value, weighted votes are cast for each of 2^k neighboring values. (In Ballard, 1986b, it is shown that k neighboring points are sufficient, but the sampling strategy must be irregular in that case.) The weights are chosen so that the weighted sum of the discrete values equals the original value. Figure 3.11 compares the two schemes for the two-dimensional case, that is, $x = (x_1, x_2)$.

This scheme has several nice properties, which are developed formally in (Ballard, 1986b).

1. It is insensitive to random measurement noise. If the measurements are corrupted by noise of mean zero then the expected interpolated value is the same as the original value.
2. It can be generalized to parameter spaces of any dimensionality.

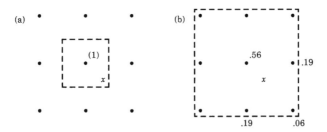

FIGURE 3.11. A comparison with the old truncation (a) vs. new interpolation (b) methods of value encoding. In the new method, receptive fields overlap, and the value is distributed among neighboring units. Also, truncation errors are eliminated: In (a) the original value cannot be recovered, whereas in (b), it can.

However, we have argued that spaces of high dimensionality ($k > 5$ − 10) are infeasible mainly because they are too expensive to represent (Ballard, 1986a).

3. If the mappings are locally linear over the grid size, that is, have a Taylor series approximation that requires only first-order terms, then the technique can be extended to handle the general case where both the voters and the votes are discretely represented.

4. The local linearity also allows the technique to be extended to general relations, that is, multiple-valued functions.

An important consequence of this model is that weights must be used to handle this encoding. For example, to continue the exposition in Figure 3.11b, a possible neuronal implementation of this model would connect the unit representing x to the neighboring units that are shown in the figure with the appropriate weights. Since x will also be represented with value units, these weights can be precomputed, as shown in Figure 3.12.

One important consequence of this scheme is that the weights can no longer be symmetric. At present this means that there is no formal convergence theorem, but two ameliorating points are: (a) such a proof may be found for the special hierarchical architectures that we are considering; and (b) a limited number of simulations using nonsymmetric weights in such systems have demonstrated them to be stable.

IMPLEMENTATION DESIGN

The generic form of the constraints is that of a ternary connection rule, as shown in Figure 3.13. Pairs of units at the kth level are connected to a unit at the $k + 1^{st}$ level. The precise connections are determined by a *connection rule*. This rule is carried out as follows. Suppose $\mathbf{x}_1$ and $\mathbf{x}_2$ are two units at level k and $\mathbf{y}$ is a unit at level $k + 1$, and there is a constraint f such that $\mathbf{y} \approx f(\mathbf{x}_1, \mathbf{x}_2)$. First a $\mathbf{y}'$ is computed such that $\mathbf{y}' = f(\mathbf{x}_1, \mathbf{x}_2)$, and then the difference between $\mathbf{y}'$ and $\mathbf{y}$ (and its neighbors) can be used to compute the connection strength according to the interpolation scheme

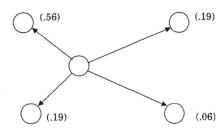

FIGURE 3.12. Weights for units can be precomputed based on the desired interpolation property.

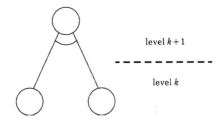

FIGURE 3.13.
Hierarchical ternary connections.

(but see discussion in the last section of this chapter). Even though this is a two-step process, the connection rule will be developed in terms of the point y' that satisfies the constraint exactly.

The overall algorithm is conceptually simple: asynchronously, each unit evaluates its input and turns on or off; when the entire network converges (in our case, after one iteration through the hierarchy), the output values of the units represent the solution to the particular problem. However, this simple description can lead to inefficient implementations, since most of the cells are off in any given instant (Ballard, 1984a).

Thus, when a processor checks its input pairs (in the case of a ternary constraint), most of the cells will be off. To take advantage of this, we use pairs of *on* units to calculate incremental inputs, and when all such pairs have been considered for any network, subtract thresholds and determine whether to turn the units on or off. This strategy is repeated for all the ternary constraints in the network. The only differences are: (a) the different constraints that relate different value cells; and (b) the set of on units at any given instant. The aforementioned strategy requires a data structure that only records on cells.

We use hash tables with collision resolution via chaining, (e.g., Horowitz & Sahni, 1976, pp. 462–469). The parameters for each table are the upper and lower limits for each component and the grain for each component. For example, the edge tables requires:

Lower	Upper	Grain Size
x_{min}	x_{max}	Δx
y_{min}	y_{max}	Δy
θ_{min}	θ_{max}	$\Delta\theta$

For each ternary constraint, two tables must be indexed to compute the index of a third. Then the input is added to the appropriate cell, as follows.

procedure Excitation__Constraint (T_1, T_2, T_3)

Foreach u in T_1 do
  Foreach v in T_2 do
    {
    w := rule (u, v, T_1, T_2)
    Increment (w, T_3)
    }

The function of *Increment* is to add the appropriate weight to the p field of the entry in the T.linetable. If there is no previous entry, an appropriate cell is added. Next the entries are thresholded, and if below threshold, deleted from the table:

procedure Threshold (T)

Foreach u in T do
  if $u <$ threshold then
    delete (u);

Specify the network of computations by specifying collections of three tables, each group having an associated update rule. The exact rules are described in Tables 3.2, 3.3, and 3.4 (in the next section).

In our simulation the aforementioned procedures are used as primitives, but the obvious extension is to introduce another level of abstraction into the simulator itself. Thus, the complete simulation at the most abstract level could be specified by the following procedure:

procedure Simulate__Newtork (Meta__Table)

foreach T_3 in Meta__Table do
  if there is a constraint relationship of the form
    $T_3 = f(T_1, T_2)$ do {Excitation__Constraint (T_1, T_2, T_3);
             If there is a threshold__constant
             of the form Threshold(T) do
             Threshold(T);
             }

POLYHEDRAL CONSTRAINTS

The geometric constraints used in the network fall into three groups that are at different hierarchical levels, as shown in Figure 3.14. Each of these levels may be further subdivided into microlevels. At the lowest level, two-dimensional constraints are used to extract points and line segments from the image. At the next (intermediate) level, three-dimensional con-

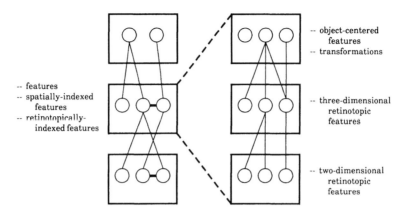

FIGURE 3.14. The constraints for recognizing polyhedra can be modeled by using "numerical" units from the middle level of the overall hierarchy defined in Figure 3.4.

straints derived from stereo are used to build a "wire-frame" representation of the scene. At the highest level, wire frames from stored representations are matched against those from the scene to detect the presence of objects. At an even higher level, object tokens are connected to their wire-frame features. This level is not implemented in the current computer model but can greatly help in recognition tasks, as will be discussed later. These three sets of macrolevels accomplish the following tasks. The first builds a two-dimensional wire-frame description of the image in terms of vertices and segments. The second matches vertices from the right and left views to build a three-dimensional description of the scene that includes three-dimensional vertices and orientation cues. Third, the vertices and orientation cues are matched against stored potential counterparts. If a rigid transformation can be computed, then the match is successful. Such a transformation is reflected in terms of rotation and transformation units.

The computer implementation uses feedforward connections only. Feedback connections require fewer microlevels and thus speed the computations. For example, in our feedforward version there are two copies of two-dimensional points for each view (see Table 3.2). In a feedback version, just one set of such units would be required, since the different constraints could be superimposed onto the same units.

Table 3.1 shows the individual units used in different layers. The specific constraints between individual layers are discussed in the following sections.

TABLE 3.1
Summary of Parameters used in Polyhedral Networks

Name	Description	Components
Laplacian	Laplacian of image intensity >	x position
L	threshold	y position
edge	photometric gradient at an	x position
e	image point x, y	y position
		θ orientation
line	two-dimensional line that spans	s_1 (see Figure 3.16)
l	the retina	s_2
2d-point	two-dimensional point	x position
x		y position
segment	a two-dimensional line segment	(x_1, y_1)
s		coordinates of one end
		(x_2, y_2)
		coordinates of the other end
3-D point	three-dimensional point	x position
X		y position
		z position
3-D segment	a three-dimensional line	(x_1, y_1, z_1)
S	segment	coordinates of one end
		(x_2, y_2, z_2)
		coordinates of the other end
orientation-frame	a pair of unit vectors derived	e_1 unit vector
O	from a polyhedral corner	e_2 unit vector
rotation	a quaternion vector	e rotation axis
r		Φ rotation amount
translation	a three-dimensional vector	ΔX change in X
t		ΔY change in Y
		ΔZ change in Z

Building the Two-Dimensional Segments

These constraints are summarized in Table 3.2.

$$l = f(e_1, e_2)$$

The first step is to build two-dimensional lines from pairs of local edges. A local edge is a unit that could receive inputs from yet more primitive levels, but in our model it is taken as the most primitive level. Edge pairs are used because in practice, the computation of the angle θ from intensity data is relatively inaccurate compared to the precision required for lines. Thus the connection rule is:

Connect each pair of colinear edge units to their
appropriate line unit. (4.1)

TABLE 3.2
Functions Used to Build the Two-Dimensional Description

Function	Description
$l = f_l(\mathbf{e}_1, \mathbf{e}_2)$	Colinear pairs of edges provide evidence for lines.
$\mathbf{x} = f_{\mathbf{x}}(l_1, l_2)$	Pairs of lines provide evidence for the 2-D point of intersection.
$\mathbf{s} = f_{\mathbf{s}}(\mathbf{x}_1, \mathbf{x}_2)$	Pairs of points provide evidence for the segment joining them.
$\mathbf{s}' = f_{\mathbf{s}'}(\mathbf{s}, \mathbf{e})$	If an appropriately oriented edge is on a segment, it provides evidence for that segment.
$\mathbf{x}' = f_{\mathbf{x}'}(\mathbf{x}, \mathbf{s}')$	A segment that has a point at one of its ends provides evidence for the point.

Figure 3.15 shows the notion of colinearity used for the edge units. The appropriate line unit is determined by the line parameters. The line parameters we used are shown in Figure 3.16.

Where (x_1, y_1, θ_1) and (x_2, y_2, θ_2) are the two edges, Equation 4.1 can be elaborated as:

$$\text{Let } \theta_a = (\theta_1 + \theta_2)/2$$
$$\text{if } (\theta_1 \approx \theta_2) \text{ and } ((\Phi + \pi \ll -\varsigma \approx \theta_a) \text{ or } ((\Phi - \pi \ll -\varsigma \approx \theta_a)$$
$$\text{then compute } s_1 \text{ and } s_2 \text{ from } (x_1, y_1) \text{ and } (x_2, y_2). \qquad (4.2)$$

$$\mathbf{x} = f_{\mathbf{x}}(l_1, l_2)$$

The next step is to use pairs of lines to build representations of two-dimensional points. Thus the rule is:

Connect each pair of lines to the point unit defined by their intersection (provided the point is on the retina).   (4.3)

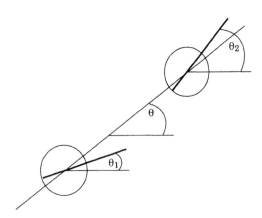

FIGURE 3.15. The colinearity constraint used to define lines in terms of edges.

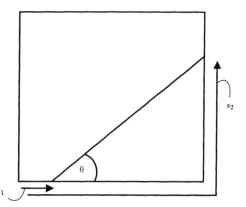

FIGURE 3.16. The parameters s_1 and s_2 are defined by the intercepts of the line with a rectangular retina as shown.

$$\mathbf{s} = f_\mathbf{s}(\mathbf{x}_1, \mathbf{x}_2)$$

Pairs of points can be used to compute segments by a simple concatenation operation. Naturally, to form a segment, the two points have to be further apart than the separation distance of the samples. Thus the connection rule is:

> Connect each pair of points x_1, x_2 to the segment that represents the concatenation of two points provided $x_1 \neq x_2$.   (4.4)

Ideally, these segments form a clique in the graph defined by the points x as vertices.

$$\mathbf{s}' = f_{\mathbf{s}'}(\mathbf{s}, \mathbf{e})$$

Naturally the segments defined by Equation 4.4 are a superset of those desired. The desired segments can be obtained by the use of the original edges. Figure 3.17 describes the constraint. The desired segments will have edge units associated with a large fraction of their length.

Since the average distance between edge units is known, the expected number of edge units per unit length of the segment can be calculated. Thus, the evidence for the segment from an edge can be scaled according to the segment length. This means that the constraint can be implemented in such a way that only segments that have edge units over a very large fraction of their length are represented. Thus the connection rule is as follows:

> If an edge unit is sufficiently close to a segment and its projection onto the line including the segment length is within the segment, then that edge unit provides evidence for the segment that is inversely proportional to the length of the segment.   (4.5)

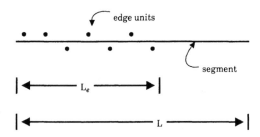

FIGURE 3.17. Filtering segments using edge units.

Where (a, b) are such that the line including the segment is given by $ax + by + 1 = 0$, the signed distance d of an edge to the line is given by

$$d = (ax + by + 1)/\sqrt{(a^2 + b^2)}$$

The point is within the segment if $0 < \lambda < 1$, where

$$x = \lambda x_1 + (1-\lambda)x_2$$

$$\mathbf{x'} = f_x(\mathbf{x}, \mathbf{L})$$

The final constraint is used to filter the points obtained by intersecting pairs of lines. The connection rule is:

> Connect a point unit and a Laplacian unit to a filtered point unit if the point unit is coincident with the Laplacian unit.   (4.6)

Building the Three-Dimensional Wire-Frame Model

These constraints are summarized in Table 3.3.

$$\mathbf{x} = f_\mathbf{x}(\mathbf{x}_L, \mathbf{x}_R)$$

TABLE 3.3
Functions Used to Build the Three-Dimensional Retinotopic
Description

Function	Description
$\mathbf{X} = f_\mathbf{x}(\mathbf{x}_L, \mathbf{x}_R)$	Points from stereo images that are nearby provide evidence for three-dimensional points.
$\mathbf{S} = f_\mathbf{S}(\mathbf{X}_1, \mathbf{X}_2)$	Pairs of three-dimensional points provide evidence for three-dimensional segments.
$\mathbf{S'} = f_{\mathbf{S'}}(\mathbf{S}, \mathbf{s})$	Two-dimensional segments provide evidence for a subset of three-dimensional segments.
$\mathbf{O} = f_\mathbf{O}(\mathbf{s}_{1'}, \mathbf{s}_{2'})$	Pairs of segments provide evidence for orientation-frames.

The first step in building a three-dimensional wire-frame representation is to match points in left (*L*) and right (*R*) stereo views. Figure 3.18 shows the geometry used.

Verging eyes allow one to have the accuracy of a large baseline while keeping the matching points proximal in retinal coordinates. The connection rule is:

Connect pairs of left and right two-dimensional point units to the appropriate three-dimensional unit if they are near each other, that is, $\|\mathbf{x}_L - \mathbf{x}_R\| < d_{separation}$. (4.7)

This constraint is specified in terms of the coordinate system for the left eye. A three-dimensional line is given by

$$\mathbf{X} = \mathbf{D} + t\mathbf{e}$$

where **e** is a unit vector in the direction of the line, $-\infty \le t \le \infty$, and **D** is a vector from the origin perpendicular to the line. For a retinal point (x, y) the line is

$$(\mathbf{D}, \mathbf{e}) = (\mathbf{O}, (x, y, -f)) \tag{4.8}$$

where f is the focal length of the eye. Equation 4.8 can be written for both

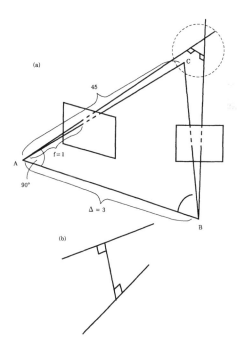

FIGURE 3.18. Matching constraint for points in stereo with vergence: (a) basic geometry; (b) detail of dotted region in a. Values for parameters are those used in the matching experiment described later in the chapter.

the left and right eyes, but then the right-eye values must be referred to the coordinate system of the left eye. So that

$$(\mathbf{D}_L, \mathbf{e}_L) = (\mathbf{O}, (x_L, y_L, -f))$$

but for the right line in terms of the coordinate system of the left,

$$(\mathbf{e}_R') = (x_R, y_R, -f)$$

$$(\mathbf{e}_R) = R_{\pi - (\alpha + \beta)} \mathbf{e}_{R'}$$

$$(\mathbf{D}_R) = \mathbf{b} - (\mathbf{b} \cdot \mathbf{e}_R) \mathbf{e}_R \qquad (4.9)$$

In these equations, R is a rotation matrix to rotate $\mathbf{e}_{R'}$ through $\Pi - (\alpha + \beta)$ about the y-axis, and $\mathbf{b}$ is the baseline vector defining the origin of the right-eye coordinate frame with respect to the left-eye system.

One problem is that, owing to errors, the lines may not intersect but only pass near each other. In this case the picked solution splits the line segment that joins the two lines and is mutually perpendicular to both of them (see inset, Figure 3.18). This may be found as (suggested by C. Quiroz):

$$(\mathbf{X}_L - \mathbf{X}_R) \cdot \mathbf{e}_L = 0$$

and

$$(\mathbf{X}_L - \mathbf{X}_R) \cdot \mathbf{e}_R = 0$$

or,

$$(\mathbf{D}_L - \mathbf{D}_R) \cdot \mathbf{e}_L + s - t \, \mathbf{e}_R \cdot \mathbf{e}_L = 0 \qquad (4.10)$$

$$(\mathbf{D}_L - \mathbf{D}_R) \cdot \mathbf{e}_R + s \, \mathbf{e}_L \cdot \mathbf{e}_R - t = 0 \qquad (4.11)$$

Matching Three-Dimensional Retinotopic Data with a Prototype

These constraints are summarized in Table 3.4.

$$\mathbf{r} = f_{\mathbf{r}}(\mathbf{O}_i, \mathbf{O}_p)$$

To develop the rotational constraint, we show how given two orientation cues O_p and O_i from the prototype and image, we can compute the rotation θ about a unit vector $\mathbf{w}$. The mathematics of quaternions (e.g., Webb, 1983) states that the rotation of one unit vector, $\mathbf{u}$, into another unit vector, $\mathbf{v}$, around a unit vector axis, $\mathbf{w}$, is given by:

$$R = V(-(\mathbf{w} \times \mathbf{v})(\mathbf{w} \times \mathbf{u})) \qquad (4.12)$$

TABLE 3.4
Functions Used in Matching Object-Centered and Three-Dimensional
Retinotopic Data

Function	Description
$\mathbf{r} = f_r(\mathbf{O}_i, \mathbf{O}_p)$	Matches between object-centered orientation cues and image-centered orientation cues provide evidence for rotation vectors.
$\mathbf{X}_{p'} = f_{\mathbf{x}'}(\mathbf{r}, \mathbf{X}_p)$	An object-centered vertex together with a rotation vector provide evidence for a rotated vertex.
$\mathbf{t} = f_t(\mathbf{X}_i, \mathbf{X}_{p'})$	Matches between an image vertex and a rotated, object-centered vertex provide evidence for a translation vector.

We will use the orientation vectors $\mathbf{e}_i$ from both the model and image as $\mathbf{u}$ and $\mathbf{v}$, respectively. How do we define $\mathbf{w}$? Since $\mathbf{w}$ must be perpendicular to both $\mathbf{u}$ and $\mathbf{v}$, it can be defined in terms of the two orientation frames as

$$\mathbf{w} = (\mathbf{e}_{1p} - \mathbf{e}_{1s}) \times (\mathbf{e}_{2p} - \mathbf{e}_{2s}) \tag{4.13}$$

In the special case of where $\mathbf{e}_{1p}$ equals $\mathbf{e}_{1s}$ and $\mathbf{e}_{2p}$ equals $\mathbf{e}_{2s}$, we arbitrarily set $\mathbf{w} = (1, 0, 0)$ and $\theta = 0$. This procedure and Equation 4.12 specify the axis of rotation.

The next step is to compute θ for the general case. The rotation from $\mathbf{u}$ to $\mathbf{v}$ is also given by

$$R = \cos(\theta/2) + \sin(\theta/2)\mathbf{w} \tag{4.14}$$

where θ is the angle of rotation around the unit vector axis $\mathbf{w}$. Thus the angle θ can be computed from Equations 4.12 and 4.14.

$$\mathbf{X}'_p = f\mathbf{X_p}(\mathbf{r}, \mathbf{X}_p)$$

Once the rotation between the protoype and scene has been established, the origins of the prototype frames can be appropriately rotated by (for details, see Webb, 1983):

$$\mathbf{X}'_p = R\,\mathbf{X}_p\,R^{-1} \tag{4.15}$$

This results in a new set of origins that only differ from their counterparts in the scene by a translation vector.

$$\mathbf{t} = f_t(\mathbf{X}'_p, \mathbf{X}'_p)$$

The translational constraint is trivially computed if the correspondence between a scene frame origin $\mathbf{X}_i$ and a rotated prototype frame origin $\mathbf{X}'_p$ is known. The answer is the difference vector

$$\mathbf{t} = \mathbf{X}'_p - \mathbf{X}_i \tag{4.16}$$

NETWORKS AND HIGH-LEVEL CONTROL

The overall goal of this chapter is to relate visual machinery to the goals of vision. We argue that different kinds of visual tasks can all be seen as using a central kernel that computes transformations between different views of geometric-frame primitives. This section reconsiders the central problems of Figure 3.4 with the view to specifying what additional control structures beyond transform computation are required.

In navigation, the main idea is to use transformational matching to compute the relationship between a current stereo view and a reference stereo view. In this case, the network can be used in two modes: discrete and continuous. The main problem to cope with is that the two views will have different numbers of features in them. If they are from nearby vantage points, then one could expect the features to be similar, but as the second view becomes more and more different, the feature content will vary to the extent that none of the original features may be present. In continuous mode, the network can be connected so that image-feature units and transform units execute object-feature units, as shown in Figure 3.19. To initialize the object frame, the identity-transform unit is turned on. This causes a copy of active units to appear in the object frame (instead of the identity transform, an object-centered transformation may be selected). Thereafter, in continuous mode, if an image-frame feature is no longer visible, its object-frame counterpart will be turned off. Vice versa, a new image feature will cause its object-centered coorespondent to be turned on. In discrete mode the navigation may be referenced to specific objects. As these become visible, a discrete switch may be made to adopt the new reference frame.

Object acquisition is similar to continuous navigation. The object in the visual scene is assumed to be segmented. One way of doing this is to use the back projection of property filters (Ballard, 1984a; Feldman & Ballard, 1982). Once this is done, and the object-centered frame is

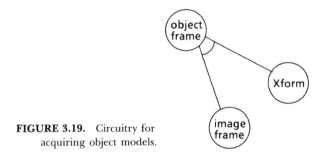

FIGURE 3.19. Circuitry for acquiring object models.

chosen, the manipulation of the object to expose all of its characteristic views will result in an internalized three-dimensional description in terms of active units. To remember this a unit must be *recruited* (Feldman, 1981; 1985) to interconnect the geometric features.

In object segmentation, we assume the active-frame feature units of the object-centered representation describe a single object. The problem is to test the visual input to see if it contains a representation of this object. If a significant portion of the object can be explained by a rigid transformation to parts of the visual field, then these parts will activate the appropriate transform units.

If several instances of the object are present, then each will be reflected as a rotation unit/translation unit-transform pair. A particular instance must be selected using some additional criterion.

For object recognition, we assume that the object already has been segmented on the basis of spatio-temporal coherence and must be identified. In this case the object network contains active units for *all* the possible objects under consideration. This set must be kept to a manageable size by other means. This situation is the inverse of the previous case except that we assume an additional object-token network (Hinton, 1981) that is connected to mutually inhibit rivals (Figure 3.20).

AN INITIAL EXPERIMENT

As an initial test of the theory, a right-angled bracket, shown in Figure 3.21, was used both as the imaged object and test object. For the memory object, the coordinates were entered manually. To make the image, this

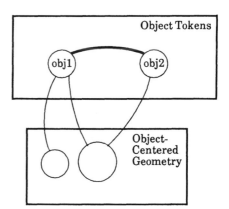

FIGURE 3.20. In recognition, an object-token network can be used that has its own constraints.

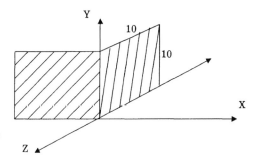

FIGURE 3.21.   Test shape used in
experiments.

object was rotated by $-45°$ about the y-axis and translated by $(0, -5, -30.9)$, using the PADL constructive solid-geometry system. Stereo pairs of images of the resultant object were made using the geometry of Figure 3.18 with $f = 1$ and $\Delta = 3$.

Table 3.5 shows the grain sizes and range for each of the parameter networks. The large-grain size reflects the fact that, for this initial experiment, interpolation coding was not used.

Table 3.6 shows the numerical results of the simulation. The actual values of parameters obtained by the simulation are compared with theoretical values expected from the model. Figures 3.22–3.26 show the results of the simulation, with active units represented as graphic tokens.

TABLE 3.5
Grain Sizes Used in Network. (Same grain is used for all components of
a parameter vector unless noted.)

Parameter		Min	Max	Δ
Edge		−128	128	256
Line		0	1024	1024
2-D vertex		−128	128	1000
2-D segment		−128	128	1000
	x	−40,000	40,000	10,000
3-D vertex	y	−40,000	40,000	10,000
	z	−40,000	0	40,000
3-D segment		Same as above	Same as above	Same as above
Orientation cue		−1.0	1.0	1000
Rotation	w	−1.0	1.0	100
	θ	−Π	Π	100
	x	−10,000	10,000	200
Translation	y	−10,000	10,000	200
	z	0	−40,000	800

TABLE 3.6
Comparison of Predicted vs. Experimental Results

A) 2-D Vertices, Left-View (x, y) Coordinates

Predicted	Experimental
(105.3, 74.7)	(102.1, 70.9)
(105.3, −74.7)	(102.5, −75.4)
(−105.3, 74.7)	(−104.0, 69.2)
(−105.3, −74.7)	(−103.6, −73.3)
(0, 91.6)	(−3.4, 87.9)
(0, −91.6)	(−3.6, −89.3)

B) 3D Vertices, (X, Y, Z) Coordinates

Predicted	Experimental
(7.0, 5.0, −37.9)	(6.6, 4.6, −36.6)
(−7.0, 5.0, −37.9)	(−7.0, 4.9, −39.2)
(7.0, −5.0, −37.9)	(6.6, −4.8, −36.7)
(−7.0, −5.0, −37.9)	(−7.0, −5.0, −39.0)
(0.0, 5.0, 30.9)	(0.3, 5.1, −32.7)
(0.0, −5.0, 30.9)	(0.2, −4.9, −31.6)

C) Transformation

	Rotation (ω, θ)
(0, 0, 0) 0°	(0, 0, 0) 10°

	Translation
(0, −5, −45)	(0, −5.6, −39.5)

FIGURE 3.22. Edge units (lower left) and line units (upper right) are displayed on the left view.

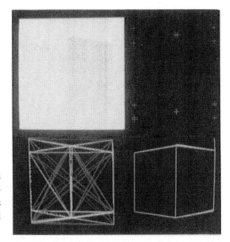

FIGURE 3.23. Upper right: line units after lateral inhibition. Upper left: two-dimensional vertices. Lower left: segments before filtering. Lower right: filtered segments.

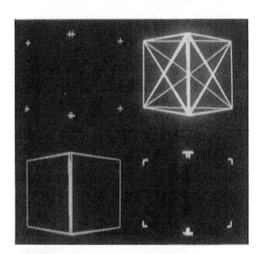

FIGURE 3.24. Upper left: three-dimensional vertices. Upper right: three-dimensional segments. Lower left: filtered three-dimensional segments. Lower right: orientation cues.

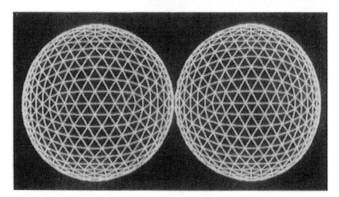

FIGURE 3.25. Units for rotation direction: the front (left) and back (right) of a geodesic showing possible rotation values.

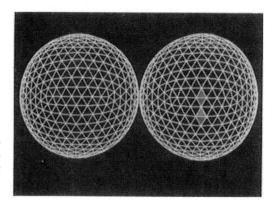

FIGURE 3.26. Units for translation direction: the front (left) and back (right) of a geodesic showing possible translation directions.

CONCLUSIONS

The goal of this chapter is to develop a computational theory of form perception that has a plausible biological implementation. The theory is incomplete since only geometric constraints are being considered. The theory describes form perception in terms of hierarchies of increasing geometric invariance. The information in these hierarchies represents small parameter descriptions of aspects of geometric shape. These hierarchies can be realized in terms of multilevel parameter networks. The processing is parallel across the spatial indices so that the time to recognize an object in the simplest case only depends on the number of levels in the network. An important implication of the high speed of processing is that it reduces the need for large amounts of active memory. This is because object-scene relations can be computed in real time when required.

The gross skeleton of the framework is borrowed from (Hinton, 1981), but differs in important aspects. The most crucial (discussed at the beginning of the chapter, is when differences in transformations and object-centered geometry are used to compute goal transformations. A second distinction is that rotation and translation are factored into separate networks in our system. While Hinton suggested an elegant three-frame system for changing contexts, we believe this can be done dynamically within one frame, as suggested in (Hrechanyk & Ballard, 1983).

The current simulation is very modest in terms of the complexity of the scene that is analyzed. It is expected that more complex examples will require some revision of the constraints being used. For example, one could compute two-dimensional segments directly from pairs of edges, and this would simplify the subsequent processing. Currently, all possible line-line intersections are processed, introducing lots of unimportant segments that are later filtered out. This could cause false segments (or ghosts) in a complicated scene. Nevertheless, the overall hierarchical organization is probably fairly stable, as there are only a limited number of ways to compute the geometric tokens using two-variable functions. Thus the number of levels in the hierarchy is likely to remain constant.

A major weakness of the current simulation is that only feedforward connections are used. This means that the system is essentially open loop and measurement errors propagate upwards through the levels. Feedback connections that enforce consistency between the networks should greatly improve the accuracy of the measurements.

The accuracy problem was exacerbated by the fact that the distributed encoding scheme was not used. Thus, the grain size of the parameter network was kept judiciously small. We expect that when the distributed scheme is implemented, this restriction could be lifted.

Symmetry played an unanticipated important role. For the simple shape used in the experiment, the projection of its parts into the orientation-cue subspace results in a nearly symmetric representation in the subspace. Consequently, many incorrect rotations of the object appear almost as good as the correct one. Although this caused no problems for our example, one can imagine that more complicated cases could produce false results due to false symmetries in the orientation-cue subspace. This issue will have to be resolved by more experimentation.

Finally, although the network is specialized to polyhedral constraints, there is no reason why it cannot be generalized to curved surfaces as well. The idea is essentially that of matching coordinate frames that can be associated easily and reliably with the objects and scene. If a way to do this is found for curved objects, then the transformational matching can be applied. We are currently working to extend our results in this direction.

ACKNOWLEDGEMENTS

This work was developed over several years during which time several people contributed to the development of the ideas expressed herein. I am especially grateful to Lydia Hrechanyk, Hiromi Tanaka, Shmuel Tomer, John Sullins, and Lucy Lin for various early implementations. Cesar Quiroz implemented the simulator primitives. Thanks also go to Jerry Feldman, Chris Brown, and members of the Rochester vision group who provided helpful critiques. Peggy Meeker handled all aspects of the preparation of this chapter.

This research was supported in part by the National Science Foundation under Grant DCR-8405720 and the National Institutes of Health under Public Health Service Grant 1R01NS22407-01.

REFERENCES

Ackley, D. H., G. E. Hinton, & T. J. Sejnowski, "A learning algorithm for Boltzmann machines," *Cognitive Science, 9*(1), 147–169, January–March 1985.

Ballard, D. H., "Generalizing the Hough transform to detect arbitrary shapes," *Pattern Recognition, 13*(2), April 1981.

Ballard, D. H., "Paramater nets," *Artificial Intelligence, 22,* 235–267, 1984a.

Ballard, D. H., "Cortical connections: Structure and function," *Brain and Behavioral Sciences, 9*(1), March 1986a.

Ballard, D. H., "Interpolation coding: A representation for numbers in neural models" (Preliminary Version), TR 175, Computer Science Department, University of Rochester, New York, May 1986b.

Ballard, D. H., "Parallel logical inference and energy minimization," TR 142, Computer Science Dept., University of Rochester, New York, March 1986c.

Ballard, D. H., & P. J. Hayes, "Parallel logical inference," *Proceedings of the Cognitive Science Conference,* Boulder, CO, June 1984.

Ballard, D. H., G. E. Hinton, & T. J. Sejnowski, "Parallel visual computation," *Nature, 306*(5938), 21–26, 3 November 1983.

Ballard, D. H., & H. Tanaka, "Frame-based form perception," *Proceedings of the 9th International Joint Conference on Artificial Intelligence,* Los Angeles, CA, August 1985.

Barlow, H. B., "Single units and sensation: A neuron doctrine for perceptual psychology?" *Perception, 1,* 371–394, 1972.

Brown, C. M., "Some mathematical and representational aspects of solid modeling," *IEEE Transactions on Pattern Analysis and Machine Intelligence, 3*(4), July 1981.

Davis, P. J. *Interpolation and Approximation.* Blaisdell Publishing Co., 1963.

Duda, R. O., & P. E. Hart, "Use of the Hough transform to detect lines and curves in pictures," *Communications of the Association for Computing Machinery 15,* 1, 11–15, January 1972.

Feldman, J. A., "Memory and change in connection networks," TR 96, Computer Science Department, University of Rochester, New York, December 1981.

Feldman, J. A., "Connectionist models and parallelism in high-level vision," *Computer Vision, Graphics, and Image Processing, 31,* 178–200, 1985.

Feldman, J. A., "Four frames suffice: a provisional model of vision and space," *The Behavioral and Brain Sciences, 8,* 265–289, June 1985.

Feldman, J. A., & D. H. Ballard, "Connectionist models and their properties," *Cognitive Science, 6,* 205–254, 1982.

Freuder, E. C., "Synthesizing constraint expressions," *Communications of the Association for Computing Machinery, 21*(11), 958–965, November 1978.

Geman, S., & D. Geman, "Stochastic relaxation, Gibbs distributions, and the Bayesian restoration of images," *IEEE Transactions on Pattern Analysis and Machine Intelligence,* January 1985.

Gibson, J. J., "The theory of affordances," in R. Shaw, J. Bransford (Eds). *Perceiving, Acting, and Knowing.* Hillsdale, NJ: Lawrence Erlbaum Associates, 1977.

Hinton, G. E., "Shape representation in parallel systems," *Proceedings of the 7th International Conference on Artificial Intelligence, 7th IJCAI,* 1088–1096, Vancouver, BC, August 1981.

Hinton, G. E., "Some demonstrations of the effects of structural descriptions in mental imagery," *Cognitive Science, 3,* 1979.

Hinton, G. E., & K. J. Lang, "Shape recognition and illusory conjunctions," *Proceedings of the 9th International Conference on Artificial Intelligence,* 252–259, Los Angeles, CA, August 1985.

Hinton, G. E., & T. J. Sejnowski, "Optimal perceptual inference," *Proceedings., IEEE Computer and Pattern Recognition Conference,* 448–453, June 1983.

Hinton, G. E., T. J. Sejnowski, & D. H. Ackley, "Boltzmann machines: Constraint satisfaction networks that learn," TR CMU-CS-84-119, Computer Science Department, Carnegie-Mellon University, May 1984.

Hopfield, J. J., "Neural networks and physical systems with collective computational abilities," *Proceedings of the National Academy of Sciences USA 79*, 2554–2558, 1982.

Hopfield, J. J., "Neurons with graded response have collective computational properties like those of two-state neurons," *Proceedings of the National Academy of Sciences, 81*, 3088–3092, May 1984.

Hopfield, J. J., & D. W. Tank, " 'Neural' computation of decision in optimization problems," to appear in *Biological Cybernetics*, 1985.

Horowitz, E., & S. Sahni. *Fundamentals of Data Structures*. Potomac, MD: Computer Science Press, Inc., 1976.

Hrechanyk, L. M., & D. H. Ballard, "Viewframes: A connectionist model of form perception," DARPA Image Understanding Workshop, Washington, DC, June 1983.

Hummel, R., & S. Zucker, "On the foundations of relaxation labeling processes," *IEEE Transactions on Patterns Analysis and Machine Intelligence*, 1983.

Jaeger, J. C., & A. M. Starfield, *An Introduction to Applied Mathematics*. Oxford Press, 1974.

Just, M. A., & P. A. Carpenter, "Cognitive coordinate systems: Accounts of mental rotation and individual differences in spatial ability," *Psychological Review, 92*(2), 137–172, April 1985.

Kirkpatrick, S., C. D. Gelatt, & M. P. Vecchi, "Optimization by simulated annealing," *Science, 220*, 671–680, 1983.

Kosslyn, S. M. *Image and Mind*. Cambridge, MA: Harvard University Press, 1980.

Li, H., M. A. Levin & R. J. LeMaster, "Fast Hough transform," *Proceedings of the 3rd Vision Workshop*, Bellaire, MI, October 1985.

Linnainmaa, S., D. Harwood, & L. S. Davis, "Pose determination of a three-dimensional object using triangle pairs," TR CAR-TR-143, Center for Automation Research, University of Maryland, College Park, August 1985.

Marr, D. *Vision*. San Francisco: W. H. Freeman Co., 1982.

Prager, J. M., "Extracting and labeling boundary segments in natural scenes," *IEEE Transactions on Pattern Analysis and Machine Intelligence, 2*(1), 16–27, January 1980.

Rosenfeld, A., R. A. Hummel, & S. W. Zucker, "Scene labelling by relaxation operations," *IEEE Transactions on Systems, Man and Cybernetics, 6*, 420, 1976.

Rumelhart, D. E., G. E. Hinton, & R. J. Williams, "Learning internal representations by error propagation," ICS Report 8506, Institute for Cognitive Science, University of California, San Diego, September 1985.

Rumelhart, D. E., & D. Zipser, "Feature discovery by competitive learning," *Cognitive Science, 9*(1), 75–112, January–March 1985.

Saund, E., "Learning continuous values in networks," *Proceedings of the American Association for Artificial Intelligence, 86*, Philadelphia, PA, August 1986.

Shepard, R. N., "Ecological constraints on internal representation: Resonant kinematics of perceiving, imagining, thinking, and dreaming," *Psychological Review, 91*, 417–447, 1984.

Silberberg, T. M., & L. S. Davis, "Some experiments in object recognition using oriented model points," CAR-TR-95, Center for Automation Research, University of Maryland, College Park, 1984.

Smolensky, P., "Foundations of harmony theory: Cognitive dynamical systems and the subsymbolic theory of information processing," in D. E. Rumelhart & J. L. McClelland (Eds). *Parallel Distributed Processing: Explorations in the Microstructure of Cognition. Vol. 1: Foundations*. Cambridge, MA: Bradford Books/MIT Press, 1986.

Stockman, G., & J. C. Esteva, "Use of geometrical constraints and clustering to determine

3D object pose," *Proceedings of the 7th International Conference on Pattern Recognition,* pp. 742–744, Montreal, Canada, 1984.

Triesman, A. M., & G. Gelade, "A feature-integration theory of attention," *Cognitive Psychology, 12,* 97–136, 1980.

Ullman, S., "Relaxation and constrained optimization by local processes," *Computer Graphics Image Processing, 10,* 115–125, 1979.

Webb, J., "Quaternions in computer vision," *Proceedings of the IEEE Conference on Computer Vision and Pattern Recognition,* Washington, DC, July 1983.

4 THE PARTS OF PERCEPTION

ALEX P. PENTLAND
Artificial Intelligence Center, SRI International
CSLI, Stanford University

To support our reasoning abilities, perception must recover environmental regularities (e.g., rigidity, "objectness," axes of symmetry) for later use by cognition. Unfortunately, the representations that are currently available were originally developed for other purposes (e.g., physics, engineering) and have so far proven unsuitable for the task of perception. In answer to this problem we present a representation that has proven competent to accurately describe an extensive variety of natural forms (e.g., people, mountains, clouds, trees), as well as man-made forms, in a succinct and natural manner. The approach taken in this representational system is to describe scene structure at a scale that is similar to our naive perceptual notion of "a part," by use of descriptions that reflect a possible formative history of the object, for example, how the object might have been constructed from lumps of clay. One absolute constraint on any theory of shape representation is that it must be possible to recover accurate descriptions from image data. We therefore present several examples of recovering such a "part" description from natural imagery, and show that this recovery process is overconstrained and, therefore, potentially quite reliable. Finally, we show that by using this shape representation we can improve man-machine communication in several contexts; this provides further evidence of the "naturalness" of the representation.

REPRESENTATION

Perception is the mind's window on the world: Its task is to recognize and report objects and relations that are important to the organism. It is this perceptual link between the *objective* environment and our *conception* of the environment that makes our thoughts meaningful; it ensures that they have some correspondence with the surrounding world.

Because the objects and relations recovered by perception are the primitives upon which all cognition is built, the particular way in which our perceptual apparatus organizes sensory data—that is, which regularities are noted and which are ignored—places strong constraints on the ways in which we can think about our environment. When perception organizes the sensory data in a way unsuited to the current task even simple problems can become nearly impossible to solve, as is illustrated by problems where you "see" the solution only when you "look" at them in the right way.

Identifying important environmental regularities and relating them to the primitive elements of cognition is, therefore, crucial to an understanding of cognitive function, and has consequently become the principal goal of research into visual function (9,10). The central problem in such research is, of course, that the sensory data underdetermines the scene structure. Image pixels, by themselves, can determine nothing. Some model of image formation and environmental structure is *required* in order to obtain *any* assertion about the viewed scene.

To construct a theory relating cognitive primitives to environmental structure, therefore, we must view visual perception as the process of recognizing image regularities that are known—on the basis of one's model of the world—to be reliably and lawfully related to cognitive primitives. The need for a model cannot be sidestepped, for it is the model that relates the theory's representations and computations to the

FIGURE 4.1: A scene described and generated by the representational system described within: tree leaves, bark, rocks, and hair are fractal surfaces. The overall shape is described by Boolean combination of appropriately deformed superquadrics. Only 56 primitives are required (fewer than 500 bytes of information) to specify this scene. The slightly cartoon-like appearance is primarily due to the lack of surface texturing.

state of the real world, and thus explains the semantics—the *meaning*—of the theory. A theory of visual function that has no model of the world also has no meaning.[1]

Models of Scene Structure

Understanding the early stages of perception as the interpretation of sensory data by use of models (knowledge) of the world has, of course, become a standard vision research paradigm. To date, however, most models have been of two kinds: high-level, *specific* models, for example, of people or houses, and low-level models of image formation, for instance, of edges. The reason research has almost exclusively focused on these two types of model is a result more of historical accident than conscious decision. The well-developed fields of optics, material science, and physics (especially photometry) have provided well worked out and easily adaptable models of image formation, while engineering, especially recent work in computer-aided design, have provided standard ways of modeling industrial parts, airplanes, and so forth.

Both the use of image formation models and specialized models has been extensively investigated. It appears to us that both types of models, although useful for many applications, encounter insuperable difficulties when applied to the problems faced by, for instance, a general purpose robot. In the next two subsections we will examine both types of models and outline their advantages and disadvantages for recovering important scene information. In the remainder of this section we motivate, develop, and investigate an alternative category of models.

Models of Image Formation

Most recent research in computational vision has focused on using pointwise models of image formation borrowed from optics, material science and physics. This research has been pursued within the general framework originally suggested by Marr (10) and by Barrow and Tenenbaum (17), in which vision proceeds through a succession of levels of represen-

---

[1] Theories of visual function, therefore, are based on models: Models of how the world is structured and of how this structure is evidenced by regularities in the image. Much vision research is *not* model based, of course: Research on the mechanisms of vision (e.g., parallel processors, neurons), or on procedures for accomplishing visual tasks (e.g., regularization or relaxation methods) need not employ models of the world. But to understand visual *function*—that is, how one can infer information about the world—it is necessary to have a model of the salient world structure and of how that structure evidences itself in the image. Only then can one understand how certain features of the image can allow recognition and recovery of the information of interest.

tation. The initial level is computed directly from local image features, and higher levels are then computed from the information contained in small regions of the preceding levels. Processing is primarily data-driven (i.e., bottom-up).

In Marr's scheme the initial level is called the "raw primal sketch," and contains a description of significant local image structure, for example, edges, lines, or flow field vectors, represented in the form of an array of feature descriptors that preserves the local two-dimensional geometry of the image. The second level is called the "2-1/2D sketch," and is intended to describe local surface properties (e.g., color, orientation) and discontinuities in a viewer-centered coordinate frame. Again, the recovered local surface properties are placed in a set of numeric arrays in registration with original image. From this point an object-centered, volumetric representation was to be computed, such as is illustrated by Figure 4.2. The rationale for this level of representation is that tasks such as navigation or object recognition seem to require description in a viewpoint-independent coordinate frame.

Despite its prevalence, there are serious problems that seem to be inherent to this research paradigm. Because scene structure is under-determined by the local image data (18), researchers have been forced to make *unverifiable* assumptions about large-scale structure (e.g., smoothness, isotropy) in order to derive useful information from their local analyses of the image. In the real world, unfortunately, such assumptions are often seriously in error: in natural scenes the image formation parameters change in fairly arbitrary ways from point to point, making any assumption about local context quite doubtful. As a result, those techniques that rely on strong assumptions such as isotropy or smoothness have proved fragile and error-prone; they are simply not useful for many natural scenes.

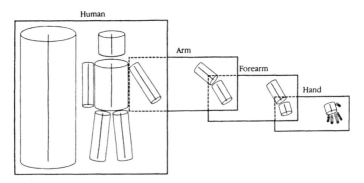

FIGURE 4.2. Marr and Nishihara's (1978) scheme for the description of biological forms.

That such difficulties have been encountered should not, perhaps, be too surprising. It is easily demonstrated (by looking through a viewing or reduction tube) that people can obtain little information about the world from a local image patch taken out of its context. It is also clear that detailed, analytic models of the image formation process are not essential to human perception; humans function quite well with range finder images (where brightness is proportional to distance rather than a function of surface orientation), electron microscope images (which are approximately the reverse of normal images), and distorted and noisy images of all kinds—not to mention paintings and drawings.

Perhaps even more fundamentally, however, even if depth maps and other maps of intrinsic surface properties could be reliably and densely computed, how useful would they be? As Witkin and Tenenbaum pointed out (19), industrial vision work using laser range data has demonstrated that the depth maps, reflectance maps, and the other maps of the 2-1/2D sketch are still basically just images. Although useful for obstacle avoidance and other very simple tasks, they still must be segmented, interpreted, and so forth before it can be used for any more sophisticated task. The conclusion to be drawn from such work is that image-like measurements of range and other surface properties contribute incrementally, in much the same way as color: They add a dimension that simplifies some decisions, but they do *not* solve the difficult problems encountered in image interpretation.

Specialized Models

The alternative to models of image formation has been engineering-style representations; for example, CAD-CAM models of specific objects that are to be identified and located. Such detailed, specific models evidence themselves in image data in an extremely complex manner, in part because the models themselves are often complex, but more importantly because it is the object's surface shape, and not the appearance of the object, that is described. As the object's orientation varies, therefore, these models produce a very large number of different pixel configurations—to say nothing of what happens when we vary the illumination and imaging conditions. As a consequence, the image regularities that allow reliable recognition across all of the allowable configurations are very subtle and complex.

The large number of possible appearances for such models makes the problem of recognizing them very difficult—unless an extremely simplified representation is employed. The most common type of simplified representation is that of a wireframe model whose components correspond to the imaged edges. Such a simplified representation permits reliable recognition of models with currently available computational resources, given that we are in a restricted environment where the descriptive power of such wireframe models is sufficient, for example, as in industrial applications. As a result systems based on CAD-like models of specific objects have provided most of the success stories in machine vision.

Despite this success, the use of an impoverished representation generally means that the flexibility, reliability and discriminability of the recognition process is limited. Thus research efforts employing specific object models have floundered whenever the number of objects to be recognized becomes large, when the objects may be largely obscured, or when there are many unknown objects also present in the scene.

An even more substantive limitation of systems that employ *only* high-level, specific models is that there is no way to learn new *types* of object: new model types must be specially entered, usually by hand, into the database of known models. This is a significant limitation, because the ability to encounter a new type of object, enter it into a catalog of known objects, and thereafter recognize it is an absolute requirement of truly general purpose vision.

Part and Process Models

Some sort of additional constraint is required to overcome the fundamental problem of insufficient information being available from the image. If sufficient constraint is not available from models of image formation, then from where? Human vision seems to function quite well as long as the imaging process preserves the basic spatial structure of the scene. It seems, therefore, that human perception must be exploiting constraints provided by the structure of the scene without reliance on quantitative, point-wise models of the image formation process. What is required, then, are models of scene structure that capture something about the larger-scale structure of our environment. We cannot, however, appeal to CAD-like models of specific objects because of the impossibility of learning new descriptions.

In response to these seemingly intractable problems some researchers have begun to search for a third type of model, one with a grain size intermediate between the point-wise models of image formation and the complex, specific models of particular objects (20,59). There is good reason to believe that it may be possible to accurately describe our world by means of such intermediate-grain models; that world can be modeled as a relatively small set of generic processes that occur again and again, with the apparent complexity of our environment being produced from this limited vocabulary by compounding these basic forms in myriad different combinations.

We have known for over a century that evolution repeats its solutions whenever possible (1), resulting in great regularities across all species: There are but a few types of limb, a few types of skin, a few types of leaf, and a few patterns of branching. An amazingly good model of a tree, for instance, is the composition of a simple branching process with three-dimensional texture processes for generating bark and leaves (21); the same branching models can also serve for rivers, veins, or coral. Similarly, it is now being discovered that inanimate forms may also be constrained by physical laws to a limited number of basic patterns (2,22). Mandelbrot has shown that such apparently complex forms such as clouds, hills, coastlines or cheese can all be described by simple patterns recursively repeated at all different scales (22), while Stevens presents strong evidence that natural textures occur in but a few basic forms (2).

It is this internal structuring in our environment that allows us to derive lawful relationships (23).[2] By causing object features to cluster into groups, this environmental structure allows us to successfully employ simplified category descriptions for commonsense reasoning (3).

It appears, then, that it may be possible to accurately model the world in terms of *parts:* macroscopic models that, in relatively simple combination, can be used to form rough-and-ready models of the objects in our world and how they behave. If we adopt this view, then the central problem of perception research is *not* Marr's scheme of successively describing images, surfaces, and volumes, with the hope that we will eventually arrive at recognition of high-level models (10). Rather, the central problem for perception is to find a set of generically applicable part-models, discover image regularities that are lawfully associated with the individual parts, and then use these regularities to recognize the content of an image as a combination of these generic primitives. This new proposal, then, is that our theory of perception can dispense entirely with these initial stages of description and begin immediately with recognition of parts models: models that are in principle much like models of houses and chairs, but that are more generally applicable and less detailed.

Because such models would be simpler than models of specific objects we would expect that we could more readily characterize how they would appear in an image. On the other hand, because they describe larger-scale structure than point-wise models of image formation, we would expect that they might not suffer from the problems of underdetermination that have forced researchers to make unrealistically strong assumptions such as smoothness or isotropy. Besides offering a good balance

---

[2]If the apparent complexity of our environment were equal to its intrinsic Kolmogorov complexity then no lawful relationships would be possible.

between complexity and reliability, such intermediate-grain parts models spark considerable interest because they describe the world in the right terms: they speak qualitatively of object's parts and of relations between parts, rather than of local surface patches or of specific objects. Thus, they can potentially provide a vocabularly for describing the world at the grain size that is most often directly useful to us (3).

The problem with forming such "parts" models is that they must be complex enough to be reliably recognizable, and yet simple enough to reasonably serve as building blocks for specific object models. Current machine vision systems, for instance, typically use rectangular solids and cylinders to model specific shapes. (see Marr & Nishihara (6), Binford (8), Agin & Binford (11), Nevatia & Binford (12), Badler & Bajcsy (13) and Brady (14)). In recent years representations like theirs have found considerable success in industrial-style machine vision systems where an exact model of the specific objects that are to be discovered in the image data is available (15,16). Unfortunately, such a representation is only capable of an extremely abstracted description of most natural and biological forms, as is illustrated in Figure 4.2. It cannot accurately and succinctly[3] describe most natural animate forms or produce a succinct description of complex inanimate forms such as clouds or mountains. Further, and perhaps more importantly, using these Platonic-solid primitives for the automatic construction of a description for an arbitrary new object has not proven possible, except[4] (as in industrial or urban imagery) when the set of objects that will be encountered is constrained to be very simple combinations of rectangular solids or cylinders (24). To support truly general purpose vision, therefore, we need to develop new modeling primitives that can be used to build descriptions of arbitrary objects and that are recognizable in standard imagery.

Our work toward this goal is the subject of the remainder of this chapter. We present a representational system that has proven competent to accurately describe an extensive variety of natural forms (e.g., people, mountains, clouds, trees), as well as man−made forms, in a succinct and natural manner. Figure 4.1 shows an example of a scene described in this representation; only 56 descriptive "parts" (about 500 bytes of information) were employed. We then present evidence that we

---

[3]If we retreat from cylinders to generalized cylinders we can, of course, describe such shapes accurately. The cost of such retreat is that we must introduce a 1-D (at least) function describing the sweeping function; which makes the representation neither succinct nor intuitively attractive.

[4]A caveat should be noted with respect to laser rangefinders and the like: In some cases the thousands of range measurements provided by these active sensors can give enough additional constraint to allow recovery of low-level, polygon-like descriptions of novel objects.

can use the special properties of this representational system to recover descriptions of specific objects from image data, and finally, we argue that these recovered descriptions are extremely useful in supporting both commonsense reasoning and man–machine communication.

A Representation For Natural Forms

The idea behind this representational system is to provide a vocabulary of models and operations that will allow us to model our world as the relatively simple composition of component "parts," parts that are reliably recognizable from image data.

The most primitive notion in this representation may be thought of as a "lump of clay," a modeling primitive that may be deformed and shaped, but which is intended to correspond roughly to our naive perceptual notion of "a part." It is worth noting that this notion of "part" agrees with that used by Konderink and van Doorn (25,26) or by Hoffman and Richards (27) in their analysis of how part boundaries impose constraints upon three-dimensional surfaces, although they did not actually propose a model of what constitutes a three-dimensional "part". For this basic modeling element we use a parameterized family of shapes known as *superquadrics* (28,29), which were originally invented by Danish mathematician Peit Hein. This family of shapes are described (adopting the notation $\cos \eta = C_\eta$, $\sin \omega = S_\omega$) by the following equation:

$$\vec{X}(\eta, \omega) = \begin{pmatrix} a_1 C_\eta^{\epsilon_1} C_\omega^{\epsilon_2} \\ a_2 C_\eta^{\epsilon_1} S_\omega^{\epsilon_2} \\ a_3 S_\eta^{\epsilon_1} \end{pmatrix} \tag{1}$$

where $X(\eta, \omega)$ is a three-dimensional vector that sweeps out a surface parameterized in latitude η and longitude ω, with the surface's shape controlled by the parameters ϵ_1 and ϵ_2. This family of functions includes cubes, cylinders, spheres, diamonds and pyramidal shapes as well as the round-edged shapes intermediate between these standard shapes. Some of these shapes are illustrated in Figure 4.3(a). Superquadrics are, therefore, a superset of the modeling primitives currently in common use.

These basic "lumps of clay" (with various symmetries and profiles) are used as prototypes that are then deformed by stretching, bending, twisting or tapering, and then combined using Boolean operations to form new, complex prototypes that may, recursively, again be subjected to deformation and Boolean combination. As an example, the back of a chair is a rounded-edge cube that has been flattened along one axis, and then bent somewhat to accommodate the rounded human form. The bottom of the chair is a similar object, but rotated 90°, and by "anding"

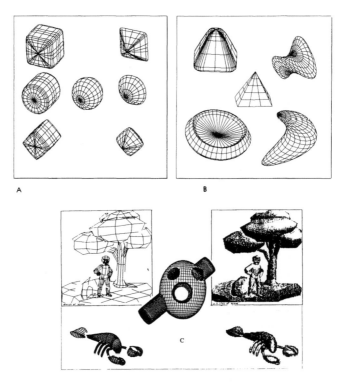

FIGURE 4.3. (a) A sampling of the basic forms allowed, (b) deformations of these forms, (c) Boolean combinations (or's and nots) of the basic forms.

these two parts together with elongated rectangular primitives describing the chair legs we obtain a complete description of the chair, as illustrated in Figure 4.4.

This descriptive language is designed to describe shapes in a manner that corresponds to a possible formative history, for example, how one would create a given shape by combining lumps of clay. Thus the description provides us with an explanation of the image data in terms of the interaction of generic formative processes. This primitive explanation can then be refined by application of specific world knowledge and context, eventually deriving causal connections, affordances, and all of the other information that makes our perceptual experience appear so rich and varied. For instance, if we have parsed the chair in Figure 4.4 into its constituent parts we could deduce that the bottom of the chair is a stable platform and thus might be useful as a seat, or we might hypothesize that the back of the chair can rigidly move relative to the supporting rod, given the evidence that they are separate "parts" and thus likely

FIGURE 4.4. A chair formed from Boolean combinations of appropriately deformed superquadrics.

separatedly formed. The reader is encouraged to consider other examples of how the knowledge of part structure can help in forming hypotheses about function.

We have found that by using such a process-oriented, possible-history
representation we force the resulting descriptions to group points that
have similar causal histories, thus obtaining "parts" that interact with the
world in a relatively simple, holistic manner. This further simplifies
many reasoning tasks, because the parameters and components that affect interactions tend to be explicitly represented rather than being some
complex or difficult-to-calculate function of the description's variables.
For instance, use of this type of representation sufficiently simplifies
questions about spatial relationships, intersection, image appearance,
and so forth that we have been able to use it to construct a real-time
three-dimensional graphical modeling system, using a Symbolics 3600
computer.[5] This system, called "SuperSketch," was used to make the
figures in this chapter.

Such descriptions may be written as a predicate calculus formula. We
may then use this description, which has a clear model-theoretic semantics, in conjunction with constraint satisfaction or theorem-proving
mechanisms, to accomplish whatever reasoning is required. Interestingly, it has been found that when adult human subjects are required to

---

[5]Real-time in this case means that a "lump" can be moved, hidden surface removal
accomplished, and drawn as a 100 polygon line drawing approximation in 1/8th of a
second, and a complex, full-color image such as Figure 4.1 can be rendered in approximately 20 seconds. The Symbolics speed is roughly comparable to a VAX 11/780, except
for being almost an order of magnitude slower on the floating-point operations that are
used heavily in this modeling system.

describe imagery verbally with completely novel content, their typical spontaneous strategy is to employ a descriptive system analogous to this one (i.e., form is described by modifying and combining prototypes (30)). The classic work by Rosch (3) supports the view that such a prototype-and-differences descriptive system is common in human reasoning: she showed that even primitive New Guinea tribesmen (who appear to have no concept of regular geometric shapes) form the geometric prototypes in much the same manner as people from other cultures and describe novel shapes in terms of differences from these prototypes.

This representational system provides a grammar of form that has surprising descriptive power. Such descriptions have the intuitively satisfying nature of the Marr and Nishihara scheme; they incorporate hierarchies of primitives with axes of symmetry. This new descriptive language, however, is considerably more powerful than other representations that have been suggested. For example, a trivial comparison is that we can describe a wider range of basic shapes, as shown in Figure 4.3(a). By allowing deformations of these shapes, we greatly expand the range of primitives allowed, as shown in Figure 4.3(b) (see also Barr (31), Hollerbach (32), Leyton (42) on describing shape using modifications of prototypes). We have, so far, required only stretching, bending, tapering, and twisting deformations to construct an extremely wide variety of objects. But the most powerful notion in this language is that of allowing (hierarchical) Boolean combination of these primitives. This intuitively attractive constructive solid modeling approach—building specific object descriptions by applying the logical set operations "and," "or," and "not" to component *parts*—introduces a language-like generative power that allows the creation of a tremendous variety of form, such as is illustrated by Figure 4.3(c) or by Figure 4.5.

Biological Forms

Biological forms such as the human body are naturally described by hierarchical Boolean combinations of the basic primitives, allowing the construction of accurate—but quite simple—descriptions of the detailed shape, as illustrated by Figure 4.5 (the slightly cartoonlike nature of these illustrations is due primarily to the lack of surface texturing). The entire human body shown in Figure 4.5, including face and hands, requires combining only 45 primitives, or approximately 400 bytes of information (these informational requirements are not a function of body position). Similarly, the description for the face requires the combination of only 19 primitives, or fewer than 150 bytes of information. The extreme brevity of these descriptions makes many otherwise difficult reasoning tasks relatively simple, for example, even NP-complete problems can be easily solved when the size of the problem is small enough.

FIGURE 4.5. Human forms described (and rendered) by use of this representational system; only 45 primitives are required for each body, approximately 400 bytes of information.

In Figure 4.5 (as in all cases examined to date) when we try to model a particular three-dimensional form we find that we are able to describe—indeed, we are almost *forced* to describe—the shape in a manner that corresponds to the organization our perceptual apparatus imposes upon the image. That is, the components of the description match one-to-one with our naive perceptual notion of the "parts" in the figure, for example, the face in Figure 4.5 is composed of primitives that correspond exactly to the cheeks, chin, nose, forehead, ears, and so forth. Figure 4.6 shows how the face is formed from the Boolean sum of several different primitives. The basic form for the head is a slightly tapered ellipsoid. To this basic form is added a somewhat cubical nose, bent pancake-like primitives for ears, bent thin ellipsoids for lips, and almond-shaped eyes, as is shown in Figure 4.6(a). Figure 4.6(b) shows the addition of rounded cheeks and a slightly pointed chin (is this Yoda from Star Wars?), and finally Figure 4.6(c) shows the addition of a squarish forehead and slightly fractalized hair. The smoothly shaded result is shown in Figure 4.6(d)—it is a reasonably accurate human head, composed of only 19 primitives, specified by slightly less than 150 bytes of information. One should remember that this representation is not in any way tailored for describing the human form: it is a general-purpose vocabulary.

The correspondence between the organization of descriptions made in this representation and human perceptual organization is important because it is strong evidence that we are on the right track. The fact that the distinctions made in this representation are very similar to those made by people makes it likely that descriptions couched in this language will be useful in understanding commonsense reasoning tasks, for example, that the vocabulary of this representation might constitute a good set

A   B   C

FIGURE 4.6. (a) shows that the basic form for the head is a slightly tapered ellipsoid; to this basic form is added a somewhat cubical nose, bent pancake-like primitives for ears, bent thin ellipsoids for lips, and almond-shaped eyes. (b) shows the addition of rounded cheeks and slightly pointed chin, and finally, (c) shows the addition of a squarish forehead and slightly fractalized hair. The smoothly shaded result is shown in (d)—it is a reasonably accurate human head, composed of only 19 primitives, specified by slightly less than 150 bytes of information.

D

of primitive predicates for theories of commonsense reasoning such as sought by the Naive Physics (33) research program.[6]

Similarly, the ability to make the right "part" distinctions offers hope that we can form qualitative descriptions of specific objects ("Ted's face") or of classes of objects ("a long, thin face") by specifying constraints on part parameters and on relations between parts, in the manner of Marr and Nishihara (6,7), Winston (46,47) or Davis (48). And, of course, such representational correspondence is also important because it provides the basis for useful man-machine interaction.

Complex Inanimate Forms

This method for representing the three-dimensional world, although excellent for biological and man-made forms, becomes awkward when applied to complex natural surfaces such as mountains or clouds. The most pronounced difficulty is that, like previously proposed representations, our superquadric lumps-of-clay representation becomes implausibly complex when confronted with the problem of representing, for example, a mountain, a crumpled newspaper, a bush, or a field of grass.

---

[6]Descriptions that correspond to a possible formative history explicitly group together parts of a form that have a similar causal history, i.e., that came about in the same manner. It appears that such groupings have a strong tendency to *continue* to act as a simple whole. Why this should be true is unclear; perhaps there are only a few basic categories of physical interaction that all may be characterized using the same definition of "part."

This makes the technique ill-suited to solving the problem of representing *classes* of such objects or determining that a particular object is member of that class.

Why is it that such introspectively simple tasks turn out to be so hard? Intuitively, the main source of difficulty is that there is too much information to deal with. Natural objects are amazingly bumpy and detailed; and classes of such objects seem to include virtually infinite variability. There is simply too much detail, and it is too variable. When we attempt to represent such objects in a detailed, quantitative manner, we are forced to an unwieldy description.

Nor does it suffice to simply introduce error tolerances into the representation (e.g., a mountain is a cone $\pm x$). For not only is such a representation misleading (do we *really* want to say that a cube is a sphere $\pm 0.25r$?), but it does not allow for the ability to distinguish between a mountain (represented as a cone $\pm x$) and a cone with a few dents in it (also represented as a cone $\pm x$).

Experiments in human perception suggest a way out of such problems. When we view a crumpled newspaper, for instance, it seems that the description we store is not accurate enough to recover every detail; rather, it seems that out of the welter of image detail people abstract a few properties such as the general "crumpledness" and a few major features of the shape (e.g., the general outline). The rest of the crumpled newspaper's structure is ignored; it is unimportant, *random*. For the purpose of describing that crumpled newspaper then, the only important constraints on shape are the crumpledness and general outline.

People escape the trap of overwhelming complexity, it seems, by varying the level of descriptive abstraction—the amount of detail captured—depending on the task. In cases like the crumpled newspaper, or when recognizing classes of objects such as "a mountain" or "a cloud," the level of abstraction is very high. Almost no specific detail is required, only that the crumpledness of the form comply with the general physical properties characteristic of that type of object. In recognizing a *specific* mountain, however, people will require that all of the major features be identical, although they typically ignore smaller details. Even though these details are "ignored," however, they must still conform to the constraints characteristic of that type of object: We would never mistake a smooth cone for a rough-surfaced mountain even if it had a generally conical shape.

The fractal model of natural surfaces (34,35) allows us to duplicate this sort of physically meaningful abstraction from the morass of details encountered in natural scenes. It lets us describe a crumpled newspaper by specifying certain structural regularities—its crumpledness, in effect—and leave the rest as variable detail. It lets us specify the qualitative shape (i.e., the surface's roughness) without (necessarily) worrying about the details.

Fractal-Based Qualitative Description.   Many naturally occurring forms are fractals[7] (22,34–36); Mandelbrot, for instance, showed that fractal surfaces are produced by several basic physical processes. One general characterization of naturally occurring fractals is that they are the end result of any physical processes that randomly modify shape through local action, that is to say, they are a generalization of random walks and Brownian motion. After innumerable repetitions, such processes will typically produce a fractal surface shape. Thus clouds, mountains, turbulent water, lightning, and even music have all been shown to have a fractal form.

During the last several years we have developed these fractal functions into a statistical model for describing complex, natural surface shapes (34,35,37) and have found that it furnishes a good description for many such surfaces. Evidence for the descriptive adequacy of this model comes from serveral sources. Recently conducted surveys of natural imagery (34–36), for instance, have found that this model accurately describes how most homogeneous textured or shaded image regions change over scale (change in resolution). The prevalence of surfaces with fractal statistics is explained by analogy to Brownian motion (the archetypical fractal function): just as when a dust mote randomly bombarded by air molecules produces a fractal Brownian random walk, the complex interaction of processes that locally modify shape produces a fractal Brownian surface.

For our current purposes, perhaps the most important fact is that one of the parameters of this statistical model (specifically, the fractal dimension of the surface) has been found to correspond very closely to people's perceptual notion of *roughness* (38,39). We have been able, for instance, to accurately predict a surface's perceptual smoothness or roughness on the basis of knowing its fractal statistics. The fractal model, therefore, gives us a way of *qualitatively* describing surface shape (34,35).

The fractal model shows how we may use physically motivated statistical description to abstract away from the overwhelming amount of detail present in many natural forms. To be useful, however, we must combine the fractal model's notion of qualitative description by physically-meaningful statistical abstraction together with the quantitative descriptive abilities of the lump-of-clay descriptive language developed in the previous sections.

---

[7]The defining characteristic of a fractal is that it has a *fractional dimension,* from which we get the word fractal.

Qualitative and Quantitative Description. We begin the task of unifying the fractal model's notion of qualitative description with the quantitative lump-of-clay description by considering the basic properties of naturally occurring examples of fractal Brownian surfaces. Such surfaces all have two important properties: (a) each segment is statistically similar to all others; (b) segments at different scales are statistically indistinguishable, that is, as we examine such a surface at greater or lesser imaging resolution its statistics (curvature, etc.) remain the same. Because of these invariances, the most important *variable* in the description of such a shape is how it varies with scale; in essence, how many large features there are relative to the number of middle-sized and smaller-sized features. For fractal shapes (and thus for many real shapes) the ratio of the number of features of one size to the number of features of the next larger size is a constant—a surprising fact that derives from the property of scale invariance. The fractal model, therefore, leads us to a statistical characterization of a surface in terms of two parameters: The surface's variance (amplitude), and the ratio between the frequency of smaller and larger features (i.e., its fractal dimension).

We may, therefore, construct fractal surfaces by using our superquadric "lumps" to describe the surface's features; specifically, we can use the recursive sum of smaller and smaller superquadric lumps to form a true fractal surface. This construction is illustrated in Figures 4.7a–c.

We start by specifying the surface's qualitative appearance—its roughness—by picking a ratio r, $0 \leq r \leq 1$, between the number of features of one size to the number of features that are twice as large. This ratio describes how the surface varies across different scales (resolutions, spatial frequency channels, etc.) and is related to the surface's fractal dimension D by $D = T + r$, where T is the topological dimension of the surface.

We then randomly place n^2 large bumps on a plane, giving the bumps a Gaussian distribution of altitude (with variance σ^2), as seen in Figure 4.7(a). We then add to that $4n^2$ bumps of half the size, and altitude variance $\sigma^2 r^2$, as shown in Figure 4.7(b). We continue with $16n^2$ bumps of one quarter the size, and altitude $\sigma^2 r^4$, then $64n^2$ bumps one eighth size, and altitude $\sigma^2 r^6$, and so forth, as shown in Figure 4.7(c). The final result, shown in Figure 4.7(c) is a true Brownian fractal shape. The validity of this construction does not depend on the particular shape of the superquadric primitives employed, the only constraint is that the sum must fill out the Fourier domain. Different shaped lumps will, however, give different appearance or texture to the resulting fractal surface; this is an important and as yet relatively uninvestigated aspect of the fractal model. Figures 4.7(d), (e) illustrate the power and generality of this construction; all of the forms and surfaces in these images can be constructed in this manner.

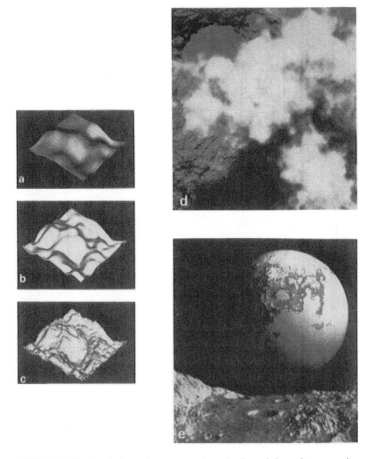

FIGURE 4.7.   (a–c) show the construction of a fractal shape by successive addition of smaller and smaller features with number of features and amplitudes described by the ratio $1/r$. All of the forms and surfaces shown in (d) and (e) (which are images by Voss and Mandelbrot, see (22)) can be generated in this manner.

When the placement and size of these superquadric lumps is random, we obtain the classical Brownian fractal surface that has been the subject of our previous research. When the larger components of this sum are matched to a particular object, however, we obtain a description of that object that is exact to the level of detail encompassed by the specified components. This makes it possible to specify a global shape while retaining a qualitative, statistical description at smaller scales: To describe a complex natural form such as a cloud or mountain, we specify the "lumps" down to the desired level of detail by fixing the larger elements of this sum, and then we specify only the fractal statistics of the smaller lumps, thus fixing the qualitative appearance of the surface. Figure 4.8 illustrates an example of such description. The overall shape is that of a sphere; to this specified large-scale shape, smaller lumps were added randomly. The smaller lumps were added with three different choices of r (i.e., three different choices of fractal statistics) resulting in three qualitatively different surfaces—each with the same basic spherical shape.

The ability to fix particular "lumps" within a given shape provides an elegant way to pass from a qualitative model of a surface to a quantitative one—or *vice versa*. We can refine a general model of the class "a mountain" to produce a model of a *particular* mountain by fixing the position and size of the largest lumps used to build the surface, while still leaving smaller details only statistically specified. Or we can take a very specific model of a shape, discard the smaller constituent lumps after calculating their statistics, and obtain a model that is less detailed than the original but which is still *qualitatively* correct.

Summary

To support our reasoning abilities perception must recover environmental regularities for later use in cognitive processes. Understanding this recovery of structure is critically important because these regularities are the building blocks of all cognitive activities. To create a theory of how perception produces meaningful cognitive building blocks we need a representation whose elements may be lawfully related to important physical regularities, and that correctly describes the perceptual organization people impose on the stimulus. Unfortunately, the representations that are currently available were originally developed for other purposes (for example, physics, engineering) and have so far proven unsuitable for the problems of perception or commonsense reasoning.

FIGURE 4.8. Spherical shapes with surface crenulations ranging from smooth (fractal dimension = topological dimension, $r \approx 0$) to rough (fractal dimension $>>$ topological dimension, $r \approx 1$).

In answer to these problems we are developing a vocabularly of models that span the space of shape possibilities. The first two elements of this models vocabulary are (a) a superquadric-based models of "parts" that are much like the "parts" that people see, and (b) a fractal-based model of three-dimensional texture, which is a statistical characterization of how Nature combines "parts" to form complex, natural surfaces. We anticipate the development of additional types of shape model as new problems are confronted.

One of the novel aspects of these models is that the descriptive strategy employed provides a possible formative history of the object, for example, how the object might have been constructed from lumps of clay. We have demonstrated that this process-oriented representational system is able to accurately describe a very wide range of natural and man-made forms in an extremely simple, and therefore useful, manner. Further, the representation can be used to support fast, qualitative approximations to determine, for example, intersection, appearance or relative position. Such qualitative reasoning is employed in SuperSketch to allow real–time movement, deformation, Boolean combination, hidden surface removal, intersection and rendering.

In the remainder of this chapter we will demonstrate that descriptions couched in this representation can be recovered from images, and that this representation can be used to facilitate man-machine communication.

PRIMITIVE PERCEPTION: RECOGNIZING MODELS

During the late 1970's and early 1980's, the dominant view of human perception has been that perception proceeds through successive levels of increasingly sophisticated representations until finally, at some point, information is transferred to our general cognitive faculties. And indeed, there *does* seem to be a gradient of sophistication in human perception, ranging from seemingly primitive inferences of shapes, textures, colors, and the like, to the apparently more sophisticated inferences of chairs, trees, affordances[8] and people's emotions. There is significant reason to believe, however, that this is not simply the flow of information through successive levels of representation.

To summarize Fodor's excellent and extended argument for this conclusion (40), we note that the sophisticated end of perception can involve virtually anything we know, and seems to blend smoothly into general cognition—for instance, we speak of perceiving abstract mathematical

---

[8]affordances are the purpose(s) of an object.

relationships of people's intentions. There is no principled reason to separate sophisticated perception from general purpose reasoning. The characteristics of primitive perception, however, are quite different from that of cognition:

- *Informational encapsulation.* Primitive perception proceeds without benefit of intimate access to the full range of our world knowledge. Most visual illusions, for instance, cannot be dispelled merely by recognizing them as illusions (41).
- *Limited extent.* The body of knowledge on which primitive perception draws is of quite limited extent, at least in comparison to our conscious world knowledge. People of all cultures seem to share a common perceptual framework (43); it is this shared framework that makes possible any communication at all.
- *Functional autonomy.* Primitive perception proceeds with little regard to the particulars of the task at hand, under at most limited voluntary control. We are capable of the same discriminations, regardless of purpose or task, except, perhaps, for a few very practiced tasks, for example, birdwatchers discriminating between different types of bird. This is not to say that we always *do* make the same discriminations (we can, after all, focus our attention), but rather that whenever we attend to a particular stimulus dimension we are always capable of making the same discriminations.

Primitive perception is at least roughly the realm of perceptual organization, that is to say, the preattentive organization of sensory data into primitives like texture, color, and form. Thus, although we often speak as if perception were a smooth series of progressively more sophisticated inferences (e.g., Marr (10)), it is more likely that there are separate, specialized mechanisms for primitive and sophisticated perception.

This leads to a conception of our perceptual apparatus as containing two distinct parts: the first, a special-purpose, perhaps innate mechanism that supports primitive perception, and the second something that closely resembles general cognition. Most of the time the sensory data is first examined by the mechanisms of primitive perception to discover instances of rigidity, parallelism, part-like groupings and other evidences of causal organization, thus providing an explanation of the image data in terms of generic formative processes. The mechanisms of sophisticated perception then use specific, learned knowledge about the world to refine this primitive, generic explanation into a detailed account of the environment.

It should be noted, however, that for at least the most practiced discriminations things seem to happen somewhat differently. When a percept, even if of a very sophisticated nature, is highly practiced or very important it appears that our minds build up a special-purpose mechanism solely for that purpose. Consider, for instance, our incredible facility at recognizing our own name, or the faces of familiar people. There may be, therefore, a sort of "compiler" for building specialized routines for these oft-repeated, important or time-critical discriminations. How much of our day-to-day perception is handled by such special-purpose routines is very much an open question.

Primitive perception, by our definition, was first seriously addressed by the Gestalt psychologists (4,5), who noticed that people seem to spontaneously impose a physically meaningful organization upon visual stimuli, through grouping, figure/ground separation, and so forth. They found that the addition of semantic context very rarely affects this spontaneous, preattentive organization of the image; somehow the visual system seems able to group an image into the correct, physically meaningful parts *before* contextual knowledge is available.

The Gestalt psychologists described this spontaneous organization as being governed by the principle of *Pragnanz*[9], however their lack of modern notions of computation limited their ability to crisply define *Pragnanz* and thus doomed them to a rather limited success. Nevertheless, their work paved the way for the two-stage model of perception that is enjoying widespread popularity in academic circles today. The first stage, which we are describing here as primitive perception, is spontaneous and preattentive. It carves the sensory data into likely meaningful parts, and presents them to the later stages of perception. The second stage of perception, which we are calling "sophisticated perception," is very little (if at all) different from our general cognitive faculty—including the ability to make very efficient, "compiled" routines, presumably by combining the outputs of primitive perception.

Recognizing Superquadric Modeling Primitives

It is our goal to provide the beginnings of a theory for our faculty of preattentive, primitive perception: to present a rigorous, mathematical definition for the vague notion of "a part" and to explain how we can, Gestalt-like, carve an image up into meaningful "parts" without need of semantic context or specific a priori knowledge. We have already described a representation that is competent to describe a wide range of natural forms and whose primitive elements seem to correspond closely to our naive notions of perceptual parts. What remains to be done is to show that these descriptive primitives can be recovered from image data.

In this section of the chapter we will use range imagery, rather than

---

[9]*Pragnanz* is normally translated as meaning "goodness of form."

intensity imagery, as the starting point for learning object descriptions. There are two reasons for taking this approach.

First, it is clear that bottom-up learning of object descriptions is perhaps the most difficult task faced by a vision system. We can make this problem somewhat easier by using a range image rather than an intensity image, because range imagery allows us to perform a simple separation of figure from ground: One "chops out" a cube of data, locates the ground plane, and the remaining data is "figure." Note, however, that even though range imagery makes the problem of finding the figure somewhat easier, all the problems of *figure segmentation* (i.e., finding the correct part structure) remain as difficult as when using intensity imagery.

The second reason for choosing to use range imagery is the similarity of this data to Marr's 2–1/2-D sketch: both are relatively dense measurements of the scene's intrinsic geometry. Thus the range-imagery techniques we develop for learning descriptions and recognizing objects are directly transferable to situations where shape–from–x and depth–from–x methods, rather than a laser rangefinder, have provided us with image-like descriptions of a scene's intrinsic geometry.

Vision as Optimization

One general way to pose the problem of learning an object description is as the process of using our shape vocabulary to find the "best" account of the data. That is, we can define the learning process as one of optimizing a description over our shape vocabulary relative to some goodness-of-fit criterion. We shall employ encoding length in this chapter as our means of evaluating an explanation of the image data, in other words, our goodness-of-fit criterion is the number of bits needed to describe the data error (evaluated by using the L_1-norm) plus the number of bits in our part description.

Minimal-length encoding is a natural way to capture the intrinsic structure of a scene by examining the image data. One can, for instance, prove that if a body of data is generated by a shape vocabulary V with parameter settings P_i, then the minimal-length encoding of that data (using V) will recover the P_i—given sufficient resolution, noise-free data, and modulo ambiguities in the vocabulary.[10]

---

[10]Briefly stated, if we have no ambiguities in the vocabulary—e.g., if we disallow situations in which one vocabulary primitive can be fitted perfectly by some combination of other vocabulary primitives—we can express the image data as an overconstrained set of equations whose variables are the generating primitive's parameters. If we change any of the parameters, the encoding is no longer accurate and therefore not minimal; if we add a primitive, the encoding is no longer minimal; consequently, because the system has no ambiguities and is overconstrained, there is no accurate encoding containing fewer primitives.

Thus, the important point about employing this approach to learn a description is that we must use a vocabulary that correctly describes the actual structure of the data. Our choice of vocabulary is based upon psychological evidence as to people's perception of the intrinsic structure of three-dimensional objects (27,42,59,63).

The primary difficulty in computing a minimal-length encoding is that it requires global optimization of a fitting function and, unfortunately, there are no efficient, general-purpose global optimization techniques for such nonlinear problems. We may, however, take advantage of the special properties of this particular problem in order to achieve an adequate solution.

The first property we may take advantage of is that we may decompose of our search for the best explanation into two phases: a local phase and a subsequent global phase. We may do this because the part models in our shape vocabulary are compact, with surfaces that are opaque to the sensor. Thus, changes that are far enough from a particular image point do not affect the description at that point. For instance, if the largest element in our shape vocabulary has a projected radius of 60 pixels, we do not have to look more than 60 or 70 pixels in any direction in order to find the part model that provides the best fit in the immediately surrounding image region.

The second property we may take advantage of is that the search for a "best fit" within a particular image region seems to be convex for parameter values near the optimal solution. Figure 4.9(a) shows a range image of a bananalike shape. Figure 4.9(b) shows the value of an L_1-norm "goodness-of-fit" functional between these range data and a three-dimensional SuperSketch "part" as each of the part's parameters are varied. At the center of each graph in Figure 4.9(b) is the exactly matching parameter value; it can be seen that our "goodness of fit" functional varies slowly as we move away from the correct parameter value (note that these graphs do not show the functional's value over the entire parameter range).

Figure 4.9, therefore, illustrates our empirical observation that finding the "best fit" within a neighborhood is a convex problem for parameter values near the optimal solution. In our experience this convex behavior obtains uniformly. The convex region surrounding the correct parameter setting is often quite broad: For instance, we can usually vary length, width, or depth by up to 50% before we leave the convex region of the parameter space. In contrast, the "goodness of fit" functional is relatively sensitive to orientation: We normally can vary rotation angles by only 10 or 15 degrees before leaving the convex region.

These two properties, together with small number of parameters in our modeling primitives, allow us to use a coarse-grained search over the entire parameter space as our optimization procedure. That is, by com-

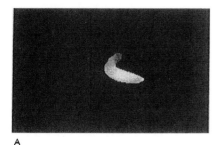

A

FIGURE 4.9. The fitting problem seems to be locally convex. (a) A range image of a banana-like shape, (b) The fit between these range data and a three-dimensional part model as the parameters of the part are varied; the correct fit occurs at the center of each graph.

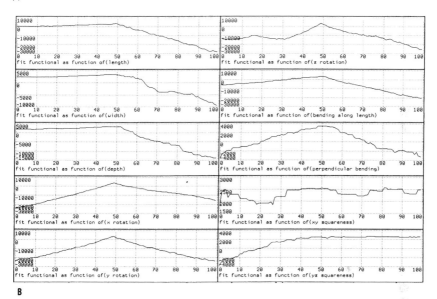

B

paring (using an L_1-norm) each combination of parameter settings with the image data surrounding each image point, we can find a small set of part models which provide the best *regional* fit to the image data. We can then search among combinations of these regional best-fits to find the best overall explanation of the image data, i.e., a minimal-length encoding of the image data in terms of our modeling primitives.

We have found that, if the (x, y, z) position parameters are excluded, about 84,000 "goodness-of-fit" evaluations are required to search the entire parameter space adequately, sampling most parameters at three different values (e.g., object widths of 10, 20, and 40 inches) and some critical parameters, such as orientation, more frequently (e.g., every 22.5 degrees)[11]. The experimental finding that our goodness–of–fit func-

---

[11]In our sampling we restrict bending to occur along at most two axes, one of which must be the longest axis, and we have typically not included tapering (it seems to make a difference only on large forms), except when using a reduced sampling in orientation.

tional varies slowly near the correct parameter setting gives us confidence that we will find a parameter setting that is within the convex region surrounding the optimum parameter setting. We may then refine the result of this coarse search by using a gradient descent algorithm.

By repeating this search for each (coarsely quantized) image position, *we can effectively carry out a coarse-grained search over the entire parameter space.* This produces a relatively small set of part models that provide the best *regional* fit to the image data. We then choose from among this set of regional fits a small set of parts that provides the best explanation (i.e., a minimal-length encoding) of the image data, and, finally, conduct a gradient descent on this final ensemble of part models.

Evaluation of the Goodness-Of-Fit Functional.   One of the key elements assuring the success of this approach is evaluation of the goodness-of-fit functional in a manner that is insensitive to occlusions and that, in addition, takes into account all the information we have about edge placement, surface shape, perspective effects, and sensor characteristics. The procedure we use is to

(1) Construct a three-dimensional SuperSketch part with the hypothesized parameters (e.g., orientation, length, squareness).

(2) Render that part by using known sensor characteristics, thereby constructing, for example, a range image, that accounts correctly for the effects of perspective, surface shape, and other known variables that affect image appearance.

(3) Histogram all of the point-by-point differences in depth between the rendered part and the image data. This produces a histogram with "buckets" at each possible offset between the hypothesized part's depth and the actual depth, so that the value in each bucket is the number of pixels at that particular offset. Note that we use the L_1-norm in this operation. While doing this, we also keep track of the number of pixels ϵ that fall off the figure entirely (when the "figure" of interest can be separated from the surrounding "ground," as is generally possible with range data).

(4) From this histogram we estimate the position p of the largest peak. This peak is the most frequent distance between the hypothesized and the measured surfaces; the number of counts in this peak is the area (in pixels) of the hypothesized part's surface that would match the image data if the part were moved in depth by a distance p. By using buckets of width σ, therefore, we can employ this histogramming technique to determine the number of pixels

μ that would match to within $\pm\sigma$ at the optimum depth positioning of the hypothesized part.

(5) Compute the value of the goodness-of-fit functional Γ for this set of parameters:

$$\Gamma = \mu - \lambda\epsilon \qquad (2)$$

The quantity $1/2\Gamma\sigma$ is our L_1-norm estimate of the total fitting error between the hypothesized part model and the observed data over the region in which the L_1-error is small enough to make a match plausible. In the following examples, $\sigma = \lambda = 4$; the procedure seems to be relatively insensitive to the value of these parameters.

By using a rendering technique that includes a full camera and sensor model, we make *explicit* all of the edge, surface, perspective, and other relations that are normally *implicit* in our model parameters. We are thus able to take into account these previously implicit relations.

By using a RANSAC-style (54) histogramming procedure, we allow large portions of the figure to be occluded without disturbing the matching process. This enables us to compute an energy functional that corresponds closely to the L_1-norm error between the image data and the hypothesized shape, while ignoring data that are due to other, occluding forms.

Refining the Initial Search. Within each region searched, the above procedure gives a "best-fitting" three-dimensional SuperSketch part model for the image data in the surrounding region. This coarse-grained global search is then followed by a gradient-descent optimization of the part's parameters versus the goodness-of-fit functional. We use a stochastic technique to avoid shallow local minima; our method is similar to the one employed by Bajcsy and Solina (64).

A single "best" explanation for the entire body of image data is then found by picking a minimal covering of the data from among the set of regionally best-fitting part models. Currently this is accomplished through a simple iterative, best-first search: We first accept the three-dimensional SuperSketch part model that accounts for the most image data, then the part that accounts for the maximum portion of the remaining data, and so forth. When we accept a part, therefore, those parts centered at nearby locations are generally excluded from further consideration because they are "covered" by the already accepted part. This search technique was chosen because, although its performance is almost always suboptimal, it is efficient and its typical-case performance is good.

This procedure, therefore, gives us a set of part models that furnishes a reasonable approximation to the minimal-length encoding of the image data in terms of our part representation. We have found, however, that it is useful to perform a final stochastic optimization on all of the parameters of this final set of parts because the histogramming technique described above is not completely insensitive to occlusion relations. We accomplish this final optimization by means of a numerical gradient algorithm that renders all the hypothesized part models together (thus completely accounting for occlusion relations) and computes the goodness-of-fit functional; the algorithm then changes one of the part's parameters and ascertains whether the fit is improved. If improvement does indeed occur, the change is accepted.

Practical Considerations. Straightforward implementation of the above operations requires about 10^9 operations per image region. The number of operations required can be reduced considerably by pruning the search space during the search, in a manner similar to that used by Bolles and Horaud (16), Goad (55), or Grimson and Lozano-Perez (56) in their model-based, global-search-and-match vision systems.

In our current implementation, this pruning is accomplished by keeping track of the current n best fits (largest Γ values) within an image region and by using their Γ values to (1) abort evaluations of Γ as soon as it becomes clear that the eventual value will be smaller than any of the current n largest Γ values (e.g., when, even if all of the remaining pixels match exactly, Γ will still be smaller than the current n best Γ values), (2) discard any parameter setting that *a priori* cannot generate a value of Γ that is larger than one of the current n best Γ values, and (3) order the search so that the above pruning techniques will be maximally effective (e.g., search over the parameter settings with the largest potential Γ values before searching over other parameter settings).

By taking advantage of these and other efficiency expedients, the examples shown here have required an average of about 10^{10} operations each, roughly two and one-half hours of CPU time on a Symbolics 3600. For industrial applications, in which bending and tapering are not typical, the search space is smaller and therefore the required computation time can be as much as $1/30^{th}$ that of the full algorithm. Because of the inherent parallelism of the technique (thousands of identical searches within each region) a full global search is expected to take only a few seconds per image with today's large, parallel computers.

Perhaps more importantly, however, a fully developed system would also make use of intensity image features such as edges and corners to prune the search space. Additionally, hierarchical coarse-to-fine techniques could be used to guide the search, thus improving efficiency and perhaps eliminating the need for gradient-descent improvement at the end of the global parameter-space search. We have not as yet had time to explore these possibilities.

Learning Object Models

One of the major advantages of the above global search technique is the certainty of convergence to a good answer (in terms of accounting for the metric properties of the data) within a fixed period of time. It may be more important, however, that we obtain a stable account of the object's *part structure*, for this is what we will use to determine the object's class identity (e.g., "gate," "car") for purposes of reasoning. Whether a model that accounts accurately for metric properties also accounts for part structure depends upon whether our shape vocabulary actually expresses a robust aspect of the object's true three-dimensional structure, as well as whether that structure is conserved under projection. This issue is one we will address in this section.

The following examples involve range imagery; for purposes of evaluation we present one synthetic example, followed by three examples using a laser range-finder attached to a vehicle moving down country roads. Some simple preprocessing of the laser rangefinder data was used to remove mixed-range pixels as well as the inherent ambiguity-interval problems of those data (57,58).

A Synthetic Data Example. The first example uses simulated range data, with approximately six-bit resolution. The purpose of this example is to demonstrate (1) the performance of the algorithm independent of special data characteristics, and (2) the ability of the technique to recover part structure despite the problems of scale and configuration.

Figure 4.10(a) shows a SuperSketch model (here and in succeeding figures we will show side views of SuperSketch models as insets placed in the lower-right-hand corner of the frame surrounding the model); Figure 4.10(b) shows a range image generated from this model. This is a fairly accurate model of the articulated human form; as such, it illustrates the necessity for a part-structure representation of the overall shape: Without such a representation, we would have to store descriptions of every possible positioning of the figure in order to recognize it as it moves about. Figure 4.10(c) shows the initial explanation of the image data, found by iterative, best-first search among the best fits at points sampled along the figure's 2-D skeleton.

The main thing to note about this initial shape description is that, although not perfect, it seems sufficiently similar to the original, generating description that we can use it to index into a database of known forms and to recognize the figure as human.

Figure 4.10(d) depicts the final learned model, the result of gradient descent from Figure 4.10(c). Figure 4.10(e) shows "blow-up" views of both the original and the learned model. Note the similarity of part structure and of part-by-part parameters.

FIGURE 4.10. (a) A SuperSketch model, (b) a range image generated from this model, (c) Initial explanation of the image data, (d) Final learned model, (e) "blow-up" views of the original model and the learned model. Note the similarity of part structure and part-by-part parameters.

150

Perhaps the major question to be asked about this procedure for recovering part structure is whether or not the recovery is *stable*, since stability in structuring the image data—i.e., in producing a *segmentation*—is the primary property required for reliable higher-level reasoning functions such as class formation and generalization (3,7,8,12,47,59,64). Some of the particulars of this example are illustrative in this regard.

Note, for instance, that the feet are described by bent primitives that account for both ankle and foot, even though in the final model the "ankle" part is not visible, having been occluded by the "calf." Such fitting of a bent primitive to two unbent parts is also observed in the right arm—here too, the upper part is occluded, by the "forearm." Although these assignments of part structure are, perhaps, not perfect, they are entirely plausible segmentations when only one view is given. Such occasional merging of connected primitives seems unavoidable with only one view; thus, we must allow for *both* possible descriptions—as one bent primitive and as two straight but connected primitives—when forming object classes or searching for similar stored models.

A more interesting case occurs in the recovery of descriptions for the hands and head, for although both head and hands are actually quite complex shapes, they are recovered as being a single, undifferentiated part. These examples show the effect of *scale;* when the image features become smaller than the range of scales searched, there is a sort of "summarizing" effect as a fit is attempted to the overall composite form. Marr and Nishihara pointed out the need for this type of "summarizing"; they proposed that we must employ a *multiscale* representation in comparing the learned model with stored models. In this example we can see how a multiscale representation, with descriptions for each distinct scale of part structure, might be combined with this recovery procedure to resolve some of the difficult problems associated with scale.

Learning Descriptions Outdoors.   The remaining examples make use of data from a time-of-flight laser range finder designed by the Environmental Research Institute of Michigan, and attached to an outdoor vehicle. This rangefinder, which collects a 256 × 64 pixel image in 0.4 seconds, has a useful range of about 128 feet and an advertised accuracy of about five percent. Its unusual imaging geometry is similar to that of a very-wide-angle lens.

Figure 4.11(a) shows a range image of the upper part of a famous industrial vision researcher, taken with this sensor. This example is interesting, especially in comparison with the synthetic data example above, in that the amount of depth information within the figure is negligible; from a practical point of view, this is merely a silhouette. Figure 4.11(b) shows the initial explanation of the image data, while

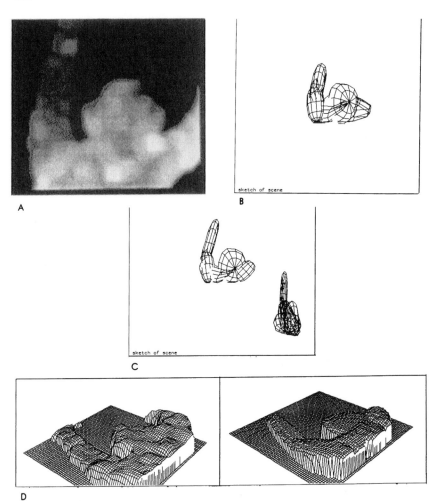

FIGURE 4.11. (a) A range image of the upper part of a famous industrial vision researcher (for practical purposes this is merely a silhouette);
(b) the initial explanation of the image data (note that the correct part
structure of his left (upraised) arm, head, and right arm are clearly present); (c) the final learned model; (d) comparison of the original range
data with a range image produced by the final learned model.

Figure 4.11(c) displays the result of gradient descent from Figure
4.11(b).

Perhaps the most salient point of this example is that a reasonable
three-dimensional part structure can be learned even from what is essentially only silhouette data; the left (upraised) arm, head, and right arm
are clearly present in the learned description. Figure 4.11(d) shows a

comparison of the original range data with a range image produced by the learned model of Figure 4.11(c). This comparison shows that the simple (70 parameter) learned description retains most of the data's original metric information, demonstrating that we have achieved a good encoding of the image data.

Figure 4.12(a) shows a range image of a gate by the side of the road.

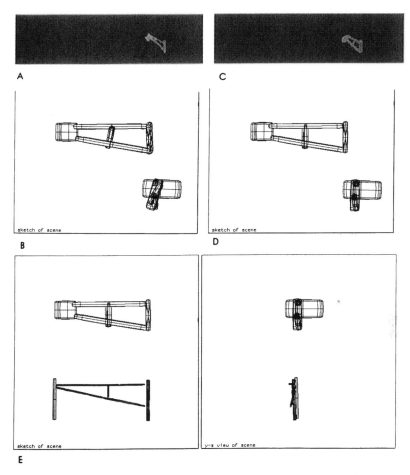

FIGURE 4.12. (a) A range image of a gate by the side of the road (our figure/ground procedure has unintentionally included a bush near the leftmost gatepost as part of the figure); (b) the final learned model; (c) a range image produced by the learned model; (d) The result of "prettifying" (b) using the domain knowledge to the effect that nearly horizontal/vertical parts are likely to be horizontal/vertical; (e) comparison of the learned model of (d) with a SuperSketch model of the gate that was constructed by hand.

Again, the data contain little more information than a silhouette; the linear elements of this figure average two pixels across. Note that our figure/ground procedure has inadvertently included a bush near the left-most gatepost as part of the figure. The most interesting aspect of this example is the small size of the imaged features; these data thus provide a severe test of noise sensitivity.

Figure 4.12(b) shows the initial explanation of the image data. Once again a reasonable part-structure description is learned, although the left gatepost is seen as a block reflecting the fact that the data include a bush as well as the gatepost. Figure 4.12(c) contains a comparison of the original range data with a range image produced by the learned model of Figure 4.12(b); here too, the learned description retains most of the data's metric information, and is thus a good encoding.

One of the advantages of having a high-level description like this part language is that it provides good "hooks" for applying domain-specific knowledge. This is illustrated by Figure 4.12(d), which shows the result of "prettifying" Figure 4.12(b) by making use of the domain knowledge that nearly horizontal or vertical parts are likely to be horizontal or vertical. Figure 4.12(e) contains a comparison of the learned model of Figure 4.12(d) with a manually constructed SuperSketch model of the gate. The thickening of the posts and bars in the learned gate can be largely attributed to preprocessing intended to remove mixed-range pixels.

Figure 4.13(a) shows a range image of a few roadside bushes. The most important aspect of this example is that it is *not* an example in which there is an obvious part structure; nor is it an example with smooth surfaces. These data, therefore, allow us to examine some of the limits of our technique's descriptive adequacy, as well as its ability to produce stable segmentations. Figure 4.13(b) shows the initial explanation of the image data, as found by iterative, best-first search among the best fits at points in a 10×10 grid covering the image data.

Figure 4.13(c) shows a range image produced by the learned model of Figure 4.13(b); the outlines of Figures 4.13(a) and (c) can be seen to be similar, thus confirming that the learned description (in this example a total of 56 parameters) retains most of the data's original metric information. Figure 4.13(d) shows a comparison of the original range data, with points closer than the median distance removed and a range image produced by the learned model of Figure 4.13(b), again with points closer than the median distance removed. This comparison shows that the *internal* structure of the learned model closely matches that of the measured range data.

This example shows that even very complex shapes can be usefully "summarized" by our shape vocabulary; thus supporting our dual claims

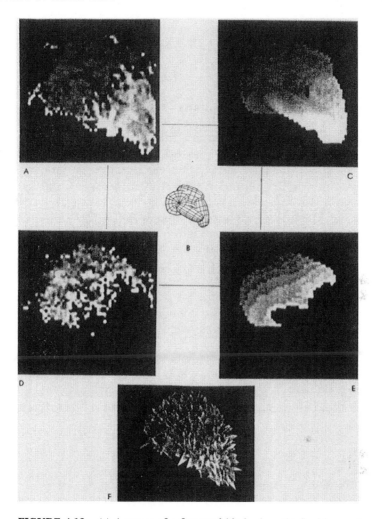

FIGURE 4.13. (a) A range of a few roadside bushes; (b) final learned model; (c) A range image produced by the learned model; (d) the original range data, with points closer than the median distance removed; (e) A range image produced by the learned model again with points closer than the median distance removed, showing the model's close match with the range data's internal structure; (f) range image produced by adding a fractal surface model to the part representation.

of descriptive adequacy and stable part structure recovery. We can improve the accuracy of the learned model somewhat by modeling the discrepancies between the recovered part structure and the range data by using a fractal surface model (34,37). The result of adding a fractal surface model to the recovered part model is shown in Figure 4.13(e). An even better description of the differences between part model and image data could be obtained by using a particle model (51) of the bush's branches and leaves.

Summary.   We have described a representation that is fairly general purpose, despite having only a small number of parameters[12]. Having this expressive power captured within a small number of parameters has allowed us to approach the problem of learning object descriptions using coarse global search to find a minimal-length encoding.

On the basis of our experiments we believe that this technique is quite robust; these examples, for instance, show that the recovery procedure is reasonably stable with respect to noise and scale. Because of the inherent parallelism of the technique (thousands of identical searches within each region) a full global search is expected to require only a few seconds per image on a Connection Machine, Cray-2, or other large, parallel computer.

We have, so far, restricted our attention to range imagery. Thus our system does not currently make use of shape cues such as edges or corners that are easily available in intensity images. One reason for choosing to concentrate on range imagery was so that we would produce an algorithm that can be directly applied to the outputs of shape–from–x and depth–from–x vision modules. We believe that our current algorithm will be effective in such an application. It seems clear, moreover, that adding intensity image information (such as edges, corner, or T-junction location) will only add to the efficiency and robustness of the algorithm.

Recognizing Fractal Surfaces

The aforementioned approach can work well for figures—even quite complex figures—presented at reasonable resolution. Unfortunately, nature is rarely so kind as to present objects in this way; we often have objects at all distances and of all sizes jumbled into one image. The result is often a situation where (if we try to describe every visible detail) the number of parameters to be recovered is larger than the number of pixels in the image, and thus our efforts at recovering a full, accurate description of the scene are *a priori* doomed to failure. This is the problem of overwhelming scene complexity; typical examples where this

---

[12]We note that *any* part structure representation must have at *least* nine parameters: three for position, three for orientation, and three for size. Our representation adds only five more parameters in order to achieve its reasonably general-purpose descriptive power. We note that the fact that we could use our modeling vocabulary to obtain accurate fits to the data in these examples lends support for its descriptive adequacy.

problem arises are images of complex natural surfaces such as mountains, clouds, or a grass covered plain.

In these cases we must—of mathematical necessity—be satisfied with
recovering an incomplete description of the scene structure; that is, a
description in which we do not try to describe every detail. Because there
is a limit to the number of parameters we can estimate from a particular
set of image data, the best we can hope to do is to describe most scene
features statistically. By choosing to describe unimportant details in an
abstract, statistical manner we can avoid the problem of scene complexity—for often only a few statistical parameters are required to accurately
summarize a great wealth of scene detail—and still have enough parameters "left over" to be able to accurately and completely describe any
important or large-scale structures.

Moreover, if we choose a *physically meaningful* statistical abstraction,
such as the fractal description introduced in the previous sections, we
will have retained important qualitative information about the mass of
detail. The fractal model of scene structure, therefore, is an important
extension to our "lump of clay" representation, for it is this statistical
model of how nature combines "lumps" to produce natural surfaces that
allows us to deal with complex scenes of mountains, grass or clouds.

To be able to recover such descriptions, however, we require techniques for (a) identifying whether or not our statistical model actually
applies to the particular image data, and (b) estimating the parameters of
the model. In the remainder of this section we will show that the fractal
model, even though it is a statistical model, can provide us with the
overconstraint needed to reliably identify portions of the scene that are
accurately described by the model, and then to estimate the parameters
of the model (i.e., fractal scaling parameter r, and amplitude).

The Mathematics of Fractal Brownian Functions. Before we can begin to
discuss recognizing fractal surfaces, we must first explicate the mathematics underlying the creation of these fractal forms. The path of a
particle exhibiting Brownian motion is the canonical example of most
naturally occurring fractals; the discussion that follows, therefore, is de-
voted exclusively to fractal Brownian functions, which are a mathematical generalization of Brownian motion.

A random function $I(x)$ is a fractal Brownian function if for all x and
Δx

$$Pr\left(\frac{I(x + \Delta x) - I(x)}{\|\Delta x\|^{1-r}} < y \right) = F(y) \tag{3}$$

where $F(y)$ is a cumulative distribution function, and the variable r is the
fractal scaling parameter (ratio) of the previous section. Note that x and

$I(x)$ can be interpreted as vector quantities, thus providing an extension to two or more topological dimensions. If the topological dimension of $I(x)$ is T, the fractal dimension D of the graph described by $I(x)$ is:

$$D = T + r \qquad (4)$$

If $r = 1/2$, and $F(y)$ comes from a zero-mean Gaussian with unit variance, then $I(x)$ is the classical Brownian function. It should be noted that very highly patterned surfaces can be Brownian fractals; all that is required is that they scale appropriately. Thus the superquadric lump-of-clay language is in one sense *orthogonal* to a fractal-based description.

Real surfaces, of course, cannot be exactly modeled by such infinite mathematical functions; in fact, they typically do not behave in a fractal manner over more than a limited range of scales. Thus we must define carefully what we mean by a "fractal surface:"

Definition. A **fractal Brownian surface** is a continuous function that obeys the statistical description given by Equation 3, with x as a two-dimensional vector at all scales (i.e., values of Δx) between some smallest (Δx_{min}) and largest (Δx_{max}) scales.

In previous papers (34,35) we have presented evidence showing that most natural surfaces are spatially isotropic fractals over scale ranges of at least $1:8$ (i.e., $\Delta x_{max}/\Delta x_{min} > 8$). This finding has since been confirmed by others (36). Note that isotropic in this sense means only that the fractal scaling parameter r is isotropic, it does not mean that the surface is not "stretched;" for example, tree bark can be a perfectly good isotropic fractal surface.

The Fractal Model and Imaging. With these definitions in hand, we can now address the problem of how homogeneous patches of a three-dimensional fractal surface appear in the 2-D image (see Kube and Pentland (60) for a more detailed exposition). We will then let $z = V_H(x, y)$ be a Fractal Brownian surface, and let $\vec{L} = (\cos \tau \sin \sigma, \sin \tau \sin \sigma, \cos \sigma)$ be the unit vector in the mean illuminant direction, where τ is the *tilt* of the illuminant (the angle the image plane component of the illuminant vector makes with the x-axis) and σ is its *slant* (the angle the illuminant vector makes with the z-axis). We will assume that the surface is Lambertian, illuminated by (possibly many) distant light sources, and not self-shadowing. In this case then the normalized image intensity $I(x, y)$ will be

$$I(x, y) = \frac{p \cos r \sin \sigma + q \sin r \sin \sigma + \cos \sigma}{(p^2 + q^2 + 1)^{1/2}} \qquad (5)$$

where

$$p = \frac{\partial}{\partial x} V_H(x, y) \tag{6}$$

$$q = \frac{\partial}{\partial y} V_H(x, y) \tag{7}$$

If we then take the Taylor series expansion of $I(x, y)$ about $p, q = 0$ through the quadratic terms[13], we obtain

$$I(x, y) \approx \cos \sigma + p \cos r \sin \sigma + q \sin r \sin \sigma - \frac{\cos \sigma}{2} (p^2 + q^2) \tag{8}$$

This expression gives an excellent approximation if $p, q \ll 1$. We note that for real surfaces, such as mountains, the maximum surface slope rarely is more than $15°$, i.e., typically $p^2 + q^2 < 0.1$. Under these conditions the linear terms of Equation 8 will dominate the power spectrum except when the average illuminant is within $\pm 6°$ of the viewer's position, i.e., when $\sin \sigma < 0.1$.

The complex Fourier spectrum $F_H(f, \theta)$ of $V_H(x, y)$ is

$$F_H(f, \theta) = f^{-\beta/2} e^{i\phi_{f,\theta}} \tag{9}$$

where ϕ is a random variable uniformly distributed on $(0, 2\pi)$, and $\phi_{f,\theta}$ is the random value "drawn" at position (f, θ) in the Fourier plane.

Now since p and q are partial derivatives of V_H, their transforms F_p and F_q are related to F_H in an elementary fashion. We can write

$$F_p(f, \theta) = 2\pi \cos \theta \, f^{1 - \beta/2} e^{i(\phi_{f,\theta} + \pi/2)} \tag{10}$$

$$F_q(f, \theta) = 2\pi \sin \theta \, f^{1 - \beta/2} e^{i(\phi_{f,\theta} + \pi/2)} \tag{11}$$

There are now two cases to consider: oblique illumination, and illumination from the viewer's position.

Case 1.   When p, q are small and the illuminant is not behind the viewer (for example, $\sin \sigma > 0.1$) then we may neglect the quadratic terms of Equation 8 and consider

$$I_1(x, y) = \cos \sigma + p \cos \tau \sin \sigma + q \sin \tau \sin \sigma \tag{12}$$

In this case, the Fourier transform of the image I_1 is (ignoring the DC term):

$$F_{I_1}(f, \theta) = 2\pi \sin \sigma \, f^{1 - \beta/2} e^{i(\phi_{f,\theta} + \pi/2)} [\cos \theta \cos \tau + \sin \theta \sin \tau]$$

---

[13]Note: in this discussion we will take $\Delta x_{min} > 0$ and Δx_{max} large.

and the power spectrum P is

$$P_{I_1}(f, \theta) = 4\pi^2 \sin^2 \sigma f^{2-\beta}[\cos \theta \cos \tau + \sin \theta \sin \tau]^2 \qquad (14)$$

This spectrum depends, as expected, upon the illuminant direction. As with the Fractal surface itself, however, the spectral falloff is isotropic: the log of the power spectrum of the image has slope $2 - \beta$ with respect to log frequency at almost all orientations (excepting a set of measure zero where $\theta = \tau \pm \pi/2$).

Case 2. When the mean illuminant vector is almost parallel to the viewing direction (i.e., $\sin \sigma \approx 0$) the quadratic terms of Equation 8 can dominate and the image of a fractional Brownian surface will look like

$$I_2(x, y) = \cos \sigma \, (1 - (p^2 + q^2)/2) \qquad (15)$$

To within a constant factor, and ignoring DC, the power spectrum F_{I_2} of this image will be the Fourier transform of the autocorrelation function $R_{p^2+q^2}$ of $p^2 + q^2$. We note that

$$P_p * P_p \approx P_p \quad P_{pq} * P_{pq} \approx P_{pq} \quad P_q * P_q \approx P_q \qquad (16)$$

and thus

$$\log P_{I_2} \propto \log P_R \propto 2 - \beta \qquad (17)$$

The conclusion, therefore, is that when the mean illumination is at the viewer's position the image will have a power spectrum falloff approximately proportional to $f^{2-\beta}$, i.e., the same relationship between surface Fractal scaling parameter and image Fractal scaling parameter that we found with oblique illumination.

Thus we have proved the following proposition: A three-dimensional fractal Brownian surface with power spectrum proportional to $f^{-\beta}$ has an image with power spectrum proportional to $f^{2-\beta}$, assuming Lambertian surface reflectance and constant illumination and albedo.

This proposition demonstrates that the fractal dimension of the three-dimensional surface dictates the fractal dimension of the image intensity surface and, of course, the dimension of the physical surface. This result has also proven to be an excellent psychophysical predictor of people's perception of three-dimensional surface roughness.[14]

---

[14]**Experimental note.** Fifteen naive subjects (mostly language researchers) were shown digitized images of eight natural textured surfaces drawn from Brodatz (52). They were asked "if you were to draw your finger horizontally along the surface pictured here, how rough or smooth would the surface feel?," i.e., they were asked to estimate the three-dimensional roughness/smoothness of the viewed surfaces. This procedure was then repeated for the vertical direction, yielding a total of sixteen roughness estimates for each subject. A scale of one (smoothest) to ten (roughest) was used to indicate three-dimensional

Simulation of the imaging process with a variety of imaging geometries and reflectance functions indicates that this result will hold quite generally; the "roughness" of the surface seems to dictate the "roughness" of the image. Thus if we know that the surface is homogeneous, then we can estimate the fractal dimension of the surface by measuring the fractal dimension of the image data. What we have developed is a method for inferring a basic property of the three-dimensional surface— its smoothness or roughness—from the image data. We no longer have to *assume* smoothness (as is often done in current bottom-up approaches to machine vision) we can *measure* it.

Properties of Fractal Descriptions.   Fractal functions must be stable over common transformations if they are to be useful as a descriptive tool. Our previous reports (34) have proven that the fractal dimension of a surface is invariant with respect to linear transformations of the data and to transformations of scale, and thus in actual practice estimates of fractal dimension have proven robust with respect to these common transforms. Stability of the fractal description is to be expected because the fractal dimension of the image is directly related to the fractal dimension of the viewed surface, which is a property of three-dimensional natural surfaces that is typically stable with respect to transformation of scale.

The fact that the fractal description is stable with respect to scale is a critically important property. After all, even though we move about in the world (and examine surfaces both foveally and peripherally) we want to compute a stable, viewer independent representation of the world. If our information about the world is not stable with respect to scale, we can have no hope of doing this.

Measurement of the Fractal Dimension

The fractal dimension of these functions can be measured either directly from the second-order statistics (dipole statistics) of $I(x)$ by use of Equation 3, or from $I(x)$'s Fourier power spectrum $P(f)$ as:

$$P(f) = kf^{2r-3} \qquad (18)$$

---

roughness/smoothness. The fractal dimension of the 2-D image was then computed along the horizontal and vertical directions by the use of Equation 18, as described in the following section, and the viewed surface's three-dimensional fractal dimension was estimated by the use of this proposition. The mean of the subject's estimates of three-dimensional roughness had an excellent 0.91 correlation ($p < 0.001$) with roughness predicted by use of the image's 2-D fractal dimension and this proposition, i.e., the three-dimensional fractal dimension predicted by use of the measured 2-D image's fractal dimension accounted for 83% of the variance in the subject's estimates of three-dimensional roughness. This result, therefore, supports the general validity of the result.

where k is a scalar constant, f is frequency, and r is as in Equation 3. Thus, we may use a linear regression on the log of the observed power spectrum as a function of f (e.g., a regression using $\log (P(f)) = (2r - 3) \log (f) + \log (k)$ for various values of f) to determine the exponent r and thus the fractal dimension.

Equation 18 suggests a method of measuring fractal dimension using physiologically-plausible linear filters. The sum of the squared response of a bandpass filter (e.g., Laplacian or center-surround filter) is proportional to the amount of power (energy) in the Fourier spectrum that lies within the filter's sensitive region. Thus if we take two filters that have equal volume in the Fourier domain and are spaced one octave of frequency apart, then the ratio of the squared response of such filters will be linearly related to the fractal dimension.

Formally, Parseval's Theorem states that the integral of squared values over the spatial domain is equal to the integral of the squared Fourier components over the frequency domain:

$$\int_{-\infty}^{\infty} \int_{-\infty}^{\infty} |V(x, y)|^2 \, dxdy = \frac{1}{4\pi^2} \int_{-\infty}^{\infty} \int_{-\infty}^{\infty} |F(f_x, f_y)|^2 \, df_x df_y \qquad (19)$$

$$= \frac{1}{4\pi^2} \int_{-\infty}^{\infty} \int_{-\infty}^{\infty} P(f_x, f_y) df_x df_y \qquad (20)$$

where $F(f_x, f_y)$ is the Fourier transform of $V(x, y)$ and $P(f_x, f_y)$ is the power spectrum. Convolution with a band-pass filter results in a signal which is restricted to a limited range of frequencies. Therefore the integral of the square of the convolved signal is proportional to the integral of the power within the original signal over this range of frequencies. Thus, by using different filters to sample the power spectrum over different bands, we can measure the fractal dimension by use of Equation 18.

To provide a simple example, let us idealize the center-surround $\nabla^2 G$ operator as having a frequency response that is a ring of radius f_0 centered around the origin of the frequency domain. Using Parseval's Theorem the integral of the squared response $R(f_0)$ is:

$$R(f_0) = \int_{-\infty}^{\infty} \int_{-\infty}^{\infty} |\nabla^2 G \otimes V(x, y)|^2 \, dxdy = \frac{1}{4\pi^2} \int_{-\infty}^{\infty} \int_{-\infty}^{\infty} \delta(f_0) P(f_x, f_y) df_x df_y \qquad (21)$$

where $\delta(f_0)$ is the response of our idealized filter (a ring a radius f_0) and P is power. Changing to polar coordinates gives:

$$R(f_0) = \frac{1}{4\pi^2} \int_0^{2\pi} P_\theta(f_0) d\theta \qquad (22)$$

Similarly, the integral of the squared response for a filter one octave higher (at radius $2f_0$) is

$$R(2f_0) = \frac{1}{4\pi^2} \int_0^{2\pi} P_\theta(2f_0)d\theta \qquad (23)$$

If the function F is fractal, i.e., it has a power spectrum as in Equation 18, then dividing Equation 23 by Equation 22 gives:

$$\frac{R(2f_0)}{R(f_0)} = 2^{2r-2} \qquad (24)$$

or

$$\log_2[R(2f_0)] - \log_2[R(f_0)] = 2r - 2 \qquad (25)$$

Thus the fractal dimension D can be obtained from r using Equation 4. See Heeger and Pentland (61) for a more detailed exposition.

Recovery Results

We have shown that the fractal dimension in the image is dependent upon that of the three-dimensional surface, thus giving us a technique for inferring a three-dimensional property of the viewed surface that closely corresponds to people's concept of roughness/smoothness. This suggests that measurement of the fractal dimension in the image will be useful in segmenting natural imagery.

Figure 4.14(a) is an aerial view of San Francisco Bay. Using Equation 24 we can measure the fractal-scaling parameter r for each pixel by use of convolutions with filters similar to those used in biological systems. This produces a sort of "fractal-dimension image," which can then be histogramed,[15] as shown in Figure 4.14(b). This histogram is then broken at the "valleys" between the modes of the histogram, and the image segmented into pixel neighborhoods belonging to one mode or another as shown by Figure 4.14(c–e).

Figure 4.14(c) shows the segmentation obtained by thresholding at the breakpoint indicated by the arrow under (b); each pixel in (c) corresponds to an 8 × 8 block of pixels in the original image. As can be seen, a good segmentation into water and land was achieved—one that cannot be obtained by thresholding on image intensity. The values to the left of the large spike in (b) have a computed fractal dimension which is less

---

[15]The example was actually accomplished using a somewhat less elegant technique: measuring the fractal dimension using a least-squares regression of the Fourier power spectrum response over an 8 × 8 block of pixels. This is functionally equivalent to the method described in the text.

164

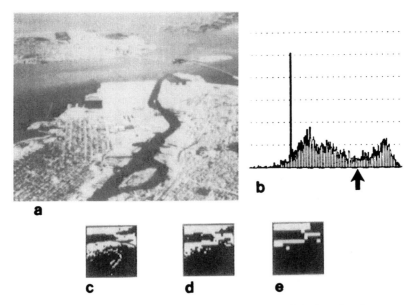

FIGURE 4.14.   (a) San Francisco Bay, (b) histogram of the fractal scaling parameter, (c)–(e) segmentations based on the fractal scaling parameter.

than the topological dimension; these points all occur along the water-land boundary and partially delineate that boundary.

To demonstrate stability over scale the original image was then averaged down, from 512 × 512 pixels into 256 × 256 and 128 × 128 pixel images, and the fractal dimension recomputed for each of the reduced images. Figures 4.14(d) and (e) illustrate the segmentations that result from using the *same* cut point as employed in the original full-resolution segmentation, demonstrating stability across wide (4 : 1) variations in scale.

Overconstraint: Testing the Applicability of the Model

Perhaps the most important characteristic of this statistical model of scene structure is that we can determine its appropriateness for particular image data—that we can know when (and when *not*) to use the model. To evaluate the applicability of the fractal model for a particular surface and its image data we need to verify (a) the homogeneity of the surface, and (b) the fractal nature of the image intensity surface. The discussion of how to verify surface homogeneity is outside of the scope of this chapter; suffice it to say that it appears that it can be accomplished by use of color information. To verify the "fractalness" of the image data we first rewrite Equation 24 to obtain the following description of the manner in which the image statistics change with scale:

$$R(kf_0)k^{2r-2} = R(f_0) \tag{26}$$

where k is the ratio between the center frequency of the first filter and the second filter.

Equation 26 is a *hypothesized* relation among the image intensities; a hypothesis that we may test statistically. If we find that Equation 26 is true of the image intensity surface within a homogeneous image region, then the proposition proved above tells us that the viewed surface must be a three-dimensional fractal Brownian surface, and thus, the fractal model is appropriate.

When we have evaluated the suitability of the fractal model for natural surfaces using, for example, the Brodatz (52) textures, we have found that for the majority of textures examined (77%) the fractal model provides a quite accurate description of how the images' statistics (spatial frequency channels, dipole statistics, etc.) change with scale. This result has since been confirmed by several other researchers.

The fact that most of the regions examined were quite well approximated by a fractal Brownian function indicates that the fractal model will often provide a useful description of natural surfaces and their images. We believe that prevalence of surfaces with fractal scaling statistics is explained by analogy to Brownian motion: Just as when a dust mote randomly bombarded by air molecules produces a fractal Brownian random walk, the complex interaction of processes that locally modify shape typically produces a fractal Brownian surface.

Summary

We have formulated the problem of vision as one of recognizing instances of the models found in a representationl vocabulary. We envision perception as proceeding by making an overconstrained, statistical determination that a particular model is applicable, and then estimating the parameters of that model. If our vocabulary of shape does in fact cover the range of shape that actually occurs, then *we will have made the best shape estimate possible with the available image data.*

In this chapter we present two models that constitute the initial stage of our attempt to collect a vocabulary of models that span the space of shape possibilities. These two models are (a) a superquadric-based models of "parts" that are much like the "parts" that people see, and (b) a fractal-based model of three-dimensional texture, which is a statistical characterization of how nature combines "parts" to form complex, natural surfaces.

This approach has let us frame the problem of vision as one in statistical decision theory: We have a range of hypotheses that we entertain, and use image data to decide among the alternatives. This gives us a rigorous framework for integrating information from motion, stereo, and so forth, together with contour, shading, and texture information without having to make additional assumptions.

Further, because we are using models of scene structure that apply to many pixels at once, we have the property of *overconstraint;* we can make an estimate of three-dimensional structure using a portion of the image data, and then we can *check* our answers using the rest of the data. This is in considerable contrast to approaches that try to apply strong, unverifiable assumptions about the nature of surfaces (e.g., that all surfaces are "smooth") in order to integrate various information sources: rather than *assuming* smoothness, we want to be able to *recognize* smoothness. This sort of overconstrained, reliable vision is possible *only* by approaching vision as the task of recognizing instances of models that account for more than a small patch of the image.

COMMUNICATION

The particular models of the world that perception uses to interpret sensory data profoundly affect all of our conceptual structures. If we stand in the center of Stonehenge, we can see either a collection of pillars, several irregular walls of pillars, or concentric circular structures with regularly-spaced pillars. This is the familiar Gestalt phenomenon of grouping; what is important about it is that *which* grouping you spontaneously see strongly influences what hypotheses you entertain when trying to deduce, for instance, the purpose of Stonehenge. Examples such as this demonstrate that the manner in which perception "carves up" the world—that is, its models of the world—strongly determine the way in which we think about the world.

The issue of perceptual models is, therefore, of more than passing interest to those interested in cognition. It seems reasonable that if we are to develop machines that are able to display commonsense reasoning abilities, for instance, we must have spatial representations that are at least roughly equivalent to those people employ in organizing their picture of the world. Similarly, if we are ever to communicate with machines about our shared environment we must develop spatial representations that are at least isomorphic to the representations that we use. We must have a representation that captures the same sorts of distinctions we make when we carve objects into parts.

Because communication depends upon having a shared representation of the situation, we can use man-machine communication as a fairly sensitive test of whether a particular representation captures the notions of difference and similarity that humans employ. The empirical (and so far informal) finding that the organization of our shape descriptions correspond closely with the human perceptual organization is, as a consequence, quite interesting: The representation seems to offer exciting possibilities for flexible, effective man-machine communication. It was, therefore, of great interest to test how effectively we could use the representation described here as a basis for communication between a computer and its operator concerning image data and three-dimensional shape.

Experiment 1: Communicating About a Digital Terrain Map

As a first experiment we took the problem of communicating with a computer about a digital terrain map (DTM), as might be done in guiding a stereo compilation process or when plotting a path through the terrain.

Figure 4.7 showed how a mountain-like surface can be built up from the combination of progressively smaller primitives. We can also take a real surface, such as the DTM of Yosemite Valley shown in Figure 4.15(a) and decompose it into a canonical lump-description by use of a minimum-complexity criterion, that is, we attempt to account for the shape with the fewest number of component parts as is possible. We can then use this lump-description to structure the pixel data in a manner that corresponds to the perceptual organization people impose upon the data, thus allowing us to communicate in a natural manner about the DTM. In this example we will use Gaussian, rather than superquadric, lumps for efficiency reasons. The difference is unimportant in this context.

Decomposition by "Bump Filtering"

We start by noting that the values in a Laplacian pyramid (50) of a surface may be viewed as the decomposition of the surface into Gaussian bumps of octave spacing, that is, if we sum Gaussians of appropriate width and amplitude equal to the values in the Laplacian pyramid, we will recover the original surface. This provides us with a computationally efficient way of parsing the surface into Gaussian bumps. We can use this decomposition to approximate the minimum complexity decomposition by forming a Laplacian pyramid of the surface, examining the entries in this pyramid for those that most closely correspond to a single bump (by looking at the neighbors of the point in both space and scale), subtracting off that bump from the original surface, and repeating this pro-

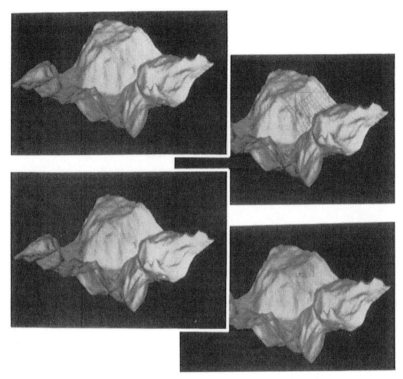

FIGURE 4.15. (a) a digital terrain map of Yosemite Valley, which is automatically decomposed into a "sketch," a description in our representational system that contains terms ("lumps") that correspond roughly to "peaks," "valleys," and "ridges," so that the parts of this description correspond closely with the perceptual organization that we impose on the scene. This is illustrated in (b), (c) and (d), which show a person pointing to a part of the image, and the computer using this sketch to determine what part of the terrain is being gestured at, and highlighting the "part" referred to by covering it with crosshatching. This decomposition of the scene into perceptually salient "parts" thus fulfills a critical requirement for effective man-machine communication: Similar representations of the scene.

cedure until no significant entries remain in the pyramid.[16] See Pentland (62) for a more detailed exposition of this algorithm.

This "Bump-Filtering" algorithm is a two-dimensional, statistical version of scale-space filtering (53). One-dimensional scale-space filtering tracked 1-D edges over a range of scale and constructed a "scale-space

---

[16]Szeliski (49) has also developed an interesting algorithm to find a canonical fractal decomposition using a Boltzmann machine architecture.

diagram" of the branching pattern of these edges as a function of scale. It was found that edges that persisted over a large range of scales corresponded roughly to perceptual "parts." Similarly, this algorithm produces a description that organizes one, two, or three-dimensional data into components that correspond to our naive perceptual notion of a "part," again by analyzing the behavior of the signal over a range of scales. We have compared Witkin's scale-space filtering with a 1-D version of this bump-filtering algorithm and found that both produce a similar description of the signal's large scale structure.

An Example: Man-Machine Communication

This "bump-sketch" allows us to structure the pixel data in a manner that corresponds to the perceptual organization we impose upon the data. It allows us to point to a part of the scene, say "that one," and have the machine know to what it is that we refer. This is illustrated in Figures 4.15 (b, c, and d), which show a user pointing at various features on Digital Terrain Map (DTM) (e.g., peaks, ridges) and the program highlighting the feature that it believes the user intended to indicate.

This program uses the bump-filtering algorithm to parse the DTM into a bump description, constructing a database of the perceptually important "parts" of the surface shape. This allows the user to interact with the DTM by simply pointing to peaks, valleys, ridges and so forth. When the user points at some feature the computer consults this database of "parts" to infer what feature the user intended to indicate, and then highlights that feature by cross-hatching.

The highlighted feature can then be edited to improve the DTM, defined as a primitive object in a path planning calculation, or used in whatever manner the user's purpose demands. As these figures illustrate, we have found a good correspondence between this program's structuring of the image and the structure people impose on the image.

Experiment 2: Building Three-Dimensional Models

The evidence presented here lends strong support to the idea that for a person constructing a three-dimensional model it may be useful to initially rough things in using this vocabulary of parts and deformations; the three-dimensional sketch produced in this manner then provides a "frame" for precise detailing. If our reasoning is correct then such a CAD tool should make the process of producing a three-dimensional design more efficient and thus cheaper.

The obvious next step, then, is to test that SuperSketch allows improved performance over the standard-representation CAD systems.

a   b

FIGURE 4.16. (a) An image of a complex industrial casting, (b) A Super-Sketch model of the casting. It required only 23 minutes to create the model shown in (b).

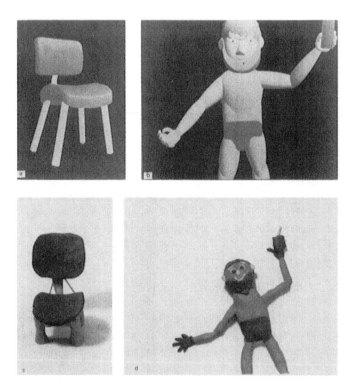

FIGURE 4.17. (a) A figure that was modeled in five minutes on Super-Sketch, a parts-and-deformations based CAD system. (b) A figure that was modeled in twenty-eight minutes on SuperSketch. (c) A clay figure that required four and one half minutes to model. (d) A clay figure that required nineteen and one half minutes to model.

One method of doing this is to describe particular three-dimensional objects and compare the elapsed time when using SuperSketch to that required when using other systems. Figure 4.16(a), for instance, shows a typical industrial casting. Figure 4.16(b) shows a SuperSketch model of it; the time required to enter this model into the computer was 23 minutes—far less than when using other, more traditional CAD systems. Such comparisons, however, suffer from inequities in raw computer power, operator experience, and the particulars of the three-dimensional shape chosen.

Another way to evaluate SuperSketch is to compare it to more traditional media. Because clay is traditionally the fastest three-dimensional "roughing-in" medium, we have chosen to compare modeling a form in clay to modeling a form using SuperSketch. Figure 4.17 shows two comparisons between modeling using clay and modeling using SuperSketch.

It took a skilled (but non-artist) operator of SuperSketch five minutes to assemble the chair in Figure 4.17(a), and twenty-eight minutes to make the image in Figure 4.17(b). Much of this speed is due to the brevity of the final descriptions: to build the scene in Figure 4.17(b) for instance, requires positioning the mouse fewer than 100 times. These same forms were then modeled in clay (by a different subject). It required four and one-half minutes for Figure 4.17(c) and nineteen and one-half minutes for Figure 4.17(d).

Thus on these two evaluation tasks the SuperSketch system performed with approximately the agility of modeling in clay. This result stands in considerable contrast to performance using traditional three-dimensional modeling systems, which might require many hours to build up a complex form such as shown in Figure 4.17(b). We believe that these comparisons illustrate how the close match between this representational system and people's perceptual organization may be able to facilitate the early "sketching" stages three-dimensional design.

SUMMARY

To support our reasoning abilities, perception must recover environmental regularities—for example, rigidity, "objectness," axes of symmetry—for later use in cognitive processes. Understanding this recovery of structure is critically important because the structural organization that perception delivers to cognition is the foundation upon which we construct our picture of the world; these regularities are the building blocks of all cognitive activities.

To create a theory of how our perceptual apparatus can produce meaningful cognitive building blocks from an array of image intensities we require a representation whose elements may be lawfully related to important physical regularities, and that correctly describes the perceptual organization people impose on the stimulus. Unfortunately, the representations that are currently available were originally developed for other purposes (e.g., physics, engineering) and have so far proven unsuitable for the problems of perception or commonsense reasoning.

For instance, the complexity of standard descriptions for such common natural forms as clouds, human faces, or trees has been a fundamental block to progress in computational psychology, artificial intelligence, and machine vision. It is a fundamental result of mathematics that one cannot recover three-dimensional shape descriptions from an image when the number of parameters to be recovered is greater than the number of pixels in the image. How, then, can we hope to understand perception when our representational tools force us into the uncomfortable position of knowing *a priori* that we cannot recover the desired descriptions from image data? Further, even if we *could* recover such descriptions, how can we hope to understand commonsense reasoning if forced to use such overly complex descriptions?

In answer to these problems we have presented a representation that has proven competent to accurately describe an extensive variety of natural forms (e.g., people, mountains, clouds, trees), as well as man-made forms, in a succinct and natural manner. The approach taken in this representational system is to describe scene structure at a scale that is more like our naive perceptual notion of "a part" than the point-wise descriptions typical of current image understanding research, and to use a description that reflects a possible formative history of the object, for example, how the object might have been constructed from lumps of clay.

Each of the component parts of this representation—superquadric "lumps," deformations, Boolean combination, and the recursive fractal construction—have been previously suggested as elements of various shape descriptions, usually for other purposes. The contribution of this chapter is to bring all of these separate descriptive elements together, and employ them as a representation for natural forms and as a theory of perceptual organization. In particular, we believe that the important contributions of this chapter are the following.

- We have demonstrated that this process-oriented representational system is able to accurately describe a very wide range of natural and man-made forms in an extremely simple, and therefore, useful manner. Further, the representation can be used to support fast, qualitative approximations to determine, for example, intersection, appearance, or relative position. Such qualitative reasoning is employed in SuperSketch and allows real-time movement, deformation, Boolean combination, hidden surface removal, intersection, and rendering.

- We have found that descriptions couched in this representation are similar to people's (naive) verbal descriptions and appear to match people's (naive) perceptual notion of "a part"; this correspondence is strong evidence that the descriptions we form will be good spatial primitives for a theory of commonsense reasoning. Additionally, we hope that this descriptive system will provide the beginnings of a rigorous, mathematical treatment of the still vaguely defined subject of human perceptual organization.

- The part-model approach to perception makes the problem of recovering shape descriptions overconstrained and therefore potentially extremely reliable, while still providing the flexibility to learn new object descriptions. Toward this end we have shown that our current descriptive vocabulary is capable of describing a wide range of natural forms and that the primitive elements of this language can be recovered from partial image data in an overconstrained and apparently noise-insensitive manner.

- And finally, we have shown that descriptions framed in the representation have markedly facilitated man-machine communication about both natural and man-made three-dimensional structures. It appears, therefore, that this representation gives us the right "control knobs" for discussing and manipulating a wide variety of three-dimensional forms.

The representational framework presented here is not complete. It seems clear that additional process-oriented modeling primitives, such as branching structures (21) or particle systems (51), will be required to accurately represent objects such as trees, hair, fire, or river rapids. Further, it seems clear that domain experts form descriptions differently than naive observers, reflecting their deeper understanding of the domain-specific formative processes and their more specific, limited purposes. Thus, accounting for expert descriptions will require additional, more specialized models. Nonetheless, we believe this descriptive system makes an important contribution toward solving current problems in perceiving and reasoning about natural forms, by allowing us to recover "part" models from image data, and by providing us with the basis for more effective man-machine communication.

ACKNOWLEDGEMENT

This research was made possible by National Science Foundation, Grant No. DCR-83-12766, by Defense Advanced Research Projects Agency contract no. MDA 903-83-C-0027, and by a grant from the Systems Development Foundation.

REFERENCES

1. Thompson, D'Arcy, (1942) *On Growth and Form,* 2d Ed. Cambridge, England: The University Press.
2. Stevens, Peter S., (1974) *Patterns in Nature.* Boston: Atlantic-Little, Brown Books.
3. Rosch, E., (1973) On the internal structure of perceptual and semantic categories. In *Cognitive Development and the Acquisition of Language,* Moore, T. E. (Ed.). New York: Academic Press.
4. Wertheimer, M., (1923) Laws of organization in perceptual forms. In *A Source Book of Gestalt Psychology,* W. D. Ellis (Ed.). New York: Harcourt Brace.
5. Johansson, G., (1950) *Configurations in Event Perception.* Stockholm: Almqvist and Wiksell.
6. Marr, D., and Nishihara, K., (1978) Representation and recognition of the spatial organization of three-dimensional shapes. *Proceedings of the Royal Society-London B,* 200:269–94.
7. Nishihara, H. K., (1981) Intensity, visible-surface and volumetric representations. *Artificial Intelligence, 17,* 265–284.
8. Binford, T. O., (1971) Visual perception by computer. *Proceeding of the IEEE Conference on Systems and Control,* Miami, December.
9. Gibson, J. J., (1979) *The Ecological Approach to Visual Perception.* Boston: Houghton Mifflin.
10. Marr, D. (1982) *Vision.* San Francisco: W. H. Freeman.
11. Agin, G. J., and Binford, T. O., (1976) Computer descriptions of curved objects. *IEEE Transactions on Pattern Analysis and Machine Intelligence, C-25,* 4, 439–449.
12. Nevatia, R., and Binford, T. O., (1977) Description and recognition of curved objects. *Artificial Intelligence, 8,* 1, 77–98.
13. Badler, N. and Bajcsy, R., (1978) Three-dimensional representations for computer graphics and computer vision. *Computer Graphics, 12,* 153–160.
14. Brady, J. M., (1982) Describing visible surfaces. In *Computer Vision Systems,* Hanson, A. and Riesman, E. (Eds.). New York: Academic Press.
15. Brooks, R., (1985) Model based 3-D interpretation of 2-D images. In *From Pixels to Predicates,* pp. 300–322. Pentland, A. (Ed.). Norwood, NJ: Ablex.
16. Bolles, B., and Haroud, R., (1985) 3DPO: An inspection system. In *From Pixels to Predicates,* pp. 359–371. Pentland, A. (Ed.). Norwood, NJ: Ablex.
17. Barrow, H. G., and Tenenbaum, J. M., (1978) Recovering intrinsic scene characteristics from images. In *Computer Vision Systems,* Hanson, A. and Riseman, E. (Eds.). New York: Academic Press.
18. Pentland, A. (1984) Local analysis of the image. *IEEE Transactions on Pattern Analysis and Machine Recognition, 6,* 2, 170–187.
19. Witkin, A. P., and Tenenbaum, J. M., (1985) On perceptual organization. In *From Pixels to Predicates,* pp. 149–169. Pentland, A. (Ed.). Norwood, NJ: Ablex.
20. Pentland, A., and Witkin, A., (1984) "On Perceptual Organization." Second Conference on Perceptual Organization, Pajaro Dunes, CA, June 12–15.
21. Smith, A. R., (1984) Plants, fractals and formal languages. In *Computer Graphics,* 18, (3), 1–11.
22. Mandelbrot, B. B., (1982) *The Fractal Geometry of Nature.* San Francisco: W. H. Freeman.

23. Georgeff, M. P., and Wallace, C. S., (1984) A general selection criterion for inductive inference. In *Proceedings of the Sixth European Conference on Artificial Intelligence,* Pisa, Italy, September 5–7.
24. Herman, M., and Kanade, T., (1985) The 3-D mosaic scene understanding system. In *From Pixels to Predicates.* pp. 359–370. Pentland, A. (Ed.). Norwood, NJ: Ablex.
25. Konderink, Jan J., and van Doorn, Andrea J., (1982) The shape of smooth objects and the way contours end. *Perception, 11,* 129–137.
26. Konderink, Jan J., and van Doorn, Andrea J., (1979) The internal representation of solid shape with respect to vision. *Biological Cybernetics, 32,* 211–216.
27. Hoffman, D., and Richards, W., (1985) Parts of recognition. In *From Pixels to Predicates,* pp. 268–294. Pentland, A. (Ed.). Norwood, NJ: Ablex.
28. Barr, A., (1981) Superquadrics and angle-preserving transformations. *IEEE Computer Graphics and Application, (1),* 1–20.
29. Kauth, R., Pentland, A., and Thomas, G., (1977). BLOB: an unsupervised clustering approach to spatial grouping. *Proceeding of the Eleventh International Symposium on Remote Sensing of the Environment,* Ann Arbor, MI, April.
30. Hobbs, J. (1985) Final Report on Commonsense Summer. SRI Artificial Intelligence Center Technical Note 370.
31. Barr, A., (1984) Global and local deformations of solid primitives. *Computer Graphics 18,* (3), 21–30.
32. Hollerbach, J. M., (1975) Hierarchical shape description of objects by selection and modification of prototypes, MIT. AI Technical Rep. 346, Cambridge, MA.
33. Hayes, P., (1985) The second naive physics manifesto. In *Formal Theories of the Commonsense World,* Hobbes, J. and Moore, R. (Eds.). Norwood, NJ: Ablex.
34. Pentland, A., (1984a), Fractal-based description of natural scenes. *IEEE Pattern Analysis and Machine Intelligence, 6,* 6, 661–674.
35. Pentland, A., (1983) Fractal-based description. *Proceedings of the International Joint Conference on Artificial Intelligence,* pp. 973–981, Karlsruhe, Germany.
36. Medioni, G. and Yasumoto, Y., (1984) A note on using the fractal dimension for segmentation, *IEEE Computer Vision Workshop,* Annapolis, MD.
37. Pentland, A., (1984b) Shading into texture. *Proceedings of the National Conference on Artificial Intelligence,* pp. 269–273, Austin, TX.
38. Pentland, A., (1984c) Fractals: A model for both texture and shading. *Optic News,* October issue, p. 71.
39. Pentland, A., (1984d) Perception of three-dimensional textures. *Investigative Opthomology and Visual Science, 25,* (3), pp. 201.
40. Fodor, J., (1982) *Modularity of Mind: An Essay on Faculty Psychology,* Cambridge, MA: MIT Press.
41. Gregory, R. L., (1970) *The Intelligent Eye.* New York: McGraw-Hill.
42. Leyton, M., (1984) Perceptual organization as nested control. *Biological Cybernetics 51,* 141–153.
43. Held, R., and Richards, W., (Eds.) (1975) *Recent Progress in Perception.* Readings from Scientific American. San Francisco: W. H. Freeman.
44. Yu, Sheng Hsuan, (1983) Implementation of shape-from-shading algorithms. Tech. Rep. on Image Understanding Research, Intelligent Systems Group, UCLA, Los Angeles, CA. DARPA Order No. 3119.
45. Roberts, L., (1965) Machine perception of three-dimensional solids. In *Optical and Electrooptical Information Processing.* Tippet, J. T., et al. (Eds.). Cambridge, MA: MIT Press.
46. Winston, P. H., (1975) Learning structural descriptions from examples. In *The Psychology of Computer Vision,* Winston, P. H. (Ed.). New York: McGraw-Hill.
47. Winston, P., Binford, T., Katz, B., and Lowry, M. (1983) *Proceedings of the National*

Conference on Artificial Intelligence (AAAI-83), pp. 433–439. Washington, DC, August 22–26.

48. Davis, E., (1983) The MERCATOR representation of spatial knowledge. *Proceedings of the Eighth International Joint Conference on Artificial Intelligence*, pp. 295–301, Karlsruhe, West Germany, August 8–12.

49. Selizski, Richard, (1985) *personal communication*.

50. Burt, P. J., and Adelson, E. H., (1983) The Laplacian pyramid as a compact image code. *IEEE Transactions on Communications, COM-31*, 4, 532–540.

51. Reeves, W. T., (1983) Particle systems—a technique for modeling a class of fuzzy objects. *ACM Transactions on Graphics 2*, 2, 91–108.

52. Brodatz, P., (1966) Textures: A photographic album for artists and designers. New York: Dover.

53. Witkin, A., (1983) Scale-space filtering. *Proceedings of the Eighth International Joint Conference on Artificial Intelligence.* Karlsruhe, W. Germany, 1019–1022.

54. Fischler, M., and Bolles, R., (1982) Random Sample Consensus: A paradigm for model fitting with applications to image analysis and automated cartography. *Communications of the ACM*, 24, (6), pp. 381–395.

55. Goad, C., (1985) A fast model-based vision system. In *From Pixels to Predicates*, pp. 371–400. Pentland, A. (Ed.). Norwood, NJ: Ablex.

56. Grimson, W. E. L., and Lozano-Perez, T., (1985) Recognition and localization of overlapping parts from sparse data in two and three dimensions. *Proc. IEEE Robotics Conference*, pp. 140–150, St. Louis, MO.

57. Fischler, M., *et al.* (1986) Knowledge-based vision techniques for the autonomous land vehicle program. SRI Project Rep. 8388. SRI International, Menlo Park, CA.

58. Barnard, S., Bolles, R., Marrimont, D., and Pentland, A., Multiple Representations for Mobile Robot Vision. *SPIE Cambridge Symposium on Optical and Optoelectronic Engineering*, October 26–31, 1986, Cambridge, MA. Available SPIE Proceedings, Vol. 727.

59. Pentland, A. Perceptual Organization and the Representation of Natural Form, *Artificial Intelligence Journal*, February 1986. 28, (2), 1–38.

60. Kube, P., and Pentland, A., (1986) On the Imaging of Fractal Surfaces. SRI Tech Note No. 390. SRI International, Menlo Park, CA.

61. Heeger, P., and Pentland, A., (1986) Measuring Fractal Dimension Using Gabor Filters. SRI Tech Note No. 391. SRI International, Menlo Park, CA.

62. Pentland, A., (1985) On Describing Complex Surfaces. *Image and Vision Computing*, 3, (4), 153–162.

63. Beiderman, I., (1985) Human image understanding: recent research and a theory. *Computer Vision, Graphics and Image Processing*, Vol 32, (1), 29–73.

64. Bajcsy, R., and Solina, F. Three-dimensional Object Representation Revisited. *First International Conf. on Computer Vision, '87*, June 8–11, London, England.

AUTHOR INDEX

⬜ SUBJECT INDEX

Printed and bound by CPI Group (UK) Ltd, Croydon, CR0 4YY

17/10/2024

01775688-0009